Modern drama in theory and practice   Volume 2

Symbolism, surrealism and the absurd

By the same author

Modern drama in theory and practice

VOLUME 2

Symbolism, surrealism and the absurd

J.L.STYAN

Franklyn Bliss Snyder Professor of English Literature
Northwestern University

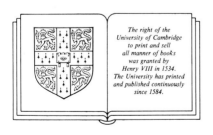

*The right of the
University of Cambridge
to print and sell
all manner of books
was granted by
Henry VIII in 1534.
The University has printed
and published continuously
since 1584.*

CAMBRIDGE UNIVERSITY PRESS
Cambridge
London · New York · New Rochelle
Melbourne · Sydney

Published by the Press Syndicate of the University of Cambridge
The Pitt Building, Trumpington Street, Cambridge CB2 1RP
32 East 57th Street, New York, NY 10022, USA
10 Stamford Road, Oakleigh, Melbourne 3166, Australia

© Cambridge University Press 1981

First published 1981
First paperback edition 1983
Reprinted 1985, 1986

Printed in Malta by Interprint Ltd

Library of Congress Cataloguing in Publication Data

Styan, J. L.
Modern drama in theory and practice.

Includes bibliographies and index.
CONTENTS: 1. Realism. – 2. Symbolism, surrealism,
and the absurd. – 3. Expressionism and epic theatre.
1. Drama – History – 20th century. 2. Theatre –
History – 20th century. I. Title.
ISBN 0 521 22737 2 volume 1 hard covers
ISBN 0 521 29628 5 volume 1 paperback
ISBN 0 521 22738 0 volume 2 hard covers
ISBN 0 521 29629 3 volume 2 paperback
ISBN 0 521 22739 9 volume 3 hard covers
ISBN 0 521 29630 7 volume 3 paperback
ISBN 0 521 23068 3 set of 3 volumes, hard covers

Contents

The dates are usually those of the first production

Illustrations

Acknowledgements

The author and publisher gratefully acknowledge the permission of the following to reproduce their illustrations in this book: Ullstein, W. Berlin (1); Document Marie-Louise et Denis Bablet, Paris (2); Schweizerische Theatersammlung, Bern (3); Administrator of the Gordon Craig Estate, London (4 and 5); Edward Craig Collection, Bledlow, Aylesbury, Bucks (6); Novosti Press Agency, London (7); British Theatre Museum at the Victoria and Albert Museum, London (8); Bildarchiv Preussischer Kulturbesits, W. Berlin (10); the courtesy of the London Festival Ballet and Alan Cunliffe (11); Dansmuseet, Stockholm (12); Fisk-Moore Studios, Canterbury (15); Mas/Gyenes, Madrid (16); Lipnitzki/Roger-Viollet, Paris (17); New York Public Library (18); Agence de Presse Bernand, Paris (19, 21, 27 and 28); © Max Waldman, 1966 (20); © Max Waldman, 1969 (29); © Max Waldman, 1969 (33); Roger Pic, Paris (22, 24, 25 and 26); Dominic, London (23); Photo Jim Crawford, courtesy of the Bread and Puppet Theater, Vermont (31) and Donald Cooper, London (34).

It has not been possible to trace the owner/copyright owner of illustrations 13 and 14: if he will write to the author or publisher, suitable acknowledgement will be made at the earliest opportunity.

Preface

It is a principle increasingly accepted that the manner of playwriting is inseparable from the kind of theatre it is written for. The new attempt of this study is to look at some of the important plays of modern times, not as isolated literary works, but in relation to their production and performance. The intention is to trace some of the interactions between playwright and performing artist (this term to include all who are involved in production: actors and directors, lighting and scenic designers), and the subject of the study is, in the widest sense, the bearing of theory on practice, and of practice on theory. Like any art form, drama is sometimes aroused by fitful rebellion, but it always builds upon the testing of ideas on an audience and the total theatre experience of the past.

The story of the theatre is one of rebellion and reaction, with new forms challenging the old, and old forms in turn providing the basis for the new. But the labels we use, realism, symbolism, and so on, too easily blanket the details of dramatic and stage history. These details are not often found in the laws of playwriting or in the manifestoes of fashionable movements, but remain to be extracted from the day-to-day dealings of the stage. We must judge less by intentions than by results, aware that theory and practice are more often in conflict than in accord: in John Gassner's words, we must recognize 'the breach between ambition and attainment'. It is necessary to turn to the promptbook and the acting edition, the *Regiebuch* and the *Modellbuch*, to notices and criticism, interviews and memoirs, as well as to the text of the play itself, to know what happened.

To adapt a concept of the art historian, E. H. Gombrich, drama originates in our reactions to the world, and not in the world itself. By this argument, the changes which an audience perceives on the stage between, say, the grim naturalism of a *Lower Depths* and the violent fantasies of Edward Bond, are changes in itself. The abiding secret of dramatic interpretation lies in its 'style', the *way of seeing* of writer, player or spectator, and style is the one ingredient, it must be supposed, which a play and its performance should ideally have in common, since it is the *sine qua non* of dramatic communication. Moreover, if an artist's perception of reality is conditioned by the age he lives in and by the medium he works with, an understanding of style will supply some of the clues to both. This study, therefore, concerned as it is with the limitations and possibilities of drama since Büchner and Wagner, Zola and Ibsen, may afford an insight into ourselves and our modes of perception.

The threads of many different styles, however, are interwoven within a single play in performance. This is especially true of this century, which can draw upon a multitude of conventions from the 'imaginary museum'. In practice, it is impossible to find a play of, say, naked realism or pure symbolism, and the best playwrights are constantly resourceful: Ibsen is a realist and a symbolist, Strindberg embraces both naturalism and expressionism, in writing a symbolist drama Pirandello becomes a progenitor of the absurd, Weiss arranges Artaudian cruelty within a Brechtian epic frame and so on. Theatre artists are similarly elastic: Meyerhold, the originator of constructivism, produced the outstanding *Government Inspector*, Jouvet showed himself master of Molière as well as of *La Machine infernale*, Barrault produced a fine *Phèdre* and was also superbly sensitive to Chekhov.

A final explanation. In order to follow a clearer path through a jungle of detail, *Modern Drama* is presented as three extended essays on realism, symbolism and expressionism, with developments in the last two into surrealism, absurdism and epic theatre. Discussions focus upon those landmark productions of modern times in order to be as specific as possible. In one way, it may seem unfortunate that these essays appear separately, artificially dividing the total theatrical scene; yet, in tracing the several competing structures of signals and responses between stage and audience, it is remarkable what continuities are revealed. At all events, my hope is to provide another aid towards a properly stage-centred dramatic criticism, using performance equally with theory as the basis for a history of the stage.

I am grateful to a Fellowship from the National Endowment

for the Humanities of the United States, as well as to Northwestern University, for giving me the opportunity to write this study. I also owe a great debt to the British Library, the Colindale Newspaper Library, the Victoria and Albert Museum and the British Theatre Centre, as well as to the Ford Curtis Theatre Collection of the Hillman Library of the University of Pittsburgh and to the Library of Northwestern University. Robert Schneideman of Northwestern University, Leonard Powlick of Wilkes-Barre University and John and Barbara Cavanagh of Mottisfont Abbey have been of material assistance to me. The staff of Cambridge University Press have been of great help from beginning to end. A larger kind of debt is owed to the scholarship of countless fine students of the modern drama, and to the creative work of an even greater number of theatre artists.

J. L. S.

1 *The symbolic in drama*

When Quince, the amateur producer in *A Midsummer Night's Dream*, assembles his actors in the palace wood for their first rehearsal of 'Pyramus and Thisbe', he finds that there are 'two hard things' for the play to get across to its audience. One is the moonlight and the other is a wall — elements of time and place, both essentials of dramatic illusion. The choice is apparently simple: shall these elements be real or symbolic? Bottom's idea is to take the obvious way and make use of the real moon by leaving open the casement window. But Quince realizes that the success of this plan depends entirely upon his power to reproduce and control the real world. The moon must rise and the clouds must clear at the right time. Nor can they readily build a wall in the great chamber and pull it down again. His more sophisticated thinking follows: somebody must represent the moon, and somebody else pretend to be a wall. In this way, day and night can be conjured at will according to the needs of the play, and the location changed as quickly as the actor can make his exit. Quince runs into some of the absurdities of dramatic symbolism when he places too much faith in it, but at least he seems to have temporarily solved the problem.

The stage has often been a great deal more than a mirror reflecting life and nature. Symbolism is never far away whenever an actor mounts his platform to imitate the world about him, since the act of putting life on exhibition is an act of reformulating reality: indeed, the existence of drama itself suggests there is an abiding need for symbolic representation. Symbolism in the theatre can therefore exist alongside realism, or it can eliminate realistic illusion entirely. It is not hard to see how the drama, which is always trying to find ways of breaking out of the temporal and spatial restrictions of its medium, moves easily from realism to symbolism, and it is significant that each of the great nineteenth-century naturalists, Ibsen,

Strindberg, Hauptmann and Chekhov, chose a more symbolic expression at the very time when he had apparently succeeded in being rigorously realistic. A symbolic stage can pass easily into surrealism and the absurd, and both the ancient and the modern theatres have shown that when the creative impulse touches the deepest feelings we all share, drama can ignore realism entirely and move into ritual.

As a technical and critical term, 'symbolism' came into specialized use with reference to poetry, and it was first employed by Stéphane Mallarmé (1842–98) and the French symbolist movement after its manifesto was published in *Figaro* in 1886. The poet's task is to find the right words to convey human feelings and ideas, and in poetic practice a verbal symbol is intended to evoke feelings and ideas greater than those the words usually stand for, suggesting a meaning beyond its immediate and concrete reality. In particular, verbal symbolism grew to be an elaborate poetic device to 'clothe thought with a sensory form'.

The style has since been associated with the work of many other French poets writing in the second half of the nineteenth century, notably Baudelaire (1821–67), Verlaine (1844–96), Rimbaud (1854–91) and Valéry (1871–1945). These poets aimed to discover the 'secret' of poetry as if it were some philosopher's stone, and they built their ideas upon a latter-day romantic theory of the mystical and the occult, the irrational and the world of fantasy and dream. A theory of symbolism seemed to sanctify the idea of art as a law unto itself, and the artist as a creature apart. Baudelaire and Rimbaud deliberately adopted a Bohemian way of life, one of drugs and debauchery, to exemplify their beliefs, expand their sensory perceptions and experience every mood to the full. In particular, they developed a theory of 'synaesthesia' in their writing, by which one sense could represent another by association (for example, a bright colour to suggest a loud sound, and vice versa). Poetry was not to obey the laws of logic, but of hallucination and the surreal, so that it should stay 'pure' and free from social relevance.

All these notions could readily be applied to the drama, but of these poets, only the less flamboyant Mallarmé went so far as to think of dramatic symbolism, and he envisaged a ritualistic form of theatre, idealized and mystical in its simplicity and impressionism. Symbolic theatre would combine all the arts and return to the simple elements of drama. Although it never reached the stage, Mallarmé conceived his poem *Hérodiade* (published in 1898) as a play.

The application of symbolism to stagecraft is straightforward, and symbols on the stage are not new. In the theatre an object or a situation can immediately suggest an idea or a feeling that is greater than itself. A storm in a play, for example, has always symbolized displeasure in heaven and the anger of the gods, and whether in high tragedy or popular melodrama, the sight and sound of thunder and lightning speak ominously to an audience anywhere. A crown is a powerful symbolic property in Shakespeare, and held between the King and Bolingbroke in *Richard II*, it unmistakably points to the disputed authority over the kingdom. Such symbols have the virtue of being unshakably traditional and almost universal in impact, like red for danger or a voyage for life itself.

A symbol can also be strong, even if personal to the poet or playwright, if its meaning and function is carefully brought out and made intelligible. In T. S. Eliot's poem *The Waste Land*, a hyacinth is made to suggest the fertility of spring, although in Strindberg's play *The Ghost Sonata* it is made to stand for the loss of the will, beautiful but suffocating and debilitating. In each case, the context settles the meaning and allows communication to proceed. But the invitation to the symbolist poet to slide into woolly, private symbolism is equally open to the playwright, and where symbolic vagueness in poetry may be suspect in the eyes of the solitary reader, in the public theatre it is irresponsible and unforgivable. At the turn of the century, some writers advanced the philosophy of 'art for art's sake' as a reason for eliminating social and political matters from their work. Even in the field of the novel, Virginia Woolf could write her damning essay 'Modern Fiction' and attack Wells, Bennett and Galsworthy as 'materialists' who could never aspire to aesthetic truth because they were concerned 'not with the spirit but with the body': 'They write of unimportant things; ... they spend immense skill and immense industry making the trivial and the transitory appear the true and the enduring.' However, there is a necessary balance to be struck between the abstract and the concrete, the true and the trivial, if the seductive perils of cloudy private symbolism are to be avoided.

At the same time, symbolism that is too specific may destroy one of its great virtues, its power to extend itself and multiply its references. A strong, resonant symbol like Chekhov's cherry orchard symbolizes in a tangle of sentiments both the family's happy past and the ugly days of serfdom; by the end of the play it has grown to mean something different to each of the characters, and it has also embraced immense social and economic changes about to take place in the future. This kind of suggestiveness can affect the whole mode of a play, which could be written and produced in a totally symbolic manner designed to persuade its audience to apprehend the action on the stage at the level chosen by the playwright. A new danger presents itself here, that of losing the audience in a forest of associations, just when the intention is for the play to be more expressive.

A recent theory of the symbolic, that of the literary critic Kenneth Burke, is associated with his idea of 'dramatism'. Burke holds that man tries to control and humanize his world by means of symbolism. Symbols and symbolic structures in art are not only typically human, he finds, but all forms of symbolism, even metaphor, must derive ultimately from the senses. Burke's realm of 'symbolicity' is one in which man finds himself in a middle area of sensory images somewhere between the purely physical and the purely abstract. Such symbolism, he maintains, is distinguished by its power to create its own language and idiom, and to express and 'discuss' itself, just as drama can determine its own poetics, and by a variety of metatheatrical liberties, seem self-consciously to dramatize the very business of conceiving and putting on a play — one thinks of Shakespeare's *A Midsummer Night's Dream* and *The Tempest* as prime examples of a dramatic structure in which the stage brilliantly explores, while it ironically smiles at, its own mode of imaginative activity.

Watching a play, therefore, may be a fundamentally symbolic act in itself, and in discussing symbolism in drama we are dealing with an elusive subject, fraught with problems yet rich in possibilities. It can be a powerful, unpredictable and explosive mode of playwriting, and it is not surprising that, at the time when naturalism was at its peak in Europe, the theatre was urgently seeking a justification in myth and ritual at another level for the visionary quality it had missed in realism.

2 Theoretical beginnings: Wagner and Nietzsche

It is impossible to pin-point the origin of the modern notion of symbolic drama, since it was a residue from an older, romantic philosophy. One outstanding source which directly influenced the modern theatre, however, was the aesthetic theory of the composer Richard Wagner (1813–83). Wagner's parallel interests in both music and drama resulted not only in the major operas *Tristan und Isolde* (1865), *Die Meistersinger* (1868) and the epic tetralogy *Der Ring des Nibelungen* (the whole work finally produced in 1876), for which he wrote both music and libretto, but also in an elaborate and obscure theory of the form and nature of 'music-drama' which he based on Schopenhauer and German metaphysics. Wagner believed music-drama to be the performing art of the future, one in which language could be extended by sound to create a fuller emotional statement. In his essay, 'The Ideas of Richard Wagner', Arthur Symons observed in 1907 that the composer's theoretical writing was especially valuable because 'it is wholly the personal expression of an artist engaged in creative work, finding out theories by the way, as he comes upon obstacles, or aids in the nature of things'. As it turned out, in Wagner's theories lay the seeds of a new romanticism, based upon the idea that 'myth' was the source of man's greatest powers as an artist.

Wagner's first great influential book, *The Art-Work of the Future* (1849), argued that art was the vital expression of instinctive life. By dance, 'tone' and poetry, man originally created a form of art in which he was himself the subject and in which he was his own agent — the work was about himself and he made it. By 'tone', Wagner meant a kind of half-speech and half-song imagined from some pre-rational time when both dance and poetry had their beginning; he believed that this tone was something like Greek choric verse, which contrived to control and bring together the movement of the body and the sound of the voice. Wagner believed that this element would once again bring dance and poetry together, and with its help man the singer and man the actor would perfect a form of ideal lyric drama, in which dance and poetry would reveal their true essence in rhythm and melody. He argued this hypothesis another way also. Music, he considered, was the most pure and sensuous form of art; Beethoven had taken music to the supreme point where only speech should follow, and Shakespeare had taken poetry to the point where only music should follow; in the art of the future, therefore, music and poetry should be combined to create the perfect drama.

In his next book, *Opera and Drama* (1851), to whose 'stubbornness of style' Wagner himself confessed, he began to write about myth as the creation of the instinctive imagination, and here defined it as 'the poem of a life-view in common'. It was inexhaustible and true for all time, and it was the dramatic poet's task to express it in action. But this book is notable for its series of loosely related propositions suggesting the theoretical connections between music and drama. For example:

1. Wagner believed that the fundamental error in opera was that 'a means of expression (music) has been made the end, while the end of expression (drama) has been made a means' (translated E. L. Burlingame).

2. He also claimed that in drama the final appeal was directly to the senses, and had meaning only when it was justified by emotional necessity: in drama, we learn and know through feeling. However, the deepest human feeling could be fully realized only in 'tone-speech' expressed by full chorus and orchestra — i.e., in a form of music.

3. The human voice was 'the oldest, truest, most beautiful organ of music', and the orchestra had 'the faculty of uttering the unspeakable'; therefore the poet's aim and the musician's expression must be indistinguishably blended.

It was this blending that led to Wagner's famous conception of the *Gesamtkunstwerk*, the 'total art-work', which he believed had not existed since the arts had been unified in ancient Greek tragedy.

Wagner continued to work over these fundamental ideas all

his life, and in *The Purpose of the Opera* (1871) pulled many of them together. The dramatic poet, he said, naturally could not play his own characters, but only outline the material upon which his actor could *improvise* — just as the composer of opera composed for an instrumentalist, who then improvised upon the music. He thought of Shakespeare's drama as an organized histrionic improvisation, the poet's initial conception magically resulting in a living art. In writing a play, the poet assumed the *possibility* of conveying his thoughts and feelings in drama, and it was in music-drama that the possibility could be realized. If the inexplicable, inspirational element in Shakespeare were perfectly complemented by the same element in Beethoven, it would produce an ideal form of expression. Just as the faculties of reason and feeling combine to make the whole man, so the media of poetry and music would join to complete the 'emotionalizing of the intellect', and create a drama richer and more perfect than either could manage alone. To Wagner's way of thinking, a musically-arranged and musically-executed histrionic performance was 'the one, indivisible, supreme creation of the mind of man', 'the most perfect art-work'.

Nothing was said directly of symbolism, but Wagner's vision of purity and idealism in art led him well away from the realism of the later nineteenth-century stage. And as he reiterated and explored the same ideas from book to book, he moved steadily towards a drama built upon archetype and myth, and upon dream and the the supernatural, mystical elements which were to dominate the symbolic drama of the twentieth century.

Wagner also explored his theories in his operatic composition, and his scores included the acting cues he wanted. Then in 1876 he built the playhouse he wanted, so that he himself could produce his music-drama in his own meticulous way. This was to become the famous Festspielhaus about a mile outside Bayreuth, a small town near Nuremberg in Bavaria. Wagner had approved of the modified apron stage of Goethe's theatre at Weimar, with its effect of bringing the audience closer to the action, but for opera he felt the stage should be more remote to accommodate a more artificial form and to increase the illusion. So at Bayreuth he set the orchestra beneath the level of the stage, and instead of the usual Victorian balconies had wedge-shaped rows of seats rising steadily from the orchestra to a gallery at the back of the house. The Festspielhaus thus became an amphitheatre. A hood covered the musicians, who were thereby rendered invisible, and a gap in its top allowed the music to be heard. One proscenium frame surrounded a second, inner proscenium, so that while the audience was unusually distanced, it was also forced to focus exclusively on a single *theatron* or looking-room. In this, Wagner's ideal world could be shown, separated from the real world of the audience. He called it his 'Mystischer Abgrund', his 'mystic abyss'.

Unfortunately, Wagner's Bayreuth reproduced the literal and pictorial kind of scene that was all too common in Victorian times: he had not matched his musical and poetic aesthetic with a visual one. When in 1951 Bayreuth reopened after the disruption of the war years, the artistic directors, Richard Wagner's grandsons Wieland and Wolfgang, wisely took advantage of all the modern theatre had learned about abstract and symbolic setting and décor. Their production policy seemed heretical to some devotees of Wagner, but to others it was appropriately flexible and imaginative.

1. Festspielhaus, Bayreuth, 1876, during the interval.

For all Wagner's far-reaching vision of a transcendental theatre, he failed to realize his notion of a perfect conjunction of the mind and the senses. It fell to others, in the beginning especially to the designers Appia and Craig, to attempt the ideal unification of the elements of theatre to achieve the overwhelming experience Wagner sought. Nevertheless, the desire to present a full emotional and spiritual experience on the stage advanced an idea of symbolism more profound, more embracing and more tremendous than anything the French lyric poets had achieved or conceived. From *The Ring* onwards, Wagner shook off the restrictions of opera's conventional arias, duets, choruses and recitatives, with their open invitation to mere individual virtuosity and showmanship, in order to design the scheme for a whole movement in which every bar, he said, would be related to a total conception, and the 'myth' at the root of the art-work could control the whole drama.

Wagner's ideas about music-drama inspired a host of theatre theorists and artists in the years that followed. One man in particular, and a fellow German, the philosopher Friedrich Nietzsche (1844–1900), was inspired to try to justify them in an ingenious, quasi-historical account of the origins of Greek tragedy, generally taken to be the beginning of western drama. If Nietzsche could account for tragedy, he would therefore have accounted for all of drama that mattered. In 1872 he published *The Birth of Tragedy from the Spirit of Music*, an argument in anthropology and aesthetic theory which has become a landmark in modern western thought.

Nietzsche believed that tragedy arose from the ritual celebration of Dionysus and was expressed in the song and dance of the dithyramb, by which man 'projected himself outside himself' as if he were a dramatic character. Dionysus represented all that was emotional and irrational in man. Meanwhile the embodiment of the dance imposed a form upon it, and this was Apollonian in its lucidity, reasonableness and harmony. Strangely anticipating Freud's theories of the id and the ego, Nietzsche argued that it was this duality and tension between the instinctive and the rational, between Dionysus and Apollo, which produced great drama.

Much of this was some way from Wagner's theory of music-drama, but Nietzsche also conveniently advanced the idea that music was Dionysiac, while the 'plastic' arts, like drama, were

Apollonian. These two forces remained in opposition until they were married in great tragedy. Like Wagner's, Nietzsche's goal was to describe a drama which expressed our 'inmost being', and justify the necessity of a dream-world. He made the point by quoting Hans Sachs, the shoemaker, in *Die Meistersinger*, III.i:

> All poems that the world has known
> are nought but truths our dreams have shown.
> (translated Frederick Jameson)

The theory in *The Birth of Tragedy*, however, was far too abstract to have much direct effect upon the practice of the modern stage, but it was clearly symptomatic of the growing impulse towards a more symbolic drama.

---

3   *Symbolic theatre: Appia and lighting design*

Tristan und Isolde (1899 and 1923)

The French-Swiss artist Adolphe François Appia (1862–1928) also took his inspiration from Wagner and conceived his ideal theatre in terms of 'musical' form; like Walter Pater, he believed that music was the condition to which the other arts aspired. Appia at first worked in the theatre in Dresden and Vienna to study the problems of three-level scenery and lighting, but he did no work at Bayreuth. Having seen Wagner's *Parsifal* there in 1882, then *Tristan und Isolde* in 1886 and *Die Meistersinger* in 1888, he found the mode of presentation far too literal in its pictorial realism for his taste. Against the three-dimensional actor, in Appia's view, two-dimensional painted scenery looked false. In its place he envisaged with extraordinary foresight a 'musical' stage design which would lift the theatre out of the Victorian age, and carry it into a mode of visual symbolism which would express the inner qualities of a play. The old immobile footlights, wing and border lights with shadows painted on the canvas had to go; in their place must come a free system of lighting from above which would throw the actors' shadows vividly upon the stage.

In thus avoiding scenic realism, Appia in fact invented rhythms and patterns more appropriate to the rendering of dreams than drama, but, as it happened, he had few opportunities to practise his theories. After scenic experiments for scenes from *Carmen* and *Manfred* in 1903, he designed for only two full-scale productions, Gluck's *Orpheus and Eurydice* in 1913 and the ballet *Echo et Narcisse* in 1919, before he finally had a chance in his old age to produce Wagner. Instead, he designed many imaginary productions, chiefly of Wagner, and set his ideas down on paper, packing his books with ideas taken from German transcendental philosophy. His fundamental works are therefore his books, *La mise en scène du drame wagnérien (Staging Wagner,* Paris, 1895), *Die Musik und die Inszenierung* (*Music and the Art of the Theatre*, Munich, 1899) and *L'oeuvre d'art vivant* (*The Work of Living Art*, Geneva, 1921). These supplied the aesthetic principles for the modern designer, and had enormous influence in European and American theatre.

Appia's achievement was to find a way of combining those arts of the stage which are usually regarded as separate, because

2. Gluck's *Orpheus and Eurydice*, 1913. Design by Appia and Dalcroze at Hellerau.

some are created in space and some in time. He saw it as the designer's task to relate and unify the visual and temporal. Musical concepts furnished him with the answers.

1. *Space.*   Even inside the proscenium arch, musical form could dictate the geometrical shapes and proportions within the acting area, so that the stage might acquire a three-dimensional and fluid property.

2. *The actor.*   The actor himself was the true measure of the effectiveness of the set, because, placed in three-dimensional space, his figure could be accentuated like a sculpture, and his rhythmic movement and gesture would be depersonalized as in the dance. Acting would seem to be, not so much an impersonation of real life, as a human equivalent to music.

3. *Costume.*   Like the set, costume was not to be considered literally, but as an extension of the mood of the actor, and always related to the set and its lighting.

4. *Setting.*   The actor is not to be placed in a setting created for its own sake: the setting must always complement the actor. For example, the audience should not see a forest with Siegfried in it, but a forest atmosphere related to Siegfried, so that the audience rivets its eyes on the actor and not on his background.

5. *Light.*   Because it was 'plastic', only light could unify the actor, the stage and the set. Thus, instead of colouring his scene with paint, the designer could brush it with controlled light, which, with its fluidity and power of nuance, could create rapid and subtle changes of colour and intensity. Expressive light and shadow would also accentuate the living qualities of the actor, and do for the drama what mood music did for Wagner —heighten the action and add a temporal dimension to the stage, making its point and moving on in time.

Appia wrote a promptbook for *Der Ring*, drawing sets for *Das Rheingold* and *Die Walküre*. In *Die Musik und die Inszenierung*, he included eighteen illustrations for *Der Ring* and *Tristan und Isolde*, and as an appendix outlined his famous plan for producing *Tristan* according to his new principles. We may now look at this.

In Wagner's score, the stage directions are brief and the 'action' is properly an inner expression of spiritual feeling. The lovers wish to die and the external world is almost irrelevant to their emotional tension, as expressed in the music. The designer, then, must support the balance of sight and sound without intruding upon the essentials of the drama. In the great love duet of the second act, Tristan and Isolde exist in a phantom world in which they declare that their passion can flower only in night and death, and it is this illusory world which the lighting, working upon the setting, must establish, so that the audience may see as the lovers see. The rule, therefore, Appia argued, is to aim at the utmost simplicity, staging the opera without superfluous detail.

The important subtleties of this second act were to be conveyed by light. A great torch set high up on a wall, stage centre, is the symbol of reality which separates Isolde from Tristan. When Isolde extinguishes the light, time stops and space is obliterated, the lovers are in each other's arms and the music takes us into their secret

3. Wagner, *Tristan und Isolde*, 1923. Design by Appia at La Scala, Milan. Act III, courtyard of the Castle Kareol, with limetree.

world. At this time, the shape of the stage setting remains blurred by shadows, and ivy-covered walls, the terrace and the trees beyond are lost in a monotonous half-light which induces an impression of death. As the actors move downstage, the audience becomes aware of the death of time, the background grows invisible and the mysterious half-light becomes uniform in tone. Against the background stage right, a pale red light representing the dawn brings in Isolde's husband King Mark with his soldiers to surprise the lovers, and the setting is cold and hard as Tristan returns to this world and challenges Melot to a duel for betraying them. Tristan allows himself to be wounded, and the red in the sky matches the red of his blood.

The various ramps and platforms upon which the actors move are essentially abstract, and the audience is aware of them only when a movement, a leap or a fall is made. Such a structure has reduced scene painting to a minimum, and creates a setting which is part of the real world from which the lovers desire release. Of greatest importance, lighting has unified the stage and the action upon it in accordance with the demands of the music. In this way the designer has subordinated his own ego to the needs of the total work. Appia also wanted to separate diffused light (from floods which were fixed) from focused light (from spots which were mobile), the former generalizing and the latter particularizing. Long before its time, he even conceived the idea of projecting scenery by slides. His proposals for staging *Tristan* are extraordinarily advanced, but by great good fortune the accessibility of the new electric light was to make his theories practicable, while the lighting technician Mariano Fortuny was simultaneously developing a way of indirect lighting.

The use of lights in a variety of combinations would eventually become equivalent to the orchestration of musical instruments, and in his book *The Stage Is Set*, Lee Simonson pointed out in 1932 that the complicated business of conducting a lighting rehearsal soon became not unlike conducting an orchestral rehearsal. Appia's ideas were not applied for many years to the opera for which they were intended, but they were applied to all kinds of drama, so that a new profession of 'lighting designer' became necessary, and the 'light plot' with its 'light cues' to match the stage action, became as important as the text itself in controlling the responses of an audience. Appia's great discovery was that the visual design of a play could express its spirit in the way that music could, and lighting for dramatic atmosphere or a character's mood became universal practice. The art of combining visual with musical effects was particularly developed in film-making. If the earlier scene-painter diminished the world to the size of the stage, Appia showed how to expand the stage to become the world.

It nevertheless remains true that combining the arts effectively for the purposes of the stage is not easily achieved. One art tends to dominate another, music smothering the detail of dramatic action, or dramatic action weakening the music to the point where it loses its power of making an efficient musical statement. Sound and light are characteristically imprecise in meaning, and where they deprive a play of particularity, the result can be a loose impression of lyricism, romanticism or fantasy.

The art which was most threatened by Appia's theories was that of the actor, and this threat came at the very time when the actor was reaching new heights in the realistic vein; perhaps as a result the actor has been a divisive force in the development of a modern aesthetic for the theatre. Appia imagined the emergence of 'musical gymnastics' in the art of acting, with music and not words controlling the actor's expression. Indeed, the rhythmic performance of the actor as dancer has made immense gains since the days of the Ballets Russes and Isadora Duncan.

One artist in particular at this time, a countryman of Appia's, advanced the art of the new performer. He was Émile Jaques-Dalcroze (1865–1950). First in Geneva in 1903 and then in Hellerau, near Dresden, in 1911. Dalcroze developed 'rhythmic gymnastics', or 'eurhythmics', as a way of educating a student in music, using the movement of his body like an instrument, on the assumption that rhythm was the physical expression of abstract time and space. It was with Dalcroze that Appia did most of his practical work after 1906, until the school at Hellerau was closed in 1914 by the war.

It was Dalcroze who fertilized Appia's ideas about the use of the human figure in a spatial dimension, and we find that concepts of rhythm and movement increasingly enter his thinking in his third book, *The Work of Living Art*. It was always necessary to set the stage as if for choreography, and, believing that the human body was a mystical representation of 'space in time and time in space', with the two brought together by movement, Appia urged the actor to dis-cover for himself the rhythm in the lines and action of the play in order to unify its spatial and temporal elements. He saw that move-ment was more exciting if it encountered physical obstacles like ramps and stairs, and if it is shown under mobile overhead lighting. His sets for Dalcroze became more constructivist, and in the Jaques-Dalcroze Institute year book *Die Schulfeste* for 1911 he wrote,

> The training through rhythmic gymnastics will make the actor especially sensitive to dimension and distance in space, corresponding to the infinite variety of sound. In voluntarily he will bring these to life on the stage and he will be bewildered by the injustice done to him by putting him, three-dimensional and living, among dead paintings on vertical canvases ... The awakening of rhythm in our-selves, in our organism, in our own flesh, is the death knell for a great part of our contemporary art, particularly the scenic art (translated Edmund Stadler).

Along with this went Appia's ideas for a radical reform of the play-house itself: all the actor needs is a space to move in, and a bare hall is sufficient to house the stage constructions and carry the overhead lighting. This would be Appia's 'cathedral of the future'.

Today there is the Fondation Adolphe Appia at Bern, but Appia had to wait until the International Theatre Exhibition of 1922 in Amsterdam before his work was recognized, although even then it is not possible to say that it was understood. Milan had opened an institute for eurhythmics like the one in Geneva, and in 1923 Arturo Toscanini commissioned him to design at last his *Tristan und Isolde* for La Scala opera house there. The plain, abstract settings were even simpler than those of the 1896 proposals, and they were not well received. They were so bald that the critic Ugo Ojetti wrote of Appia as a Calvinist, and thought the garden in act III looked like a prison yard and its lime-tree seemed to be diseased and dying. Cosima Wagner, who had compared Appia's earlier sketches to those of Nansen at the North Pole, thought his ideas those of a madman. Critics and audience alike expected the stage to be richly decorated in the way grand opera had always been, and even the stage technicians were obstructive. Happily, Toscanini kept the production in the repertoire, although Appia continued to meet with similar opposition for his work on *Das Rheingold* in 1924, *Die Walküre* in 1925 and Aeschylus's *Prometheus* in the Basel Stadttheater. Out of respect for Wagner the composer, Appia explained, he had ignored the wishes of Wagner the producer. Being a pioneer is never easy, and it is especially difficult in a field in which tradition dies hard and which requires the absolute cooperation of so many different people.

4   *Symbolic theatre: Craig and stage design*

The Moscow 'Hamlet' (1912)

The Englishman Edward Gordon Craig (1872–1966), son of the great actress Ellen Terry, was eight years younger than Appia, and by 1899 had produced an experimental *Dido and Aeneas* by Purcell when Appia was still theorizing. Yet it is an extraordinary coincidence that these two innovators should have arrived independently at a common theory of revolutionary proportions. Craig did not meet Appia until 1914. In 1917 he wrote to Appia, 'To me there is far more vivid life and drama in one of your great studies for scenes than in anything else known to me in our theatre of Europe.' Both exhibited their work in Amsterdam in 1922. In comparison with Appia, Craig developed a less rigorous philosophy of the theatre, and Lee Simonson was not alone in finding his theories 'windy' and his talent 'inflated'. Like Appia's, Craig's theatre practice was surprisingly limited: after an eight-year apprenticeship as an actor with Henry Irving, whom he idealized, Craig worked as a designer sporadically in London, Berlin, Florence, Moscow and Copenhagen as he acquired a European reputation. Nevertheless, he exercised enormous influence, particularly through his book *The Art of the Theatre* (1905, expanded in 1911), in which he showed how the theatre could be released from nineteenth-century realism and returned to a poetic drama. He finally settled in Florence, where his periodical *The Mask* provided a forum for his ideas from 1908 to 1929. Writing in this over a variety of signatures, he became the prophet of the new movement.

Like Appia, Craig believed in the need to create a production as a whole, and held therefore that all its parts, including the contribution of the actor, should be subordinated to one man's conception, that of the director. Like Appia, he began where all theorists of the theatre in those days began, by denouncing realism. The actor should not impersonate, but present and interpret, a character; not imitate and reproduce nature like a photographer, but create as an artist. He therefore advocated the 'abolition' of the actor in the traditional sense as being 'the means by which a debased stage realism is produced and flourishes'. For the old concept of the actor, he substituted that of the '*Über-marionette*', the name compounded from German and French. The term was invented to describe a super-puppet, not a large doll, but a creature whose perfect stillness of body and gravity of expression could transform an actor into a giant, a beautiful god, a divine image. This idea derived from the Oriental and Greek theatres, and implied a masked performer working in a ritualistic theatre which had no use for the personality, the 'ego', of the actor. Through the *Über-marionette*, audiences would be promised 'a return to their ancient joy in ceremonies'. The intense discipline in the work of the Japanese *Noh* or the Indian actor seems to have been behind Craig's thinking.

From his love for Italian Renaissance painting, Craig conceived the art of the theatre, therefore, as built of kinetic light and movement, not of words alone: 'A drama is not to be read, but to be seen upon the stage.' Like Appia, he saw drama as composed of all the elements of 'action, words, line, colour, rhythm', each making its appeal to the eyes and the ears. In practice, his approach was quite subjective — after the realist Otto Brahm had studied a Craig design for *Venice Preserved*, he dared to ask, 'Where is the door?', only to receive the answer, 'There is no door; there is a way in and a way out.' Craig worked to reproduce his 'sense' of a play, explaining, 'I let my scenes grow out of not merely the play, but from broad sweeps of thought which the play has conjured up in me.' Thus, the *Hamlet* mood was one of 'a lonely soul in a dark place', and the rugged fjords of Ibsen's *Brand* were to symbolize the moral implacability of the title character.

Like Appia, Craig was at bottom a designer, but not always a practical one. For Craig, the scene was 'an atmosphere, not a locality', and he aimed at the simplicity and severity of vertical lines, which, mixed with shadow, could carry the eye beyond the limits of the stage to make its height and space eloquent. Craig's famous assertion was,

> Remember that on a sheet of paper which is but two inches square you can make a line which seems to tower miles in

4. Sophocles, *Electra*, 1905. Design by Craig.

the air, and you can do the same on your stage, for it is all
a matter of proportion.

The truth of this is questionable, because while a pencil mark is anything you want it to be, the actor's proportions are fixed. When in
1906 Craig designed 30-foot high windows for Ibsen's *Rosmersholm,*
Eleanora Duse is reported to have said that she felt like a stagehand
who had walked on stage by mistake: However, the simple principle
that vertical lines dwarf the actor and horizontal ones enlarge him
has been pursued profitably in the modern theatre ever since.

Craig's notion of the *Über-marionette* was particularly in conflict
with the psychological detail of realistic acting sought by naturalistic
directors like Stanislavsky, yet these two apparent adversaries came
together to produce *Hamlet* at the Moscow Art Theatre (MAT) in
1912. By 1908, Stanislavsky had grown aware that his special skills
in realistic theatre could not answer the demands of a poetic or
symbolic drama, and he bravely invited Europe's leading symbolist
to Moscow. For his part, Craig was looking for any good opportunity
to try out his ideas. But their method of working hardly helped their
relationship. Craig would give his orders and leave Stanislavsky to
carry them out while he went off to Florence to work up some more
ideas. Meanwhile, Stanislavsky naturally and necessarily reduced
Craig's vision to what would work, or what an audience might
accept, or what the talents of his actors could accommodate; and he
soon fell back on the tried psychological methods he knew best. This
process went on for three and a half years with increasing irritation
on both sides.

The production seemed doomed from the start, and the Russian
actors could not satisfy Craig. It seemed that the simple strength he
wanted could be supplied neither by the old declamatory style, nor
by the new realism. In the familiar MAT way, Stanislavsky and his
colleague Nemirovich-Danchenko had researched medieval castles
to make a Gothic setting, but Craig thought quite differently in terms
of abstract shapes to match his mystical thinking. In the event, the
scene was furnished with great moveable screens which could be
placed on the stage in a large variety of positions. These screens
were Craig's notorious invention designed to offer 'a thousand
scenes in one', and they had had a trial with Yeats and Lady Gregory
in the Abbey Theatre, Dublin, in 1910. Craig had wanted no curtain,

and instead called for visible scene-setters who would make the audience conscious of a symbolic performance; however, in Moscow, the screens were so precarious that the curtains had to be drawn every time the set was changed. They had light wooden frames fitted with grey transparent canvas and reversible hinges; they also had a great tendency to topple over. On the first night of the Moscow *Hamlet*, it is said that they fell like dominoes. (Scenic screens have since been better used by the Japanese designer Isamu Noguchi for John Gielgud's *King Lear* in London in 1955.)

Craig visualized his Prince of Denmark as a giant of a man in both body and mind, with leonine hair like a snow-capped mountain —strangely like Craig's own flowing locks. He was to be a truly Shakespearian *Über-marionette*. Craig thought of him as a figure isolated against the gaudy, insincere court, and the first court scene

5. Shakespeare, *Hamlet*. Woodcut by Craig, 1909. Hamlet greeting the Actors.

was to be represented as 'Hamlet's nightmare'. The court itself was to be so many pallid faces seen through holes cut in a huge golden cloth, which was to appear to stream down like the trains of the King and Queen on their high thrones. Stanislavsky could not manage this, but pleased Craig by arranging a golden pyramid of courtiers, with the King at its peak speaking like an automaton. The idea of a monolithic monarch did not work so well for the play scene, where the King was so remote from the audience that it could not see his face, thus defeating the object. The conception behind these devices was that of a 'monodrama' in which the audience was to see only as if with Hamlet's eyes. Stanislavsky argued that realism had to return to the other characters when Hamlet was not on stage, so Craig decided to keep the Prince as a silent presence in scenes in which he was not required. At one time, Craig conceived a 'bright golden figure' as Hamlet's daemon, and at another, he wanted a figure of death to enter to music, so that the play should be understood as a struggle between the material and the spiritual. Trying to cope with the demands of his part, Kachalov, the actor playing Hamlet, naturally found it distracting to be haunted on the stage by an *alter ego* who had no lines, nor any part in the action.

6. Shakespeare, *Hamlet*, 1912. Model of stage setting, design by Craig.

As for the other characters, Craig thought of the King as masked with a large head, a blazing eye and enormous hands like an eagle's talons. Ophelia was to flit across the scene with a pretty face, child-like and stupid: in Craig's view, Hamlet's love was for an imaginary girl, whereas Stanislavsky took the conventional view of her as a sympathetic victim, rightly believing that if Ophelia were played by a fool, it would diminish Hamlet's stature as a man. Stanislavsky wanted the secondary characters played with the realism of every-day detail, whereas Craig wanted them to behave like puppets —he tried to teach them lighter voice tones with the aid of musical instru-ments, and to have them stand as silhouettes with waxen arms and faces. He accordingly sketched their costumes for sculptural and statuesque effect. The Ghost was to appear in ethereal silhouette on a high platform, with Hamlet symbolically below in heavy, earth-bound garments. The Players were to fly in through windows on wires, like Chinese acrobats. The figures of the dumbshow were to be seen as huge shadows thrown on a backdrop. In her mad scene, Ophelia would stand still, playing against the earlier background of the masked court.

7. Shakespeare, *Hamlet*, 1912. Production at the Moscow Art Theatre by Stanislavsky, design by Craig. Final scene.

This legendary production of the new symbolist theatre also had the proverbial mixed reception, although its fame kept it running for more than 400 performances. Those who had come to expect either the new true-to-life psychological realism of the MAT, or the traditional declamatory brooding of the nineteenth-century's gloomy Dane, were disappointed. Most of the complaints were at the expense of the design, in which Craig's endless screens appeared to stifle the play. More perceptively, some saw that the abstract setting was out of key with the traditional acting. But theatre people had their eyes truly opened, and were genuinely impressed by what the new stagecraft could do. Craig's name conjured up dreams of a visionary theatre for years to come, and his suggestion for the manipulation of time and space on the stage slowly took hold. If no major dramatist sprang up to meet the challenge, many twentieth-century plays could not have been conceived without the possibilities of Craig's new principles of design.

5   *Symbolist drama: Ibsen to Maeterlinck and Lugné-Poe*

Hedda Gabler (1890), *Pelléas and Mélisande* (1893)

Before the end of the century, both the advocates of naturalism and of symbolism were claiming Ibsen as master, and taking up hardened positions in opposition to each other. The naturalists regarded the symbolists as romantic and decadent, and the symbolists scorned the naturalists as political and materialistic. Freudian psychology curiously provided support for both sides, the laying bare of character and the influences upon it urging a realistic treatment, and the validity of dreams justifying a symbolic representation. Yet Ibsen had used symbolism at least as early as *Brand* (1866), and his mature plays drew indivisibly upon both conventions. A glance at *The Wild Duck* (1884), *Rosmersholm* (1886), *The Lady from the Sea* (1888) and *Hedda Gabler* (1890) shows, not a simple transition from social realism to symbolic vision, but an increasing depth and complexity stemming from their mutual enrichment.

In a letter of 2 September 1884, Ibsen wrote that his new play, *The Wild Duck*, represented a departure from his earlier way of writing, and a new direction for playwrights to follow. He was undoubtedly referring to the calculated infusion of symbolic elements into the play. He was concerned that the lighting should match the darkening mood of each act; major characters, for all the realistic variety of semi-comic detail in their make-up, stand almost diagrammatically opposed to each other in attitude; although still based in realism, the scene is provocatively set with symbolic items like Hjalmar's photographic apparatus and the mysterious attic door; the dialogue contains oblique suggestions about sight and blindness, and how to save the wild duck, all of which aim to underscore the play's theme of getting at the truth; but binding the play together is the wild duck itself, an elusive symbol of guilt and one of wide application —it almost has a symbolic life of its own. It in not surprising that contemporary audiences were baffled by the play's dialectical element, and found its symbols intrusive. In Paris, the audience at the first production made its feelings known by quacking like ducks.

The plays which followed increasingly cover Ibsen's realistic surface with symbolic suggestion, increasingly probe irrational states of mind, and seek to articulate psychic phenomena to the point of straining the limits of realistic theatre. *The Lady from the Sea* even includes an unnamed character of unaccountably supernatural qualities, 'The Stranger', intended to personify the sea and embody Ellida's desire for spiritual freedom. Purely symbolic characters, 'dream' characters, will appear in Ibsen again, like Hilde of *The Master Builder* (1892), who is chiefly a figment of the wishful imagination of the title character.

Hedda Gabler is a study of how a predatory woman and others in the play feed on each other to promote a self-image. In this play symbolic elements proliferate: the season of the year; the portrait of General Gabler; his pistols, which symbolize Hedda's yearning to have a man's freedom and to escape from her domestic prison, together with what they suggest of her destructiveness, matching her 'steel-grey' eyes; Lövborg's manuscript, representing a life's achievement, a legacy to time, like a child; Thea's fair hair to accompany her weak face, and Hedda's jealousy of it; the stove on the stage, linking

the manuscript and the hair, both of which Hedda has the impulse
to burn; the vine-leaves of Hedda's romantic imagining, and her idea
of a beautiful death. All these symbols are wonderfully integrated
with the most intricate character studies Ibsen had yet achieved, and
we are lucky to have the extensive notes he made in preparation for
writing his first draft. He noted, for example, Hedda's fear of scandal
mixed with her passionate desire to shock, and her demoniacal urge
to influence a man, countered by her contempt for him after her success; the double nature of Lövborg, in love with Thea but at the same
time driven beyond all limits by his desire for Hedda; and more.
Ibsen claimed that he created his characters only after long daily
association with them.

   Yet the luminous presence of symbolic suggestion in this and
the last plays insists that Ibsen's work had moved decisively towards
a poetic drama: the white horses of *Rosmersholm*, the climbing of
towers in *The Master Builder*, the crutch in *Little Eyolf* (1894), Rubek's
statue in *When We Dead Awaken* (1899) are inescapable. His plays
became 'extended metaphors' indeed. However, when a translation
of *The Master Builder* was circulated round the theatre managers in
London, they found it simply unintelligible, and everywhere audiences at the first productions of the later plays found them impenetrable.
The author himself tended to disclaim a symbolic intention, believing that his critics sought it where it did not exist —life was full of
symbols, he said, and so therefore were his plays. While Maeterlinck
declared that *The Master Builder* was the first masterpiece of the
new movement, and Ibsen's work was claimed for poetry by virtue
of its symbolic content, Ibsen himself particularly detested
Maeterlinck's brazenly overt symbolism. In *Ibsen —a dissenting view*
(1977), Ronald Gray has recently ventured to question whether Ibsen
successfully married realism and symbolism, finding the symbols of
the later plays to be 'useless additions, attempts at giving greater
portentousness, distractions from the human relations with which
he seems to be concerned'. But in the 1890s the symbolist movement
in the theatre was growing vigorously, and Ibsen was greeted as the
leader, particularly in France, even though the keen new directors
scarcely found his more verbal and less visual style much of an
invitation to develop their techniques.

   In English productions, the technical problem for Elizabeth

Robins and Marion Lea, who decided to produce *Hedda Gabler* themselves, turned chiefly on how to speak the lines of the unplayable
translations put in their hands. In Europe, the problem which faced
the symbolist director was how to convey the irrational. Ibsen was
played as if his characters were not quite real people, their speeches
recited slowly and their movements barely perceptible. When
Meyerhold directed *Hedda Gabler* at the Kommissarzhevskaya
Theatre in Moscow in 1906, he pursued the symbolist principle of
suiting colour to character and mood. Marc Slonim described the
set in his *Russian Theatre from the Empire to the Soviets*:

> The stage seemed filled with bluish-green-silver mist. The
> background was blue. On the right side, a huge transom,
> the whole height of the stage, represented a window. Under-
> neath stuck out the leaves of a black rhododendron. Outside
> the window, the air was greenish-blue. In the last act, the
> twinkling of stars pierced the bluish mist. On the left, the
> whole wall was occupied by a huge tapestry representing a
> silvery gold woman with a deer. Silver lace decorated the
> top and the wings of the stage. Greenish-blue carpet covered
> the floor. The furniture, including a grand piano, was white.
> Green-white vases held large white chrysanthemums. White
> furs were thrown over a strangely shaped sofa, on which
> Hedda reclined — in a sea-watery green dress. It shimmered
> and flowed at her every movement, and she resembled a
> sea serpent with shiny scales (pp. 196–7).

Michael Meyer has pointed out, however, that symbolism in drama
is often more effective if played with the simplest realism.

Partly in reaction after the spiritual depression following
the Franco-Prussian War, Paris became the centre of the movement
for symbolist drama, as it was for symbolist poetry. Théodore de
Banville was among the first to reject realistic theatre by turning to
classical myth, which he dramatized in a lyrical mode. While
Stéphane Mallarmé became the spokesman for the new movement,
his friend Villiers de L'Isle-Adam (1838–89) was among the first
to achieve a dramatic embodiment of spiritual values in his
Wagnerian play *Axël*, written over a period of twenty years, but not
produced until 1894 after his death. The romantic hero of the title

lives a life of solitude in a castle in the Black Forest, and when the finds love in the arms of the lovely but mysterious Sara, they immortalize their union in death, like Tristan and Isolde. Villiers's mysticism was vastly admired by Yeats in Ireland and Maeterlinck in Belgium.

Maurice Maeterlinck (1862–1949) similarly plunged his plays into mystery by his vaguely medieval subjects and his heavily allegorical way of writing. He was among those, like Gordon Craig, who thought that the contemporary style of acting was too realistic for poetic drama: symbolism was at odds with the merely human. He believed that the Greeks dressed their actors in masks to rid them of the domination of the senses and the limitation of living in time present.

Maeterlinck's way of evoking a mystical experience and a subconscious mood in dramatic form is partly explained by his theory of a 'static' theatre. In his essay 'Le Tragique quotidien' ('Everyday Tragedy') from *Le Trésor des humbles* (*The Treasure of the Humble*, 1896), he declared that the poet's task was to reveal the mysterious and invisible qualities of life, its grandeur and its misery, which have nothing to do with realism. If we stay on a realistic level, we remain ignorant of the eternal world, and therefore of the true meaning of existence and destiny, of life and death. The poet must deal with what is unseen, superhuman and infinite. Maeterlinck pointed to the tragedies of Aeschylus as examples of a drama in which there is no movement, no event, only 'psychological action'. By such arguments, symbolist drama widened to embrace all theatrical manifestations of dream and fantasy: after all, weren't dreams the stuff of which theatre is made?

In practice, Maeterlinck's early plays were laden with a sense of doom. His has been called a drama of silences, composed of bloodless, shadowy characters, an immobile scene, a disconnected, allusive and repetitive prose dialogue broken by long pauses, and smothered in symbols which turned up in everything from forests to footsteps. His three well-known one-act 'puppet' plays, *L'Intruse* (*The Intruder*), *Les Aveugles* (*The Blind*, both 1890) and *L'Intérieur* (*Interior*, 1894), were heavy with fear and death.

The scene for *Les Aveugles*, for example, is an island, and there we are to see 'a very ancient forest, eternal of aspect, beneath a sky profoundly starred'. On the stage sit six blind old men and, facing them, six blind women, one with a child. The child can see, but it cannot speak. All are waiting, not unlike the characters in Samuel Beckett's *Waiting for Godot*, for some godly person to come and be their guide. Unhappily, the priest they wait for is there among them already, although he is dead:

> His head and the upper part of his body, slightly thrown
> back and mortally still, are leaning against the bole of an
> oak tree, huge and cavernous. His face is fearfully pale and
> of an inalterable waxen lividity; his violet lips are parted.
> His eyes, dumb and fixed, no longer gaze at the visible side
> of eternity, and seem bleeding beneath a multitude of im-
> memorial sorrows and of tears ... (translated Laurence
> Alma Tadema).

So they sit, wrapped in the shadows of 'great funereal trees, yews, weeping willows, cypresses'.

> FIRST BLIND MAN. Is he not coming yet?
> SECOND BLIND MAN. You have waked me!
> FIRST BLIND MAN. I was asleep too.
> THIRD BLIND MAN. I was asleep too.
> FIRST BLIND MAN. Is he not coming yet?
> SECOND BLIND MAN. I hear nothing coming.
> THIRD BLIND MAN. It must be about time to go back to the
> asylum.

The tone of Beckett's play may be more witty, but the point may not be too different. Have some of Maeterlinck's ideas been fully real- ized only recently in the work of Artaud and Beckett, or in surrealis- tic films like Alain Resnais's haunting *Last Year in Marienbad* (1961)?

Maeterlinck resorted to an indeterminate medieval world of dream and fantasy to achieve the distance from reality he wanted, and *Pelléas et Mélisande* (1893) is typical of his next series of obscurely metaphysical tragedies designed to express the inexpressible. In a forest near a castle, Mélisande is a young and beautiful girl dis- covered crying by a spring. She has been tricked into marriage by the older of two brothers, Golaud. When the younger brother, Pelléas, is brushed by her long hair as she combs it at a window, he caresses it and falls in love with her. The tragic consequence is that Pelléas is slain by Golaud — in joy and defiance of death, the lovers had kissed each other distractedly by the spring as Golaud rushed upon them. Mélisande dies of a broken heart. It is now embarrassing to read the lines of this ineffable and slightly immoral tale, for what was once judged immortal now seems hollow, and only Debussy's music for the operatic version of 1902 survives. It is hard to believe from the evidence of this play that Maeterlinck in his time influenced writers as profound as Strindberg (*Easter, Swanwhite*) and Synge (*Riders to the Sea*).

Maeterlinck suffered in part the fate of the irresponsible element in the symbolist movement, and his popularity as its leader was short-lived. Any success he had was essentially dependent upon the invention of a wholly different style of production from that of realism. In Paris, both Ibsen and Maeterlinck owed a great deal to the support of the symbolist actor and director Aurélien-Marie Lugné-Poe (1869–1940). Lugné lectured urgently in their cause, and produced *L'Intruse* and *Les Aveugles* in the Théâtre d'Art in 1891. This theatre had been founded in Montparnasse in 1890 by the symbolist poet and director Paul Fort as an answer to Antoine's realism, and to provide a house for Maeterlinck and other symbolist playwrights. When it closed in 1893, Lugné took it over to try out new ways of poetic production. In this way he founded his successful company of the Théâtre de l'Oeuvre, opening with *Pelléas et Mélisande* and *Rosmersholm*, in which Lugné himself played Golaud and Rosmer. This company continued to bring to Paris a truly cosmopolitan avant-garde drama, which included Strindberg's *The Father* and *Creditors*, and Oscar Wilde's French *Salomé*, until its demise in 1929.

The production of *Pelléas et Mélisande* was given one matinee performance at the Théâtre des Bouffes-Parisiens. Lugné found that the play fell into eighteen tableaux, and planned each as a decorated picture. He designed the costumes to evoke the middle ages, and the painter Paul Vogler painted the scenery like a dream world — a vast, archaic hall, a thick forest, a backdrop like an ancient tapestry. Under Lugné's lighting, time and place seemed indefinite, and Maeterlinck's emphasis on nature, dusk and night, the moon and the wind, added powerfully to the atmosphere. The actors appeared as phantoms in the moonlight, their characters generalized and embodying abstract concepts, their gestures simplified to the slow movement of hands and arms to lend special weight to each line, and their speech half chanted and touched with

8. Maeterlinck, *Pelléas et Mélisande*, 1893. Production at the Vaudeville Theatre, London, with Mrs Patrick Campbell and Sarah Bernhardt, 1904.

hesitations and repetitions. The result was impressive — unlike anything seen on the stage before —and the critics swung between rapture and sarcasm. Lugné-Poe had created an historic moment for modern drama. Unfortunately, little pictorial record of his work remains.

The London production of *Pelléas et Mélisande* was at the Vaudeville in 1904. The cast was altogether distinguished, as befitted a great new poet, with Mrs Patrick Campbell as Mélisande, supported by the Shakespearians Martin Harvey and Forbes-Robertson. The costumes were said to have been 'inspired' by the Pre-Raphaelite painter Burne-Jones, who had re-created the dream world of the so-called 'Golden Age' on his luscious canvases.

Maeterlinck's story teaches a painful lesson. His incantatory, half-articulate dialogue was early recognized for its musical qualities, and in 1905, well before he had heard Debussy's arrangement of *Pelléas et Mélisande*, the music critic Ernest Newman pointed out that a passage in *Joyzelle* (1903) 'reads almost exactly like a libretto without its music':

> JOYZELLE. Je t'embrassais la nuit, quand j'embrassais mes
> rêves...
>
> (I used to embrace you at night when I
> embraced my dreams)
> LANCÉOR. Je n'ai pas eu de doute...
> (I knew no doubt)
> JOYZELLE. Je n'ai pas eu de crainte...
> (I knew no fear)
> LANCÉOR. Et tout m'est accordé...
> (And everything is granted me)
> JOYZELLE. Et tout me rend heureuse!...
> (And everything makes me happy!)

Newman went on to argue that Maeterlinck's verbal cloudiness needed to be set to music before it could convey its full meaning, and believed that it was the opera-libretto element in Maeterlinck's plays that accounted for 'many of those curious scenes in which the characters keep on reiterating apparently insignificant words, to the intense annoyance of the man in the street, who cannot see the meaning of it at all'. Newman prophesied correctly, for

Maeterlinck has appealed to many composers of widely different persuasions, among them Debussy, Fauré, Schönberg and Sibelius, and, if anywhere, his plays live today only in the work of those composers who went imaginatively beyond him. The Debussy is occasionally revived, and proves that music is a better vehicle for some kinds of symbolism than drama.

After the excitement generated by the early symbolists had waned, and Lugné-Poe had broken with them in 1899, he was responsible for making known the religious plays of the French diplomat Paul Claudel (1868–1955), who, like his director, was a friend and disciple of Mallarmé and influenced by Rimbaud. The Théâtre de l'Oeuvre made Claudel's name with *L'Otage* (*The Hostage*, 1911) and especially *L'Annonce faite à Marie* (*The Tidings Brought to Mary*, 1912), done after the style of a medieval mystery. The auto-biographical *Partage de midi* (*Break of Noon*) was first published in 1906, and then rewritten for Jean-Louis Barrault's production of 1948. *Le Soulier de satin* (*The Satin Slipper*), a vast play of the Spanish Renaissance, was written between 1919 and 1924, but had to wait for Barrault's production at the Comédie-Française in 1943. These revivals should tell us something about continuity in French symbolist production. All of Claudel's plays dramatize his Catholic faith, and repeat in a variety of ways the theme of human love transformed into the spiritual and divine; to that extent they have had only limited sectarian appeal outside France. Their style and tone is symbolist, lyrical and ritualistic, with little action and much poetry. They introduce music, which, according to Claudel's 1930 lecture 'Le Drame et la musique', is intended to touch off the poetic speech by counterpoint, as in the *Kabuki* theatre, rather than swallow the performer, as in Wagner. The symbolist directors in France and America also found that the cosmic quality in Claudel's themes lent itself to spectacular staging.

Moscow also tried to find a style for symbolism in the early years of the twentieth century. The mystical and spiritual mood, however, called for a wholly different approach to production which left the realists in the MAT at a loss. Stanislavsky, who had produced Maeterlinck's one-act plays in 1904 none too successfully, was exercised by the difficulty of creating detailed characterization in a play based only on abstractions – it went against his whole training and sense of theatre. Yet he was attracted to the idea of simplification, stylizing and impressionism on the stage, and he generously left it to Meyerhold at the Povarskaya Street Theatre-Studio, an offshoot of the MAT, to work out an appropriate stage technique for the new symbolist drama.

Meyerhold has described his anti-realistic experiments during the 1905 rehearsals for Maeterlinck's *La Mort de Tintagiles* (*The Death of Tintagiles*, 1894) for the Theatre-Studio. As it happened, the production was another doubtful success, and never shown to the public; it was also one cause of the break between the two great directors. Following Wagner, Meyerhold argued that for such a play, designer and composer must be in especially close accord with the director, and all three responsive to the mood of the play. He aimed to achieve a harmony of spiritual feeling and a quiet grandeur by majestic, statuesque acting and a calm, cold mode of speech free from tremolo or emotional tension. The lines would be spoken to music, and the voices would be distinct and pure in sound to create the 'inner thrill' of a 'mystic tremor'. The play was to be performed against a simple canvas background with a few ornamental flats, in order to emphasize the actors' iconographic gestures in the manner of a fresco. All movement and gesture were to be stylized, made up of poses and glances — Meyerhold described this kind of acting as 'plastic'. The result appears to have been the strangely abstracted style typical of symbolist productions, and the opposite of everything the realistic theatre stood for. Unfortunately, Meyerhold's solution did not solve the problem facing the live actor who was merely absorbed into the pattern, and felt unable to contribute anything of his own.

What may we conclude about this initial phase of symbolist theatre? Maeterlinck's first play, *La Princesse Maleine* (1889) had been greeted by the playwright Octave Mirbeau with an enthusiastic review in *Le Figaro* of 24 August 1890, in which he declared the play to be 'the greatest work of genius of our time . . . comparable, and — shall I dare say it? — superior in beauty to whatever is most beautiful in Shakespeare'. But Maeterlinck's limitations as a vapid poet and a sterile philosopher were soon apparent. New plays continued to proliferate from his pen, but they always returned to the same elusive, fragmentary notions of life and death, and others of the eternal verities which swam into view. Every summer, Maeterlinck would retire to the Abbaye of Saint Wandrille, a glorious old place of cloisters and ruins, chapels and vaults, just the spot where the poet might imagine his medieval ladies passing their time. Needless to say, they were soon no longer acceptable on the increasingly cynical stages of the twentieth century.

6 *Symbolist drama after Maeterlinck*

Salomé (1896), *The Life of Man* (1907)

The influence of French symbolist drama spread quickly. In England, Oscar Wilde (1854–1900) considered his florid *Salomé*, first published in French in 1893 and produced in Paris in 1896, to be his most important play. In his two quasi-Platonic dialogues of 1891 given the title "The Critic as Artist', Wilde had set out the rarefied aesthetic he had acquired from John Ruskin and Walter Pater. 'The world is made by the singer for the dreamer', he declared:

> When one looks back upon the life that was so vivid in its emotional intensity, and filled with such fervent moments of ecstasy or of joy, it all seems to be a dream and an illusion.

The idea that to be a dreamer was tantamount to saying the writer was irresponsible did not enter his mind:

> Yes: I am a dreamer. For a dreamer is one who can only find his way by moonlight, and his punishment is that he sees the dawn before the rest of the world.

Literature was the perfect expression of life, and emotion for the sake of emotion was the aim of art. So it was that Wilde reached his dangerous conclusion, that 'All art is immoral.' This kind of thinking was a long way from Wagner's, but it had nothing to do with the unhappy story of the play's production in Britain.

Salomé is the tale of the eighteen-year-old princess of Judea, beautiful and sensual. This was a mixture which had made her story appeal to a number of French symbolists, helping to earn them the name 'decadents'. Salomé desires the prophet Jokanaan, who spurns her love. When her stepfather King Herod wishes her to dance for him, she agrees to do so only if in return he will give her the prophet's head on a platter. The climax of the play is therefore her dance of death and lust, but when she has kissed the dead lips, Herod in loathing has her executed immediately by his guards, who crush her to death under their shields. So exotic and erotic a play could hardly fail to catch the attention of the rest of Europe.

Wilde was living in Paris after 1891, and he wrote the play in simple French (which its detractors consider to be 'phrase-book' French) as a gesture of admiration for French culture. The play has been compared with a beautiful fresco, in its repetitions and generally static quality done after the manner of Maeterlinck. Its symbolist character further emerged in the initial discussions about its décor. Graham Robertson suggested that every costume should be in a different shade of yellow, 'from clearest lemon to deep orange', all to be set against 'a great empty sky of deepest violet'. Wilde imagined the play to be one of odours, and wanted braziers of perfume to stand in the orchestra pit: 'Think: the scented clouds rising and partly veiling the stage from time to time ... a new perfume for each emotion'. Charles Ricketts, the 1906 designer, proposed a black floor upon which Salomé's feet would move 'like white doves', and the sky should be a rich turquoise blue, with gilded strips of Japanese matting hanging high over terraces on the stage and suggesting an aerial tent. Herod and Herodias would be dressed in blood-red, and Salomé in gold or silver. Wilde, however, wanted her in green, 'like a poisonous lizard', and Sarah Bernhardt, who was to have played the first Salomé, wanted her hair to be powdered blue. When the final decision was made, Bernhardt, with characteristic economy, said she would have to use the old costumes from an earlier production, *Cléopâtre*. So much for 'syn-aesthesia' and the symbolist requirement of matching up character, mood and colour.

The play did not really need more decoration. It already bore the symbolist stamp richly enough. The leit-motifs of colour and symbol were vivid in the white moon and red blood, and the play was built up musically with incantatory repetitions, paralysing silences and alternating shouts and whispers. Moreover, *Salomé*'s strongest moments on the stage were powerfully ritualistic, as when the strong black arm of the King's executioner rises slowly from the cistern, lifting Jokanaan's head on its silver platter, or when

9. Wilde, *Salomé*, 1894. Drawing by Aubrey Beardsley: 'The Climax'.

the King's guards rush down upon Salomé and crush her beneath their shields.

Wilde was, of course, delighted when Sarah Bernhardt agreed to play the lead in the first production, planned for the Palace Theatre, London, in 1892. The play was in full rehearsal when the Lord Chamberlain, then Britain's authority for stage censorship, invoked the law which had suppressed the medieval mystery plays three hundred years before, that Biblical characters must not be represented on the public stage. If this judgment contributed to the questionable reputation of the author and his play, it also contributed to its success everywhere in Europe. Lugné-Poe was the first to take advantage of the play's availability, and presented it at the Théâtre de l'Oeuvre in 1896, with Lina Muntz as the first Salomé and himself as Herod. This occurred when Wilde was in prison in Reading, and he never saw a production. The play was produced in Germany in 1901, and had many subsequent productions there, including one by Max Reinhardt in his Kleines Theater in Berlin. London had a first, private production given by the New Stage Club in 1905, with Millicent Murby as Salomé and Robert Farquharson as Herod. That year New York also saw it in a public production, although the papers responded with very guarded notices; 'decadent stuff' was the pronouncement of the *Tribune*. In 1905 also, Richard Strauss wrote his opera after the play. Back in England, the Independent Theatre manager who did so much to promote Ibsen, J. T. Grein, in 1918 risked his savings in a lawsuit in which he tried to defend the play, and lost. The censor finally gave way in 1927 in the face of increasing criticism of his office and a defiant production by Terence Gray at his Festival Theatre, Cambridge. *Salomé* had its first public performance in London at the Gate Theatre in 1929, thirty years after the death of its author.

Oscar Wilde is now best known for one of the best Victorian farces, *The Importance of Being Earnest* (1895). In 1891 he had written, 'In every sphere of life Form is the beginning of things. The rhythmic harmonious gestures of dancing convey, Plato tells us, both rhythm and harmony into the mind.' We see nowadays that even farce has musical form, and that even *The Importance* is operatic — at least to judge from George Alexander's promptbook for its first production at the St James's Theatre, in which he

arranged the stage to emphasize the play's duets, trios, quartets, sep-
tets and arias. And when W. H. Auden reviewed Wilde's *Letters* in
The New Yorker for March 1963, he claimed that this play was 'the
only pure verbal opera in English'. It represented, he said, 'a
verbal universe in which the characters are determined by the kinds
of things they say, and the plot is nothing but a succession of
opportunities to say them'. Which might be one definition of a
symbolist drama.

In Germany, Gerhart Hauptmann (1862–1946), who had
begun by writing powerful plays of social criticsm in the naturalistic
vein like *Die Weber* (*The Weavers*, 1892), used his compassion for
the poor and oppressed to bring fire to an evocative symbolist drama
which reached a wider audience. Echoing Maeterlinck, the romantic fantasies *Hanneles Himmelfahrt* (*The Assumption of
Hannele*, 1893, *Die versunkene Glocke* (*The Sunken Bell*, 1896) and
Und Pippa tanzt (*And Pippa Dances*, 1906) include visionary scenes in
lyrical verse which are quite the opposite of objective reporting, but
which draw freely upon the new symbolism to express their author's
discontent.

Hannele, for example, is a 'dream poem' taken from Hans

10. Hauptmann, *The Assumption of Hannele*, 1893. Production at
Dresden, 1894.

Andersen's story of the little match girl. It is set vividly in a village workhouse in winter. Hannele is a girl of fourteen who has tried to drown herself to escape her drunken stepfather. In her fever she suffers hallucinations, and these provide Hauptmann with his cue to shift from prose to verse. She sees her dead father and mother, and, like a wish-fulfilment, has a vision of her own death as a saint. The vision mixes Christian images with those of the fairy tales she knows, and a figure of a man who is half fairy prince and half Jesus Christ, punishes her stepfather and prepares her for heaven. The sentimentality of this play is not made less melodramatic by its grim setting. The symbolism in *The Sunken Bell*, a 'fairy tale' in verse, grows more elusive still, and *Pippa*, which tells of a beautiful Italian girl whose dancing incites a destructive desire in all who watch her, moves from realism to wild fantasy. Both of these plays develop the simple pattern of a dream in which the symbolism means what one chooses it to mean.

In Russia, Leonid Andreyev (1871–1919) was influenced enough by Maeterlinck to write *The Life of Man* (1907). This is thought to have been the first symbolist play in Russian, and it brought Andreyev immediate recognition. Nameless characters move on his stage, including the ominous 'Someone in Gray', a divine figure of fate. The play is a series of scenes depicting man's sorry progress from birth to death, and Someone in Gray remains on stage throughout the performance, holding a lighted candle that slowly burns away.

The Life of Man is important because it represents the Moscow Art Theatre's first attempt at the new style of production. In his autobiography, Konstantin Stanislavsky admits that it was out of character for the MAT to put on this kind of play when they had made their name as the most realistic company in Europe, and although the production was successful, he did not consider that they had reached their goal of 'entrance into the spheres of the abstract'. Stanislavsky tells how he had intended a setting of black velvet for Maeterlinck's *The Blue Bird*, but it turned out to be right for *The Life of Man*. The velvet killed the three-dimensional quality of the stage by absorbing all rays of light. This had the effect of introducing the presence of death to the stage and suiting the pessimism of Andreyev's 'gloomy genius'. Against this background,

Someone in Gray seemed even more ghostly, and the life of man was given the appearance of 'accidentality, ghostliness and evanescence'. The scenery was made out of ropes, which marked the contours of the room, its windows and doors, tables and chairs, as if the stage were a piece of black paper with the scenery drawn on it with white lines, which lent the scene 'a fearsome and endless depth'. The characters, who wore costumes of black velvet outlined with white lines, represented only 'schemes for people'; their voices did not sound as if they were alive, but as if they were recorded; and their black clothing against a black ground enabled them to appear suddenly on the forestage, and to disappear as quickly into 'endless space'.

In the best symbolist manner, the stage changed its colour and mood from scene to scene. The white of scene 1 changed to rose for the youth and wedded happiness of scene 2; as Man grew affluent in scene 3, so the tone of the setting became golden. Lifeless dancers spinning to a ghostly orchestra, against a foreground of 'deformities' of old men and women, brought in the despair of scene 4, when the couple lost their child. The last scene, in which Man meets a drunken death, was 'a continuous nightmare', according to Stanislavsky:

> Black figures in long cloaks, like rats with tails, crawling across the floor, their cronelike whispering, coughing and grumbling create horror and fearful premonition. . . At the moment of the death of Man, a multitude of tremendous human figures that reach the ceiling grow from nowhere, there is a bacchanale of flying and creeping deformities, which symbolizes the death agony . . . Only in the bottomless and endless darkness there again grows the tremendous figure of Someone in Gray, which pronounces in a fateful, steely and unescapable voice, once and forever, the death sentence of all humanity (translated J. J. Robbins).

All this first brought Andreyev an accusation of blasphemy from the Russian Church, and, later, a charge of bourgeois thinking from the Soviet government.

In Austria, Hugo von Hofmannsthal (1874—1929) turned from writing lyric poetry to symbolist playwriting. Because his

intention was to fuse words with music in order to create a
symbolist ideal of drama as a private vision, he called his first
one-act plays *'lyrische Dramen'*, 'lyrical plays', and it is not
surprising that his lyrical talents eventually resulted in a series
of libretti for Richard Strauss's operas, of which the best known is
Der Rosenkavalier (1911).

Hofmannsthal wrote often of the symbolist's aims. In an early
essay on 'Poetry and Life' (1896), he explained that the poet
tries to evoke 'a state of soul', and in 'The Stage as Dream Image'
(1903), he developed the idea that both life and the stage shared a
dreamlike quality. Dreams themselves displayed a dramatic
economy which could be of service to the stage. He believed that
only on the stage, in art, could one find 'truth': 'all other things are
parables and reflections in a mirror'. In his prologue to Sophocles's
Antigone, Hofmannsthal embodied a 'Spirit of Tragedy'. As she steps
from the palace door and slowly descends the steps wearing a flowing robe surrounded by a milky, shimmering light, she is addressed
by a Student, who speaks of the theatre as an extension of life:

> Phantom is what you are,
> hatched by this unaccountable place, by this
> uncertain light, by these deceptive walls,
> the legions of the dreams which nest in it. . .

To which she replies,

>   I infuse
> each heart with solitude as in a desert,
> I make time stop, all agitation cease.
> What happens here is not within time's power.
>   (translated Christopher Middleton)

Here also lies the symbolist's desire for impersonality in the arts,
which troubled Hofmannsthal until he could reconcile it with
what was valid in the human personality. But he decided that
Shakespeare and Molière and Calderón had all reconciled art and
dream with reality, and in 1918 he worked on the problem of this
dualism as expressed in Calderón's masterpiece, *Life Is a Dream*.
This he eventually turned into a play of his own, *Der Turm* (*The
Tower*, in two versions, 1925 and 1927).

Hofmannsthal followed Maeterlinck in creating a mystic theatre of forests and castles. He borrowed repeatedly from Greek myth (Oedipus, Electra, Alcestis), transforming its subjects into dramatic images of his own psyche. And his development as a playwright owes much to his association with his fellow-country-man, the director Max Reinhardt, who had the skill to exploit Hofmannsthal's visionary qualities. Together they founded the Salzburg Festival in 1920, which opened with Hofmannsthal's highly original modernization of the medieval morality play *Jedermann* (*Everyman*, 1911), and in Reinhardt's hands became a huge outdoor pageant set in Salzburg's cathedral square. The two repeated their success in 1922 with another adaptation from Calderón, *Das grosse Salzburger Welttheater* (*The Salzburg Great Theatre of the World*). Reinhardt's work will be more appropriately discussed in volume 3.

In the 1890s, August Strindberg (1849—1912) was also in Paris, searching for ways to expand his naturalistic conception of drama to reveal the reality beneath surface appearances. He found a new stimulus in French symbolist thinking. Drawing also on the ideas of the Swedish philosopher Swedenborg, and the musical theories of Wagner, Strindberg began to conceive plays as fantasies inducing hypnotic emotion, structured no longer as well-made plays, but by the laws of musical form. 'Dream play' was the name he gave his first attempts of this sort, the trilogy *To Damascus* (1897—1904) and *A Dream Play* (1902), because with their operatic rhythms and symbolic suggestion, they expressed the inner states of the soul and the activities of the subconscious mind. In the hands of the artist, these subjects could expand to become the troubles of mankind as a whole. They could represent, Strindberg said in his celebrated preface to *A Dream Play*, 'the disconnected but apparently logical form of a dream', in which 'time and space do not exist', and where 'everything is possible and probable'.

Strindberg also came to know something of Maeterlinck's static drama, with its freedom from 'the violence of anecdote'. In a letter of April 1901, Strindberg wrote without hesitation, 'If you want to understand my future work properly, please read Maeterlinck's *Le Trésor des humbles*, one of the greatest books I have ever read.' Maeterlinck's manner of symbolism is especially felt in

Strindberg's tender morality play *Easter* (1901), in which the saintly
sixteen-year-old Eleanora is a childlike visionary who symbolizes
the desire of the human spirit to bring happiness to others.
Strindberg's interest in occult religion is felt in this play as the
action progresses formally through the, Christian calendar from
Maundy Thursday to Good Friday, and finally to Easter Eve and the
Resurrection. His musical ideas are reflected in the play's three acts,
each of which captures a specific mood by opening with an appropriate passage from Haydn's *The Seven Words of the Redeemer*. *Swanwhite*
(written in 1902 and produced in 1908), for which Sibelius wrote
the music, is a folk-tale whose wicked king and queen are changed
from evil to good by the purity of Swanwhite's love for a handsome
prince; it is set in a medieval castle after the style of Maeterlinck.
Maeterlinck's influence is also felt in the religious folk fantasy, *The
Crown-Bride* (published 1904, produced 1906). Of this play Strindberg
wrote in a letter of February 1901 that it was 'an attempt on my part
to penetrate into Maeterlinck's wonderful realm of beauty, omitting
analyses, questions and viewpoints, seeking only beauty in depiction
and mood'. It is remarkable what a large number of first-rate
plays were touched off by a second-rate playwright.

Strindberg returned to the subjectivity of the dream plays in
1907, when he began to write his five *Kammarspel* ('chamber
plays') for his Intima Teatern ('Intimate Theatre'), which he formed
in Stockholm with the actor and director August Falck. These plays,
with their musical form and their neglect of realistic plot and character, are clearly indebted to symbolist theory. They are dream
fantasies which explore the abiding theme of appearances and reality. The best known of them, *The Ghost Sonata* (1907), together with
A Dream Play, were to be of immeasurable importance, not only for
the development of symbolism and surrealism in the 1920s, both
of which looked back gratefully to Strindberg, but also for another
offshoot from Strindberg's extraordinary *oeuvre*, expressionism. The
case is that Strindberg's dream plays and chamber plays, claimed
for their own by symbolist and expressionist alike, are a point of
division in the modern theatre, and Strindberg's work itself is a great
watershed. These plays will contribute to the beginning of another
major development in modern drama, that of expressionism, and to
the third volume of this book.

7   Jarry, precursor of surrealism in France

Ubu roi (1896)

One kind of theatrical symbolism in France took off in an irrational, irreverent direction from the start, as if subversion was implicit in the original symbolist formula. Just as some symbolist poetry had struck a note of illogic and the bizarre with acrobatic imagery and *non sequiturs* of thought and feeling, the non-realistic stage constituted an open invitation to transform reality into dream and nightmare and projections of violent satire. At the age of twenty-three, Alfred Jarry (1873–1907) found a way of breaking completely with both earth-bound realism and the romantic self-conceit of some of the symbolists.

Lugné-Poe, whose Théâtre de l'Oeuvre was ready to dare anything, had the distinction of presenting Jarry's symbolic farce *Ubu roi ou les Polonais* for two momentous performances at the Nouveau-Théâtre in 1896. The play was announced as a *comédie guignolesque*, because it was to be played as if by puppets, and it enacted the regicide of the King of Poland at the hands of two obscene puppet-monsters of greed and stupidity. These were Papa Ubu and his wife, who were faintly reminiscent of Macbeth and his lady. In form and content the play was an unprecedented piece of impertinent theatre, a wild burlesque of the romantic historical drama, although it has retained its appeal longer than any burlesque has the right to expect. The French light comedian and comic playwright Sacha Guitry could not identify its genre, but went so far as to pronounce,

> The question whether or not [*Ubu roi*] is a masterpiece
> seems to me idle. I believe it is a masterpiece of its kind.
> You will ask, what is its kind? That is very difficult to
> define, for it is neither strictly humour nor strictly parody.
> It is not related to any other form of literature... If I were
> forced to classify this phenomenon, I should put it first

among excessive caricatures, ranking it with the most original and powerful burlesques of all time (translated Barbara Wright).

Jarry was a familiar eccentric in Bohemian Montmartre. He lived in poverty, and wore old trousers tucked inside his socks like a cyclist, and a pair of carpet slippers with the toes out. Yet, incongruously, he was always seen carrying a pair of loaded pistols, and wearing an erect phallus capped by a little velvet hat — perhaps to spare the blushes of the ladies. Wherever he went, he was heard reciting lines from the play he had been composing and revising over and over again since his days at the *lycée*, the school where, with some friends, Jarry had once presented a puppet play in mockery of a teacher they disliked. Lugné had read a published version of *Ubu* with dismay, but encouraging comments from friends persuaded him to produce it.

Jarry was explicit in his instructions. There was to be a minimum of décor, which was to consist of a single set, or even a plain backcloth. This would do away with the raising and lowering of a curtain during the continuous action. The multitude of entrances and exits in the play would be accompanied by incidental music to be written by Claude Terrasse, who would also conduct a little orchestra in the wings. The set was to be designed by Sérusier and Bonnard in such a way as to show the interior and the exterior of a room simultaneously, and simultaneously contrast a torrid and an arctic location. The effect was aggressively unreal, childlike and grotesque. On the left side of the stage was painted a large bed with a chamber-pot underneath it, and a tree standing in snow at its foot. The wall on the right side was painted with palm trees, one having a boa constrictor coiled round it, side by side with a gallows from which hung a skeleton. All this was backed by a view of the sea and the countryside. Against the upstage wall stood a fire-place with a clock and a candelabrum on the mantelpiece. However, the whole frame of this fireplace was made to open in the middle like a door through which the characters could come and go. As if to match the confusion of all these visual suggestions, the location of the action constantly changes from house to palace, then to the mountains and back, and then from Poland to Russia, the change being indicated each time by an old man in white beard and evening dress who hung a placard on a nail in full view of the audience. In every sense, this set was wonderfully timeless and placeless.

Lugné read Jarry's elaborate production notes in despair, and wisely left him to direct the play himself. Perhaps impressed by the episodic nature of the scenes in *Peer Gynt*, one of the few modern plays he admired, Jarry had put together a string of incidents intended to follow one another in rapid succession like the items in a music-hall bill. The performance was to last no more than three-quarters of an hour, and was to be neatly stylized and economical. Since the characters had been conceived as puppets, so were they to be played, moving with mechanical gestures and wearing masks of Jarry's own design. In this way the characters were to eliminate some of their human attributes, and like caricatures embody powerful symbolic ideas. The first Père Ubu was gross, with a bald, pear-shaped head and a huge stomach. His mask had a nose like an elephant's trunk, and he wore a bowler hat, and later in the play a crown, on the top of all. A cane stuck out of his pocket and a bottle dangled at his side. When he became king, he carried a lavatory brush for a sceptre. The well-known Firmin Gémier of the Comédie-Français who played the part, spoke on two notes without inflection or emphasis, in deliberate imitation of Jarry's own manner of speaking, and made weird gestures with his hands and feet. Mère Ubu, played by Louise France, wore the dress of a concièrge sur-mounted by a vulgar pink hat smothered in flowers and feathers. The intention was not so much to amuse the audience as to insult it.

Among the gimmicks, or '*trucs*', which Jarry introduced into the performance were forty life-sized, fully costumed wicker figures to represent the Nobles, Financiers and Magistrates of act III. In the text, these characters were to have been pushed down a trap, but in performance they were toppled into the pit, much to the perplexity of the audience. It cost a fortune to make these figures, so Lugné stored them in the theatre for a long time, in the hope that he would find some other use for them; he never did. The cavalry charge of act IV was accomplished by the use of so many cardboard horses. And the problem of crowd scenes was solved by having no crowds: a single soldier was reviewed by Ubu as his army, and a single soldier did all the fighting when Ubu cries, 'What a gang, what a retreat!'

It should be recorded that when Peter Brook's international company successfully presented a composite *Ubu* at the Théâtre du Bouffes du Nord in Paris in 1977, with Andréas Katsulas as Père Ubu and Michèle Collison as Mère Ubu, it was acceptably performed virtually without masks or costumes. There was also a minimum of props, and the players improvised scenes with two large cable-drums, a few sticks and bricks, and a fake fur rug. The Russians waged a delightful war on Ubu by tossing high-bouncing rubber balls at him — which may suggest the light-hearted spirit of the whole production. Brook showed his ingenuity by using the same dirty fur rug as a bedspread, as Ubu's royal ermine and even as a bear which swallows a man whole and afterwards tosses out his hat and a bone. The play took on the appearance of a romp, a game of childlike invention.

The performance of the original *Ubu roi* was a very special occasion. It was played to a full house made up of Jarry's friends, a few genuine avant-garde critics and many who came expecting to be scandalized. The audience divided readily into rival parties, made up of those supporting Ubu, led by Henry Bauer of *L'Echo*, and those against him, led by Henri Fouquier of *Le Figaro*. One group would applaud ostentatiously, which prompted the other group to cry out indignantly and jump to its feet in protest.

The author himself introduced the play dressed in a baggy suit, his neck wrapped in a chiffon scarf and his powdered white face heavily painted. Jarry placed his notes on a table set on the stage and covered in old sacking, and for ten minutes spoke in a toneless voice. He apologized for the orchestra, which he said he had hoped would consist of trombone and percussion, and then in disconnected sentences hinted at what was to come. Finally Gémier as Ubu walked downstage to the audience and spoke the immortal first word of the play's scatological, Rabelaisian dialogue — *'Merdre'* ('shit' with an added 'r'). This produced an immediate uproar which lasted for fifteen minutes, and many people in the audience walked out at this stage. The word is repeated no less than thirty-three times throughout the play, and every time it was followed by an ever greater roar of rage and laughter. However, Gémier shouted above the noise, and eventually his fine comic performance held the attention of those who were left, so that something of the satirical spirit of the play came across.

Although it was hardly Jarry's concern to legislate for the theatre of the future, this unique event bore stranger fruit. He defended the play in *La Revue Blanche* in January 1897, by insisting that the only justification for a play was to show something on the stage which could not be read in a book. For him, the stage was a mirror which must distort the characters in proportion to their vices, just as the masks distorted the features. Ubu was a clown intended to convey his stupidity with all the confidence of his ignorance, and to exhibit gluttony, brutality, cupidity, coarseness and cowardice. But the debate which followed *Ubu roi* would not soon die. Fouquier in *Le Figaro* had considered the play such a bore that 'it implied the downfall of a symbolic tyranny called *Ubu roi*'. However, Romain Coolus in *La Revue Blanche* considered it an historic evening: 'La folle, c'extraordinaire soirée!' In everyday conversation, Ubu became the symbol for bourgeois stupidity in everything from art to politics, and in its ridicule of war even appeared to prophesy the events following 1914. 'The smell of Ubu is everywhere.' Jarry henceforth signed his letters 'Père Ubu' and used the royal 'we', but, succumbing to alcohol and ether, he died at the early age of thirty-four. His last request was for a toothpick.

In *The Banquet Years*, Roger Shattuck records that the symbolist poet Mallarmé entirely approved of Jarry as 'a sure, sober, dramatic sculptor' and of *Ubu* as 'in the best taste', and he wrote a letter to Jarry congratulating him. It also happened that W. B. Yeats and Arthur Symons were present on the first night, and both were impressed by the play, if a little troubled by its implications. Yeats wrote in his autobiography,

> Feeling bound to support the most spirited party, we have
> shouted for the play, but that night at the Hotel Corneille
> I am very sad, for comedy, objectivity, has displayed its
> growing power once more. I say, 'After Stéphane Mallarmé,
> after Paul Verlaine, after Gustave Moreau, after Puvis de
> Chavannes, after our own verse, after all our subtle colour
> and nervous rhythm, after the faint mixed tints of Conder,
> what more is possible? After us the Savage God, (p. 234).

The claims for *Ubu* were exaggerated, although a private and subjective use of the theatre medium temporarily took hold in Paris. This was the beginning of a counter-culture which would display many manifestations of artistic anarchy, and preach a variety of loosely related philosophies, or antiphilosophies, of life and art.

One legacy from Jarry was the ironically named cult of 'Pataphysics'. The word was first introduced casually into a conversation between Ubu and one Professor Achras, distinguished collector of polyhedrons, in the preface to Jarry's first book, *Les Minutes de Sable Mémorial* (1890):

> UBU.   Remember that you are addressing a celebrated
>   pataphysician.
> ACHRAS. Excuse me, Sir, you said?
> UBU.   Pataphysician. Pataphysics is a branch of science
>   which we have invented and for which a crying
>   need is generally experienced.

Pataphysics was 'the science of imaginary solutions', dealing with 'the laws which govern exceptions' and exploring 'the world beyond metaphysics'. In scoring the things of this world, Jarry offered himself as a victim of the world's absurdity. He worked on this Universal Science from 1894 to 1898, intending to incorporate it in the unfinished story, *Les Gestes et Opinions du Docteur Faustroll, Pataphysicien*, an account of a journey from one symbolic island to another through the region aptly named Ethernity. The 'Collège de Pataphysique' was, however, not founded until 1949, when a few enthusiasts, who included the absurdist playwright Ionesco, designed its rules, invested its officers and devised the first issue of *Les Cahiers du Collège de Pataphysique*, which was published in April 1950. It was the College which first recognized Ionesco's *La Cantatrice chauve* (*The Bald Soprano*, 1952) and Boris Vian's *Les Bâtisseurs d'empire* (*The Empire Builders*, 1959). The College of Pataphysics announced itself as an institution which refused to serve any purpose, refused to save mankind, 'or, what is even more unusual, the World'.

Alfred Jarry wrote two more plays, *Ubu cocu* (*Ubu Cuckolded*, 1898) and *Ubu enchaîné* (*Ubu in Chains*, 1900). He saw neither of these produced. *Faustroll* was not published until four years after he died. But his cause was soon espoused by the surrealist Apollinaire, and, immediately after the First World War, by André Breton. The greater artist Jean Cocteau also took up Jarry's approach to playwriting, and in this way the outrageous *Ubu* may be linked with the development of surrealism and absurdism on the modern stage.

8 *Dada and surrealism in France: Tzara to Cocteau*

The Wedding on the Eiffel Tower (1921)

In the 1910s, the air was thick with idiosyncratic manifestoes for the reform of the arts, those of Cubism, Futurism, and many others. Each sought a public, but few discovered dramatic talent. In Craig's periodical *The Mask*, no. VI, 1913, Filippo Tommaso Marinetti (1876–1944), founder of Italian Futurism, advocated the style of the music-hall as the model for a new drama, considering its comic distortions, its unromantic eccentricities and its grotesque parodies the best way to destroy 'the solemn, the sacred, the serious, the sublime of Art with a capital A'. Futurist plays were brief to a fault (Marinetti's *Clair de lune* lasts only two or three minutes) and were skittish as only music-hall skits can be.

Tristan Tzara (1896–1963) and André Breton (1896–1966) are credited with the invention and promotion of dada, a movement designed to show its disciples' disgust with the senseless values of modern society, as chiefly represented by the appalling trench warfare of the First World War, like the Franco-German battle of Verdun. In 1916, Tzara had retreated to neutral Switzerland, neutral but right in the centre of war-torn Europe. There in Zürich he set about inventing forms of senseless art with the sole intention of shocking his audience. Through dada he proclaimed the necessity for chaos; nothing was sacred; all order, all systems, all social conventions and manners would be abolished. In the second dada manifesto, it was stated that the chief purpose of a dada exhibition was to bring about the utmost degree of misunderstanding between the performer and his audience. All the dada artists, by profession chiefly poets and painters, let the world know that art needed to be violently shaken up.

Tzara's public proclamations were in fact accompanied by violent gestures and bloodcurdling screams and whistles in order to emphasize his points. A poetry-reading would consist of reciting a newspaper article to the wild accompaniment of bells and rattles; a copy of the Mona Lisa would be given a moustache with elaborate ceremony. When, a year later, Tzara transferred his organization to Paris, he continued to put out his manifestoes and pursue the same policy of attacking the artistic establishment, as well as the newest vogues of Cubism and Futurism. The dada festivals of Zürich and Paris continued until 1921.

The movement was treated, at best, as a great joke. However, from this distance we can see that dada was not entirely nihilist, as many believed. Rather, it delivered to the art of the twentieth century a needed jolt, preparatory to its further growth and development. If politically dada wanted to change the establishment, aesthetically it wanted to change how people perceived the world about them. Its final goal was to bring down the barricades of form and idea which art and tradition had erected between the artist and the public. Tzara sought to return to simplicity and spontaneity, and to enhance the values of the personal and the subjective. To do this, he had to disorientate the spectator — and perhaps the artist too. And dada's greatest claim to a positive virtue is, paradoxically, that it was a *thoughtful* movement: it takes some effort of the intellect to upset rational thinking, and to recognize what is completely incongruous in nature and art requires not a little ingenuity.

Nevertheless, surrealism, which evolved from dada, was the great invention of the age. If dada chiefly tried to denounce art by disrupting it, surrealism refined the application of dadaist principles by exploring through the arts all the mysteries of the irrational mind. The rational control of our perceptions was to be disturbed and questioned by whatever means could be devised, and to do so the surrealist artist would use elements of surprise, the involuntary and the unconscious. Pure dada had wanted only *chance* to rule human activity; surrealism was more purposeful and wanted to *arrange* the derangement of the senses. Most people think of surrealism as the work of the Catalan painter Salvador Dali — in the words of

Maurice Richardson, 'with all those bent watches, truncated phallic limbs on crutches, mammiferous chests of drawers, set against the landscape of his native peninsular of Cadaqués' (*The Times Literary Supplement*, 13 January 1978) — the formless exploitation of the genre. Some may have met surrealism in the film, whose editing process lends itself to the irrational juxtaposition of images: in 1939, Joseph Cornell abused a typical Hollywood melodrama of the 1930s by speeding it up, cutting it to twenty-four minutes and replacing its serious soundtrack with Latin American music — a bit of fun. But at its best, surrealism was a way of carefully dislocating logical thinking, confounding causality and argument, and disarranging time and space for everyone to *understand*. The consequent disorder may even have the effect of lifting its audience on to a new, heightened, 'poetic' level of perception. In the art of the film, the surrealist Luis Buñuel's work is universally well regarded as a characteristic form of black comedy.

André Breton's first manifesto was put out in 1924, and his version of surrealism soon replaced Tzara's dada. A former medical student, Breton injected Freudian psychology into his arguments, and advocated his own brand of artistic anarchy, made up of words and images culled from free association. This was 'automatic writing'. Breton demanded that a work of surrealist art should be a window through which the viewer could look upon some inner landscape of the mind. His approach lent a new importance to dreams, fantasies and hallucinations, and notable precursors could now include anyone from Hieronymus Bosch to Lewis Carroll — anyone who was egocentric enough and drew sufficiently upon the subconscious. At this stage in the story, surrealism had become more than a movement in modern art: it could be viewed almost as a way of life.

Surrealist connections with the stage are necessarily somewhat uncertain. Illogic, which is static rather than dramatic, can play no final part, needless to say, in good drama; Freud himself would have insisted that even bad dreams had a point. But the search for an elusive 'reality' or a personal 'identity' in the fantasies of trance and dream, and in the violent expression of the subconscious mind, went on in one way or another for a generation, and inevitably touched those who wrote for the stage.

Surrealism in the theatre emerged chiefly in Paris, and particularly in the plays of Apollinaire and Cocteau. Little of dada or surrealism reached London or New York. It was as late as 1936 before Londoners even saw anything of French surrealism: this was the date of the International Surrealist Exhibition, designed by Roland Penrose at the New Burlington Galleries. The show was intended to shock. Dali himself appeared wearing a diver's helmet (and nearly suffocated before it could be removed), and a young lady promenaded the floor with a bunch of roses on her shoulders instead of a head. Except for the very few who had a French or German interest in modern art, the public was universally hostile. By the time of the second surrealist exhibition at the Hayward Gallery in 1978, the subject was treated as a matter of history only, and foreign history at that.

In Paris it was different. 1917 saw the production of two notable plays directly indebted to Jarry's *Ubu* and to dada. These were *Les Mamelles de Tirésias* (*The Breasts of Tiresias*) by Apollinaire and *Parade* by Cocteau, and they ushered in a decade of French surrealistic theatre. Like *Ubu*, surrealist plays were made up of many quick scenes, and they introduced characters wearing masks and moving like mechanical robots. Like the Italian Futurists, the French surrealists eschewed everything conventional, but unlike the Futurists, they tried to bring some order and reason into their idiom of performance, deploying surrealistic devices in order to reveal, even moralistically, what they considered to be the reality of life and what was important about it.

Guillaume Apollinaire (1880–1918) had begun his *Les Mamelles de Tirésias* in 1903, when he had first met Jarry, and he took the satirical side of *Ubu*'s burlesque seriously. The play is written in verse, in two acts and fourteen scenes, but it retains the unity of place and time, and even tells a reasonable story about feminism in Zanzibar, where the women have refused to bear children. It could be thought of even as a burlesque of a problem play about women's liberation. But the action is replete with Ubuesque *trucs*. The rebellious heroine Thérèse wears red and blue balloons for breasts, which she lets fly on strings before exploding them; later, they become balls which she tosses to the audience, so that she can become Tirésias, sprouting a moustache and a beard at the same time. The people of Zanzibar, like the armies in *Ubu*, are represented by a single actor who responds by banging pots and pans and anything else that makes a noise. One character is a newspaper woman incarcerated in a kiosk which sings and dances and waves its arms. Asides are spoken by megaphone, and the dialogue itself is made up of newspaper headlines delivered in the voice-tones of a newspaper-seller. Clearly, every device is intended to subvert the realism of the well-made play, and in his preface Apollinaire claimed that by his attack on realism he had returned to nature. Hence, he arrived at his notion of surrealism: 'When man wished to imitate walking he invented the wheel, which bears no resemblance to a leg.

11. Cocteau, *Parade*, 1917. Design by Picasso.

In this way he has unconsciously created surrealism'. Apollinaire denied that there was any symbolism in the play, and when it was first produced at the Théâtre Maubel, it was given the subtitle, 'Un drame surréalist', the first use of the word.

Jean Cocteau (1889–1963) was not only versatile in trying his hand at every artistic medium, but he also experimented endlessly in the media he chose; it is understandable if the criticism that he was a showman has clung. His gift of creating striking and unique visual images can be seen in play and film alike. 'Astonish me!', demanded Diaghilev, and Cocteau responded with *Parade*, the first of many attempts to astonish his audiences. When it was performed at the Théâtre du Châtelet, he ironically called it a 'ballet réaliste'. It was danced by Diaghilev's Russian Ballet, as choreographed by Leonid Massine, and it was this that tended to suppress any dialogue Cocteau had supplied in his libretto. The music was by Eric Satie and the ballet had a mobile Cubist set by Picasso. This collaboration by a trio of highly temperamental avant-garde artists made it a miracle that a performance of *Parade* ever took place. The idea was to set illusion against reality, and the 'parade' of the title referred to the bizarre display outside a circus tent before the show, designed to lure spectators inside to see the 'reality'. The side-show consisted of three Managers encased in scenery, with a cast of two acrobats, a Chinese prestidigitator and 'a little American girl', who looked like Mary Pickford in a sailor suit about to face *The Perils of Pauline*. The dancing was accompanied by outrageous sound-effects produced by sirens, whistles and typewriters, and the dancers were made to seem like unreal, Craig-like pieces of moving machinery inside the frame of the stage. The audience was denied a view of what was really inside the tent, and was scandalously made to feel it was part of the grotesque show it was watching. The production was received with the customary mixture of cheers and catcalls, and was also followed by public insults and lawsuits. But this was Cocteau's début, and *Parade* ensured that his reputation was truly launched.

Like any playwright, Cocteau was searching for a style to match his content, and in his surrealistic plays the two are certainly inseparable. He believed that the action in his next play was pictorial, and he explained that he was trying to substitute what he called 'poésie de théâtre', 'theatre poetry', for the usual poetry *in* the theatre, the poetry being in the structure of the play rather than in its language. Hence, he emphasized visual and theatrical effects at the expense of words. *Les Mariés de la Tour Eiffel* (*The Wedding on the Eiffel Tower*), produced in 1921 at the Théâtre des Champs-Élysées, was designed as another ballet, choreographed this time by Cocteau himself with Jean Borlin, and danced by the new Swedish ballet under Rolfe de Maré. This play, however, reclaims the text, which asserts much more control over the performance: while the performers mime the action in masks, two music-hall compères, dressed as gramophones with horns for mouths, recite the lines and narrate what is happening. This arrangement produces the singular effect of dissociation between actor and character, an effect which Brecht would pursue on a later occasion for other reasons (see volume 3).

The set by Irène Lagut consisted of the bellows of a giant camera arranged to one side on the first landing of the Eiffel Tower, with the front of the camera opening like a door for the entrance of the characters. On the backcloth was painted a suggestion, a 'bird's-eye view', of Paris, seen through the girders of the tower. The costumes and masks were by Jean Victor-Hugo, and the play begins with an ostrich marching across the stage, chased by a hunter. A photographer later explains that the last time he said, 'Watch the birdie', it was this ostrich that stepped out of the camera. After this, whenever the photographer tries to take a picture of the wedding party, some new creature jumps out, including a lion and a bathing beauty from Trouville. Finally, a little fat boy emerges, representing the newlyweds' future offspring, who proceeds to throw macaroons at the guests. There is more nonsense along these lines, until the whole wedding party disappears into the camera to the count of five. So much for the play's action.

With a foretaste of Ionesco, the dialogue is a series of clichés ('cliché' in French signifies both a commonplace and a snapshot), spoken by the gramophones quickly and loudly. It is accompanied sarcastically by a variety of contrapuntal funeral marches, waltzes and other musical forms, arranged for parody by Georges Auric, Darius Milhaud, Francis Poulenc, Germaine Tailleferre and other

12. Cocteau, *The Wedding on the Eiffel Tower*, 1921. Production by the Swedish Ballet at the Théâtre des Champs-Élysées, design by Irène Lagut.

composers of the 'Six', as they came to be known. The whole play had the effect of a preposterous dream, madly irreverent and wildly comic. In his preface of 1922, Cocteau declared that instead of trying to lessen the absurdity of life, he had emphasized it: 'I try to paint *more truly than the truth*' (Cocteau's italics). He wanted to 'rejuvenate the commonplace', and present it in such a light that it 'recaptures its youth'. If his play seems elementary, he asks, 'Aren't we still in school? Aren't we still deciphering what is elementary?' Accused of buffoonery, he cites Molière in his own defence: 'The attitude of the buffoon is the only one that allows certain audacities.'

This remarkable preface comes near to advancing Cocteau's theory of symbolism. 'The true symbol is never planned', he says; 'it emerges by itself':

> In a fairyland, the fairies do not appear. They walk invisibly there. To mortal eyes they can appear only on the terra firma of everyday. The unsophisticated mind is more likely than the others to see the fairies, for it will not oppose to the marvellous the resistance of the hardheaded.

He reported that it was the candour of *Les Mariés* that caused it initially to be mistaken for a piece of esoteric writing — apparently what is mysterious inspires a kind of fear in the public. But in this play, he insists,

> I renounce mystery, I illuminate everything, I underline everything. Sunday vacuity, human livestock, ready-made expressions, dissociation of ideas into flesh and bone, the fierce cruelty of childhood, the miraculous poetry of daily life: these are my play (translated Dudley Fitts).

And Cocteau suggests that a line by the photographer might do well for his epigraph: 'Since these mysteries are beyond me, let's pretend that I arranged them all the time.'

As it turned out, the first performance of *Les Mariés* went largely unheard because Tzara and his dadaist followers chose to shout 'Long live Dada!' one after another throughout the evening. For the rest, the play was received with the usual uproar of hisses and cheers, and the author was not exactly pleased. In his preface, he attacks those who refuse to go along with an experiment, who stay 'outside':

> In the case of a new work, the first impression so shocks, ir-
> ritates, angers the spectator that he will not enter. He is
> repelled from its true nature by its face, by the unfamiliar out-
> ward appearance which distracts him as would a clown
> grimacing at the door.

Cocteau records that the correspondent of *Débuts* was the only critic
to accord *Les Mariés* the praise of having any *wit*.

In later years, Cocteau attracted great directors to his service,
Jouvet for *La Machine infernale* in 1924, Pitoëff for *Orphée* in 1926.
While Cocteau continued to mix music and mime, ballet dancing
and circus acrobatics, his dramatic work grew more substantial. Yet
it is a nice irony that some of his best writing for the stage, like *Les
Parents terribles* (1938), was in the vein of psychological realism. For
while he declared his opposition to realism, he also considered
that Jarry's *Ubu* and Apollinaire's *Les Mamelles de Tirésias* consisted
at the same time of symbolism and a species of drama *à thèse*, that
they had successfully merged symbolism and realism. It could well
be true that a play which manages to draw upon both symbolism
and realism is likely to be the more universal and durable.

Alfred Jarry's legacy to the French theatre was understandably
unpredictable. *Ubu* liberated the theatre from outworn conventions
without proposing new ones. No doubt surrealism and automatic
writing were a dead end, but another beginning would be made
when Artaud founded the Théâtre Alfred-Jarry in 1927, and yet
another in 1949 when Eugène Ionesco formed the Collège de Pataphysique in the master's honour. The surrealistic creations of the
'theatre of cruelty' and the 'theatre of the absurd' were yet to come.

9 Symbolist drama in English: Yeats and Japanese, Noh, drama

At the Hawk's Well (1916)

With the Irish poet William Butler Yeats (1865–1939), the idea of symbolism in drama takes on a profoundly new character. Well before he was aware of the French *symbolistes*, Yeats had encountered symbolism for himself in reading Boehme, Blake and Swedenborg, and he had recognized the possibilities of the occult as a member of the society of 'The Hermetic Students'. When he was introduced to the French movement by Arthur Symons, what he learned only corroborated much that he knew already. More than this, Yeats's concept of symbolism assumed a religious dimension the French knew nothing of. It was not merely a technique, but a belief.

In *Symbolism and Implications*, Robert O'Driscoll has recently summarized usefully the difference between the materialist and the symbolist, a difference which underlines the kind of religious faith implied in Yeats's position. The materialist believes there is no difference between the natural and the spiritual order; his knowledge comes from observing the external world through his senses. The symbolist does believe there is a difference, an absolute difference, between nature and the spirit; for him, the world is the external expression of what lies hidden in the mind. At the centre of the universe is the 'universal mood', the truth of God, of which everything in art and nature is an expression or embodiment. Blake believed that by means of symbolism we could enter the universality of God, and Yeats believed that symbolism was 'a hand pointing the way into some divine labyrinth'. Both believed that symbols had the power to evoke the world beyond the senses, and reveal the inner elements of rhythm and pattern that distinguish one living form from another.

This was elevated thinking indeed, suggesting that Yeats wanted a different order of literature. And it is true that he had decided that literature had sunk to become merely a criticism of external life, rather than a revelation of the invisible world of the spirit. It was for symbolism to alter the substance, form and style of litera-ture and art. Such a 'symbolic apocalypse', Yeats felt, could come in Ireland through the legend and lore of its peasantry, for whom, he wrote in 1888, 'everything is a symbol' and instinct does the work of reason. So he began collecting Irish folklore, publishing a collec-tion in 1893 under the provocative title, *The Celtic Twilight*, and began to think of poetic drama as the highest form of literature towards which he should aim.

Yeats was attracted to symbolism and the occult at the very time when the need was also felt for an Irish national drama to challenge Dublin's commercial theatre. He had read Mallarmé and Valéry, and had seen Jarry and Maeterlinck on the Paris stage (and questioned the latter's sincerity). Like his French counterparts, he also instinctively rejected realism. He had seen *A Doll's House* in London in 1889, and in 1894 had watched *Arms and the Man* in rehearsal: he had hated both. He found the characters in *Ghosts* less than life-size, and regarded Ibsen and Shaw as bourgeois moralists and reformers — mere logicians whose colourless dialogue was lacking in poetic vision and exhilaration. 'Art is art because it is not nature', Yeats said. Everything he saw on the modern stage turned him back to Irish folklore.

Yeats saw drama as 'a moment of intense life', a simplifica-tion and a concentration of character and action. There, in 1904, spoke Yeats the symbolist. To match this intensity, he called for the vivid and beautiful language which he believed Gaelic and the Irish peasant tongue possessed. He believed that kings and queens would yet people the stage again, 'masterful spirits' who would reveal the true reality, that of the soul: 'Has not the long decline of the arts been but the shadow of declining faith in an unseen reality?' The limited life of the play, simple in form and style, could evoke the rich imagined life behind it. This would be ensured, because, unlike the Moscow Art Theatre and the French Théâtre-Libre, the Irish national theatre would be a writer's and not a direc-tor's theatre.

With Lady Gregory, as we saw in volume 1, Yeats set out

to run a 'People's Theatre', but he had soon to admit that his personal demands could not be satisfied within the Abbey Theatre. It was not enough to bring the Irish folk-world to the city of Dublin: Yeats wished to extend and explore it more subjectively as a form of poetic drama. He went so far as to declare that he wanted 'an unpopular theatre and an audience like a secret society where admission is by favour and never to many', perhaps some fifty people of the same mind in a large drawing-room, an audience ready to appreciate the subtleties belonging to a poetic theatre. He was certainly not going to find fifty such kindred spirits in the Abbey audience.

Yeats's early verse plays like *The Countess Cathleen* (1892) and *The Land of Heart's Desire* (1894) had been lyrical, romantic and nationalistic. They had been as mystical and moody as Maeterlinck, mixing a little symbolism of the broadest kind with their Irish myth. Yeats pursued this kind of mixture with rather more symbolism and in a tragic and heroic vein in *On Baile's Strand* (1904) and *Deirdre* (1906), and these plays saw the start of a fundamental change. Gordon Craig designed the costumes for the former, and in 1906 sent Yeats a set of his famous screens for the Abbey. Yeats admired the simplification of scene and colour in Craig's work, recognizing that the actors themselves could harmonize with such décor, and so concentrate the attention of the audience on the spoken word. A background of trees and hills, for example, could be painted as an unrealistic, decorative pattern and be quite un-obtrusive.

Yeats wanted maximum attention to be given to the speaking of his lines, and insisted that the voice express a 'continually varied music', at times using the pure notes of song itself. He was delighted with the half-tone chanting achieved by the actress Florence Farr, and the Abbey actors Frank and William Fay helped him to train his players in verse-speaking. Yeats also wanted his actors to learn how to stand still on the stage, using only graceful gestures to comple-ment the lines. Lady Gregory suggested that they should rehearse with plates on their heads, and Yeats had the idea of putting them in barrels which would then be pushed on wheels about the stage by a pole, as the action required: 'We must get rid of everything that is restless', he said, 'everything that draws attention away from the sound of the voice'. He might have asked the actors themselves — he could hardly have hit upon a more distracting device than that of an actor in a barrel, even if he did anticipate a tendency in the plays of Samuel Beckett. Worse still, the intoning of the verse slowed down the plays to the point of lifelessness.

Yeats spoke increasingly of an ideal of lyrical but 'passionless' drama, and in 'The Tragic Theatre' (1910) he wrote of ways to exclude the 'impure' elements of realism and comedy, and to lessen the contemporaneity of character. For these he would substitute, 'rhythm, balance, pattern, images that remind us of vast passions, the vagueness of past times, all the chimeras that haunt the edge of trance'. Personal emotion was to be expressed through the play's form, with symbolism 'handled by the generations', masks 'from whose eyes the disembodied looks', and a style 'that remembers many masters, that it may escape contemporary suggestion'. By such means, the actors would 'greaten till they are humanity itself' and 'we feel our minds expand convulsively or spread out slowly like some moon-brightened image-crowded sea'. Although characteristically oblique, a poem in itself, this majestic essay must be read in its entirety.

Then in about 1916, Yeats discovered Oriental drama. In his essay 'Certain Noble Plays of Japan', he reported that with the help of Japanese plays translated by Ernest Fenollosa and finished by Ezra Pound, 'I have invented a form of drama, distinguished, indirect, and symbolic, and having no need of mob or Press to pay its way — an aristocratic form'. Yeats had been studying the *Noh* play, and although he had never seen a *Noh* performance, he enthusiastically embraced its severe ritualism and its elements of music, dance and poetry, that unification of the arts so dear to the hearts of the symbolists. 'It is natural that I go to Asia for a stage convention, for more formal faces, for a chorus that has no part in the action, and perhaps for those movements of the body copied from the marionette shows of the fourteenth century.' He was particularly taken with the simplification characteristic of *Noh* drama. He did not see this as a mere economy, but as a way of recovering something of the importance of the actor's voice and the verse he spoke. In other forms of staging, the play seemed to be 'behind a veil', with the contrast in light and darkness, and the distance between the actor and the audience, destroying the intimacy of the theatre.

Craig and the *Noh* drama also encouraged Yeats with the use of masks. He had visited Edmund Dulac's studio, where he saw the mask to be worn by his character Cuchulain, half-Greek and half-Asiatic, and argued that such a mask would help his work attain 'the distance from life which can make credible strange events, elaborate words'.

> The players wear masks and found their movements upon those of puppets . . . a swift or a slow movement and a long or a short stillness, and then another movement. They sing as much as they speak, and there is a chorus which describes the scene and interprets their thought and never becomes as in the Greek theatre a part of the action. At the climax, instead of the disordered passion of nature, there is a dance, a series of positions and movements which may represent a battle, or a marriage, or the pain of a ghost in the Buddhist Purgatory. . . The interest is not in the human form but in the rhythm to which it moves, and the triumph of their art is to express the rhythm in its intensity.

Yeats had apparently found a form of impersonalized and stylized drama which could help distance his art, for 'this distance, once chosen, must be firmly held against a pushing world'.

The play which brought together all these techniques was *At the Hawk's Well,* the first of Yeats's *Four Plays for Dancers.* It was produced in 1916 along the imagined lines of a *Noh* play, with music by Edmund Dulac for bamboo flute, harp or zither, drum and gong. Dulac also designed the masks and costumes, and the choreography was by Itow, a Japanese dancer who also danced the part of the Hawk with 'minute intensity of movement'. The first performance was in London in Lady Cunard's drawing-room, and only those who cared for poetry were invited. It was played upon the floor of the room, and the actors entered by the same door as the audience. Yeats reported that everyone was pleased with the production, but that when it was later played before some 300 people 'my muses were but half welcome'.

At the Hawk's Well is a short play in verse, telling the story of the young Cuchulain and his wish to drink from the well of immortality. The stage was to be 'any bare space' backed by a patterned screen representing a lonely place that 'the salt sea wind has swept bare'. Two lanterns stand on posts at the corners of the acting area. A chorus of three Musicians, with their faces made up like masks, begin the action with a careful ritual:

The First Musician carries with him a folded black cloth and

13. Yeats, *At the Hawk's Well*, 1916. Costume design by Edmund Dulac for Old Man.

goes to the centre of the stage towards the front and stands motionless, the folded cloth hanging from between his hands. The two other Musicians enter and, after standing a moment at either side of the stage, go towards him and slowly unfold the cloth, singing as they do so. . . As they unfold the cloth, they

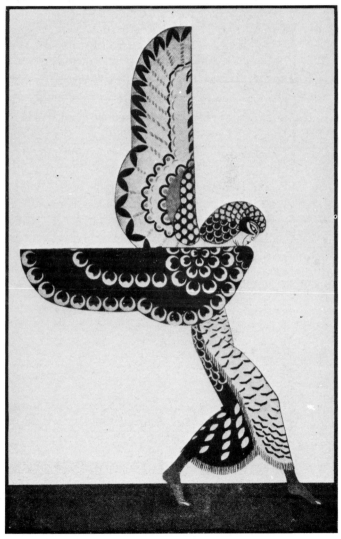

14. Yeats, *At the Hawk's Well*, 1916. Costume design by Edmund Dulac for the Guardian of the Well.

go backward a little so that the stretched cloth and the wall make a triangle with the First Musician at the apex supporting the centre of the cloth. On the black cloth is a gold pattern suggesting a hawk. The Second and Third Musicians now slowly fold up the cloth again, pacing with a rhythmic movement of the arms towards the First Musician and singing.

The Guardian of the Well, covered with a black cloak and her face also made up like a mask, crouches on the ground. Beside her, a square of blue cloth represents the well. The Musicians chant their lines and with their instruments accompany the movements of the players so that they seem to be marionettes jerked by the music.

A fearful figure in the mask of an Old Man has been to the well unsuccessfully for fifty years, and he now stands motionlessly to one side with bowed head. To a tap of the drum he raises his head, and to another he comes downstage and moves his hands as if he is making a fire. Cuchulain, masked like a Young Man, enters without fear, whereupon the Guardian of the Well lets out a cry like a hawk and throws off her cloak to reveal a hawk's costume. She dances before the two men until the Old Man falls asleep and Cuchulain is entranced. Suddenly the Musicians cry out and strike the gong to symbolize the noise of battle. At this, Cuchulain recovers his wits and, still mortal, goes off impulsively with his spear to fight:

> He has lost what may not be found
> Till men heap his burial-mound.

A hero's immortality will be gained only by heroism. Finally, the Musicians again perform the ritual of unfolding and folding the cloth.

In a subsequent note on the first performance of the play, Yeats considered that he had made a great advance in simplicity.

> My blunder has been that I did not discover in my youth
> that my theatre must be the ancient theatre that can be
> made by unrolling a carpet or making out a place with a
> stick or setting a screen against the wall. It has been a
> great gain to get rid of scenery, to substitute for a crude
> landscape painted upon canvas three performers who, sit-

ting before the wall or a patterned screen, describe landscape or event, and accompany movement with drum and
gong, or deepen the emotion of the words with zither or
flute. Painted scenery after all is unnecessary to my friends
and to myself, for our imagination kept living by the arts
can imagine a mountain covered with thorn-trees in a
drawing-room without any great trouble.

But none of this would be of consequence without the poetry of
Yeats.

Into this stark visual setting he set gems of packed allusive
poetry written in a spare, hard verse. The play was strong and
simple, and had the unity of a single mood. Its action was dreamlike and unreal, and each character in its inhuman, abstracting
mask, seeming only to change with the light that fell upon it, represented a single state of mind. In such an artificial framework, the only
drama lies in placing age beside youth, weakness beside strength,
fear and disillusion beside resolution and zest for life. At best, the
play achieved a remoteness and timelessness; at worst, it remained
a static lyric poem. When Yeats was no longer required to satisfy
the needs of the public stage, all the weaknesses of the symbolist and
idealist theatre were free to flourish. He had adopted the Japanese
conventions without the saving grace of the accepted and time-
honoured Japanese tradition. In spite of a friendly drawing-room,
Yeats shared no common ground with his audience, and the *Noh*
drama was interesting chiefly as a novelty. In his *Poetry and Drama*,
T. S. Eliot decided that Yeats's *Plays for Dancers* solved no problems
for the modern verse dramatist.

Nevertheless, the debate goes on. The common view is that
expressed by hardly an impartial witness, Sean O'Casey, who
thought the plays too bloodless. He considered that *At the Hawk's
Well* as performed in a Dublin drawing-room was an artificial flower
in a poetical conventicle, and he wondered with some amusement
what would have happened had Fluther Good bounded in from
The Plough and the Stars, full of drink and roaring for a fight. Yet
dedicated experimental groups continued to produce Yeats's symbolist plays: John Jay of the Trinity Players Theatre and James
Flannery of the Project Theatre, Dublin. The Lyric Theatre, Belfast,
holds the record for having produced all of Yeats's plays.

Symbolist drama in English: Eliot and religious drama

Murder in the Cathedral (1935)

Yeats continued to experiment with a symbolist drama for a private, minority theatre long after the form had taken other directions in Paris and elsewhere, and it was sad for him, and damaging for the Irish movement, that he increasingly ignored trends in the public theatre. The history of the attempt by T. S. Eliot (1888–1965) to revive a verse drama in England at a time when western theatre was growing ever more international also reflects a certain theatrical parochialism, which we can see now accounts in part for the failure of good poets like Yeats and Eliot to have any significant dramatic influence on others.

Theatre history will acknowledge that Eliot deliberately set himself the all but elusive goal of writing a successful poetic drama for the twentieth-century audience. He had at first fallen under the spell of the French symbolist poets, Laforgue, Rimbaud, Verlaine, Corbière and Apollinaire, and he was not unaware of symbolist drama in Paris. He was also appreciative of what poetry in the theatre had achieved in the past, and in 1920 he published *The Sacred Wood*, a collection of critical essays in which he demonstrated his interest in why the Elizabethan verse drama had succeeded and the problems of introducing poetry into the modern theatre. Like Yeats, Eliot found the realistic drama formless, and in 'Four Elizabethan Dramatists' went so far as to protest that in such drama 'the human being intrudes'. But he believed that there was no point in writing a play in verse if prose would do, and continued to puzzle over the way verse in a play 'must justify itself dramatically'. The issue was precisely what was 'dramatic' about verse written for the stage.

Like other earlier aspiring verse dramatists, Eliot kept Shakespeare, master of them all, at the back of his mind, and wondered at the ease with which he had appealed to so wide an audience. Without actually regurgitating the ancient fallacy that Shakespeare's plays included coarse material for the groundlings and philosophy for the lords, Eliot nevertheless explained the matter in *The Use of Poetry and the Use of Criticism* (1933) in a not dissimilar way.

> In a play of Shakespeare you get several levels of significance. For the simplest auditor there is the plot, for the more thoughtful the character and conflict of character, for the more literary the words and phrasing, for the more musically sensitive the rhythm, and for auditors of greater sensitiveness and understanding a meaning which reveals itself gradually.

A play for the public stage, in other words, could satisfy the superficial needs of the box-office and the more profound requirements of an educated audience if it could incorporate a multiplicity of levels of appreciation. Eliot was apparently groping for the workings of a symbolism which could treat a Christian martyrdom as if it were a murder (the first title for *Murder in the Cathedral* was *The Archbishop Murder Case*), and in *The Family Reunion* the subject of sin and expiation as if it were a matter of crime and punishment.

In the case of *Murder in the Cathedral,* the degree of symbolism was an issue accentuated by the circumstances of the play's composition. George Bell, Bishop of Chichester, had founded the Religious Drama Society in 1929, with E. Martin Browne as director of productions, following the success of John Masefield's play *The Coming of Christ* at the Canterbury Festival of Music and Drama in 1928. Bishop Bell was responsible for encouraging and commissioning plays from an unexpectedly large number of verse playwrights in the 1930s — Christopher Fry, Christopher Hassall, Duncan Jones, Norman Nicholson, Anne Ridler, Dorothy Sayers, Charles Williams — and when he invited Eliot to write his first full-length play on a religious subject, *Murder in the Cathedral* was the result. The issue was at its most acute. By what means could a popular, if middle-class, audience, unaccustomed to much religion in or out of the theatre, be seduced into sitting through a religious play? If going to a Christian play were not exactly a substitute for worship, could it be a substitute for 'entertainment'?

Directed by Martin Browne in the Chapter House of Canterbury Cathedral in 1935 (and afterwards in the Mercury Theatre), *Murder in the Cathedral* tells the story of the martyrdom in the twelfth century of the archbishop Thomas à Becket, played by Robert Speaight. The writing drew successfully on earlier forms: the liturgies of the Church, the characters of medieval morality drama, the versification of *Everyman* (revived in recent years by William Poel), and an Aeschylean tragic chorus representing the common world of the women of Canterbury, whose incantatory speeches were designed to guide the emotional responses of the audience. Since the play was written for a chapel or a church (the first open stage with a permanent set, as it were, in Britain), much of the ritual was well suited to the setting. The simple religious symbolism of the priest and the tempters was not disturbing to the audience, who could attend to the proceedings like a congregation to a church

15. Eliot, *Murder in the Cathedral*, 1935. Production by E. Martin Browne at the Mercury Theatre, London, with Robert Speaight as Becket.

service. Because the play was set in a remote period of history, the actors could wear costumes and speak unnaturally in verse without question. Indeed, under such artificial circumstances, the content of this play could never have provided a true test of the possibilities of a modern verse drama.

Eliot's real achievement in this play was to find a symbolic action in Thomas's martyrdom which a devout member of the audience could apply to himself. In adopting St Thomas Aquinas's *via negativa*, the way to reach God through the rejection of material and temporal things, and by assuming the validity of man's original sin and need for atonement, Eliot proposes Becket as representative of a society in which all are sinful. It may be thought that a larger-than-life figure like the archbishop of history and legend is not an obvious one with whom any 'type of the common man' can readily identify: even a less likely contender than Eliot's Sweeney with his mechanical and mundane view of life as 'birth, copulation and death'. But we are to recognize in Becket's story 'the eternal design':

> A Christian martyrdom is never an accident, for saints are
> not made by accident. Still less is a Christian martyrdom
> the effect of a man's will to become a saint, as man by
> willing and contriving may become a ruler of men. A
> martyrdom is always the design of God, for His love of
> men, to warn them and to lead them, to bring them back
> to His ways. It is never the design of man; for the true
> martyr is he who has become the instrument of God, who
> has lost his will in the will of God, and who no longer
> desires anything for himself, not even the glory of being a
> martyr.

We are to recognize this design well before we ask the question spoken like a detective by the Fourth Knight: 'Who killed the Archbishop?' Insofar as we have just seen the Knights kill him, the psychological implication of this question is now that Thomas brought it on himself in his pride. The audience, with the Women of Canterbury, are invited to solve the crime, and in this way a piece of medieval history is given a contemporary dimension. In *T. S. Eliot between Two Worlds*, David Ward reports that in the original performances the accusation that Thomas was courting martyrdom for the sake of personal glory produced murmurs of agreement from the audience.

However, like any non-dramatic poet, Eliot spoke essentially only through a single character, Thomas himself. The Christian martyrdom was offered and accepted as history and as truth, and there is no real conflict between stage and audience. Even with the rhythmic and kinaesthetic choruses and the variety of stress and rhyme in the verse, Eliot failed to produce a drama any less static than Yeats's. The intense symbolism of the Mass was not necessarily more viable than the refinement of the *Noh*.

Eliot quickly recognized that those elements which worked well for *Murder in the Cathedral* could not easily lend themselves to a religious play in a modern setting. In *Poetry and Drama* (1951), he explained that:

> What we have to do is to bring poetry into the world in
> which the audience lives and to which it returns when it
> leaves the theatre; not to transport the audience into some
> imaginary world totally unlike its own, an unreal world
> in which poetry is tolerated.

It may be that in deciding this, Eliot made his fatal mistake — that of rejecting the primary advantage the physical theatre can bring to the art of drama, the use of just 'some imaginary world totally unlike its own'.

Murder in the Cathedral moved from the Mercury Theatre to the Duchess Theatre and ran for nearly a year; it was equally well received in America, France and Germany. For important reasons, Eliot's next play did not fare so well. This was his Orestes play, *The Family Reunion* (1939), and this and his Heracles play, *The Cocktail Party* (1949), attempted to put verse dialogue into a modern situation. To avoid the charge that the poet was merely writing the unnatural language appropriate to a costume drama and an unrepresentative audience, a country-house setting was substituted for a chapter-house, and Harry Monchensey of *The Family Reunion* and Celia Coplestone and her friends in *The Cocktail Party* were offered as representative sinners. Harry's compassionate aunt Agatha clarifies his role:

It is possible
You are the consciousness of your unhappy family,
Its bird sent flying through the purgatorial flame.
Indeed it is possible.

However, Eliot's concern for the ubiquity of his play led him to introduce parallels with the *Oresteia* of Aeschylus, and he found himself calling up the Greek Furies as symbols of retribution. Unfortunately, a drawing-room set on the modern proscenium stage is ill-suited to accommodate such alien creatures, as Eliot reported in his lecture of 1951, *Poetry and Drama*:

> We tried every possible manner of presenting them. We put them on the stage, and they looked like uninvited guests who had strayed in from a fancy dress ball. We concealed them behind gauze, and they suggested a still out of a Walt Disney film. We made them dimmer, and they looked like shrubbery just outside the window. I have seen other expedients tried: I have seen them signalling from across the garden, or swarming on to the stage like a football team, and they are never right. They never succeed in being either Greek goddesses or modern spooks. But their failure is merely a symptom of the failure to adjust the ancient with the modern (p. 30).

The Family Reunion was revived after the war in 1947 at the Mercury Theatre with scarcely better success.

Eliot's later plays seemed prosaic to the extent that their dialogue approximated to ordinary speech and their situations imitated English middle-class drawing-room comedy. As it happens, there is nothing more prosaic than English middle-class drawing-room comedy in the whole history of the stage. Thus, where Yeats's mistake was to eschew the current commercial fashion, Eliot's was to embrace it more warmly. The solution to a modern verse drama may lie somewhere between these extremes.

11 *Pirandello and the* teatro grottesco

Six Characters in Search of an Author (1921)

In Paris in 1923, the startling Italian play *Sei personaggi in cerca d'autore* (*Six Characters in Search of an Author*) by Luigi Pirandello (1867–1936) was published in *Les Cahiers dramatiques* and presented by Georges Pitoëff at the Théâtre des Champs-Élysées. The audience was moderately accustomed to the surprises of symbolist drama, but was not prepared for the play's insistent reversal of theatrical expectations. As had been done in Rome, the 'Actors' entered casually in their everyday clothes through the house, the province of the spectators, and climbed on to an undressed stage. When it was the moment for the 'Characters' to enter, they were flooded with a green light and amazingly lowered to the stage from above, as if they had dropped from the sky: they were actually riding in an old cage-lift previously used for scenery. Paris was wildly enthusiastic, and the author was subsequently honoured by the French government. It was the beginning of an unusually individual and idiosyncratic influence on playwriting everywhere, but particularly in France and America. What we can now recognize as the uniquely Pirandellian element in symbolism is visible in Crommelynck, Anouilh and Genêt, and in Thornton Wilder and Tennessee Williams. It may also account for much of that irrational and consciously theatrical perspective seen in post-war theatre of the absurd.

Six Characters had had a *succès de scandale* in 1921 in Rome, a city not generally considered to be a theatre capital. Directed by Dario Niccodemi at the Teatro Valle, it had been played in an atmosphere of pandemonium, with spectators, critics and actors shouting abuse at one another: *Manicomio!* (Madhouse!) *Buffone!* (Buffoon!) Fighting broke out in the house, and was carried on to the stage and even into the boxes. When, at the end of the play, the author made a timid appearance on the stage, the noise doubled. Nor did the crowd outside the theatre show any sign of dispersing. Pirandello and his daughter Lietta waited for an hour, and then left by a back alley; recognized under a lamppost, they were attacked with whistles and insults until they escaped in a taxi with the crowd throwing coins after them. The heated debate continued through the night. Naturally, the play's reputation spread rapidly, and soon afterwards it was successfully published. Four months later the same production was put on in the Teatro Manzoni in Milan, this time with the audience listening religiously to every word. In 1922 the play was produced in London by Kommisarjevsky and in New York by Brock Pemberton. In 1924 Reinhardt presented it in Berlin, and by 1925 it had been translated into twenty-five languages, including Japanese. It was universally recognized that a new force, not merely a new playwright or a new style, had appeared in the theatre.

Although Pirandello's last plays incline towards myth and symbolism, the best work with which he startled the world of the theatre is so individual as to be hard to identify with a specific movement. In his rejection of realism, as well as of Gabriele d'Annunzio's latter-day romanticism, as a satisfying mode for a future theatre, he appears to borrow from expressionism, surrealism and absurdism; in some ways he seems to link himself with Marinetti's Futurism; in others he seems to be expressing a new-found freedom simply by playing theatre games. But Pirandello does not quite cast off Ibsen. The great Norwegian had met with the usual mixed reception in Rome, and Pirandello had come to his defence. Much of the narrative element buried in Pirandello's plays indeed suggests Ibsen's kind of retrospective drama, like the handling of the inner scene of the milliner's shop in *Six Characters*. His attack on the actors' style of performance in this play also recalls Ibsen's denunciation of the nineteenth-century commercial theatre. But the connection ends there, for in this play and in others, time is fragmented as cleverly as in any symbolist drama, and cause and effect obey the laws only of the imagination. In the last analysis, the evolution of Pirandello's dramatic thinking can be explained only by the growth of his own consciousness of the world in which he lived.

He had begun as a prolific writer of poems and stories, and at his death he had written 232 stories, 7 novels and 44 plays. As early as 1898 he had outlined in the periodical *Il Marzocco* what he considered good modern dramatic dialogue should consist of. Not claiming it to be his own concept, he identified such dialogue as *'azione parlata'*, 'spoken action'. He argued that drama differed from narrative in that the lines in a play must be individual to the character that speaks them, and by their special kinaesthetic quality make him move and live. From this it followed that a playwright should not first choose his plot and then fit his characters to it, but do the opposite. Art is life, said Pirandello, and a play does not make people; rather, people make a play. A play's appropriate style, therefore, should arise from free, living, individual characters conceived in the spirit of their chosen story. The playwright's greatest problem, he contended, is to marry the living character with its function in the plot. These points Pirandello was to elaborate again and again, and especially twenty-five years later in his famous preface to *Six Characters*.

As Professor of Italian in Rome, he published in 1908 his most profound statement on the theory of the *teatro grottesco*, the 'grotesque theatre'. This was the long essay *L'umorismo*, only recently translated into English for the first time as *On Humor*, although 'humourism' would be accurate. The book is a collection of ideas and insights, and, especially in part II, constitutes a synthesis of Pirandello's thinking about the kind of comedy he intended to write. The comic, he believed, has as its basis 'the perception of the opposite'; humour, however, does not try to make you laugh, but instead gives you 'the *feeling* of the opposite', *'il sentimento del contrario'*. He is making the distinction here between the intellect and the emotions, and humour is of the emotions. It stems from the spontaneous reflection of conflicting images in a work of art, so that the humourist is a person constantly off-key, 'like a violin and double bass at the same time', a man whose reflection is like 'icy water' in which feeling plunges and extinguishes itself. The feeling of the opposite arises from the work itself, in which the reflection has caused a violent eruption: 'Every feeling, every thought, or every impulse that arises in the humorist immediately splits into its contrary' (translated A. Illiano and D. P. Testa).

This kind of irony becomes transcendental, Pirandello believed, when the writer sees his role as one of tearing off masks to reveal reality. Such action can also be the source of tragic anguish, for in certain moments of inner silence, perhaps in a flash of madness, the writer senses a void in human existence, senses that life itself is illusory, no less. 'If Cleopatra's nose had been longer', wondered Pirandello, 'who knows what might have happened to the world?' That little 'if' can be inserted like a wedge into anything that happens, and so destroy all reason behind the life we live. For Pirandello, the thought was terrifying.

By 1917, Pirandello's wife had become insanely jealous, accusing him even of incest with his own daughter. In that year he wrote a letter to his son, the writer Stefano Landi, in which he projected a novel about six characters who were obsessed with their story of incest and sibling murder, and sought an author who would express their terrible thoughts and feelings. In this idea Pirandello embodied both his own sense of being obsessed with creative material which demanded realization, and his theory that a character should have a free life of its own. Even then the idea was not quite new: he had written two stories about such *'personaggi'* before, *'La tragedia d'un personaggio'* in 1911 and *'Colloqui coi personaggi'* in 1915.

In all his best plays, the central philosophical comedies, Pirandello pursued the elusive identity, the 'reality', of the free character. *Così è (se vi pare)* (*Right You Are, If You Think So*, 1916), written in six days, was his first major play to question whether the truth could ever be known about other people. *Six Characters*, written in three weeks in 1921, and *Enrico IV* (*Henry IV*), written in two weeks in 1922, further probed the relationship between objective and subjective knowledge of the personality, and brought their author international recognition. *Ciascuno a suo modo* (*Each in His Own Way*, 1924) and *Questa sera si recita a soggetto* (*Tonight We Improvise*, 1930) completed the 'trilogy of the theatre in the theatre' begun by *Six Characters*, these three plays using the physical presence of the medium, its actors and spectators, to break up even more our comfortable attitude towards reality. Although Luigi Chiarelli's play *La maschera e il volto* (*The Mask and the Face*, written in 1913 and produced in 1916) is usually given the credit for having initiated the Italian *teatro grottesco*, because it dealt with social appearances and pretences, it was Pirandello who provided a genuine test of an audience's sense of reality, and it was *Six Characters* which finally shattered the conventions of realism.

Pirandello wrote his remarkable preface to *Six Characters* in 1925, long after the play had proved itself on the stage, and after he had had time to reflect. He picked up his former theme by insisting that the play dealt with the creative process itself, with the activity in his mind of his 'nimble little maidservant' called Fantasy, a creature that was 'a little puckish and malicious'. The Characters, he wrote, had entered his imagination, each crying out to be heard, and his play was written out of the need to give them life – they had obsessed him. He wrote his play, not for the simple pleasure of it, but because the Characters had acquired for him a special power, a 'universal value'. So they became the characters in his play, and although their story was a tragic one, their attempt to put it on the stage was essentially comic. When it comes to it, the six Characters may have found Pirandello, but they fail to find the author they want, and, instead, have to make do with a second-rate director from a second-rate company.

While Pirandello designated 'fantasy' as the source of his inspiration, we might be inclined to call this method of writing symbolist. He declared that he hated symbolic art, which in its need to be allegorical destroyed all spontaneity. Symbolism began with an idea, and only then began to find an appropriate 'image' for the stage representation of the idea. Pirandello's writing, however, began with the image, and so remained 'alive and free', creating on the stage a nice combination of the fantastic and the realistic. His creatures, born of fantasy, asserted the passions of real life, as, like life, they came alive on the stage. We can see that by his dramatic gift, Pirandello had effectively found a way to give the abstractions of symbolism the reality the stage demands.

The Characters express, of course, passions which had been buried in their author. They are identified and reveal themselves in part by what they stand for: the Father, the Stepdaughter and the Son are realized as 'mind', the Mother as 'nature'; in part by the degree of their realization as characters: the Father and the Step-daughter are more rounded than the others. Again, this mixes symbolism and realism. The Father is aware of his incompleteness, and so seeks an author; the Mother is unaware that she is incomplete and not alive, and so is totally fictional, fixed and passive in her own world. But all these creatures of art live forever in their moment of passion, 'embalmed alive in its incorruptible form'. Mme Pace differs from the others in that she makes her entrance without logical motivation of any kind; as Pirandello explained it, she represents 'a sudden change in the level of reality of the scene'. The level of reality assumed by any symbolic stage is not fixed.

Yet little of this matters if it cannot be conveyed to an audience and does not stretch its perception of reality. Pirandello's greatest achievement is to make an audience itself experience the pathos and humour of human self-deception and the relativity of truth. His subjects have the appearance of being abstract and his dialogue of being static, but in performance the drama is very much alive in the mind of its auditors. The conflicting accounts of sanity and madness in the principals in *Right You Are* deceive the audience as much as the townspeople who hear them. *Henry IV* leaves us as much in doubt about the hero's sanity as those on the stage, and we suffer the same fluctuations of belief and disbelief. The playwright's task is to flex the aesthetic distance between the illusion on the stage and the reality in the auditorium, matching the doubts in our minds with the stage action in order to create a dialectic of feeling by which we contradict ourselves.

Six Characters begins with a complete deception. The audience comes into the theatre, and, seeing a rehearsal in progress, is to assume it is in the same world of reality as that it has just left outside. That Pirandello was pleased with the success of this tactic is suggested by its expansion between the first and final versions of the play (1921 and 1925), apparently changed in rehearsal and the light of production. Because of the absence in America of an English translation of the 1925 text, eminent critics like Francis Fergusson, Wylie Sypher and Robert Brustein seem to have been unaware of the changes Pirandello made. The revision begins with the hammering of nails as the stage crew goes about its work, and the customary edge of the audience's anticipation is completely blunted. It was a detail like this that so irritated the Roman audience on the first night. The Actors enter casually, and the Director comes through the auditorium, the world of the audience itself, as does the Leading Lady, who enters late with her pet dog. Only after this indecisive opening does the play seem to begin, and then it is another play that is rehearsed, disarmingly an earlier one by Pirandello, *Il giuoco delle parti* (*The Rules of the Game*, 1918). The Actors proceed to make sarcastic comments about the author's reputation as a playwright of the obscure, self-deflating jokes which the audience may be expected to approve. When the Characters enter, they do not do so from backstage, but, in the final version, from the house also, that is, as if from the real world. In the first version, they stand briefly 'in a tenuous light' to suggest their origin in fantasy, but by 1925 Pirandello recommended that they wear light masks. This device is now generally omitted from production because it inhibits the audience's subsequent ability to believe in the reality of the Characters. When Mme Pace enters unannounced (and with a red wig in the new version), the Actors no longer stand back stupefied, but rush wildly off the stage in fear, thereby associating themselves in their anxiety with the audience in its uncertainty.

The scene in the milliner's shop between the Father and the Stepdaughter was also expanded brilliantly in the final version to accentuate the 'touched up' style of the Actors as they repeat the performance of the Characters. Pirandello also asked that the high pitch of the Prompter's voice be heard throughout the scene, speaking monotonously a little ahead of the Actors as he would have done in the nineteenth-century theatre, thus lending their voices the unreal air of an echo or a bad recording. When the Director rehearses the Actors in how to express particular feelings, he does so by taking their place and repeating some of the lines yet a third time, so that the repetition itself makes the words seem incongruous. Meanwhile, increasing laughter is forced from the Characters at what they hear, and prompts the audience to respond in the same way.

The shock ending of *Six Characters* underwent an even greater extension. In 1925, Pirandello omitted the long passage near the end of the first part of the play, and does not disclose the fate of the children until the end. In this way the drowning of the Girl and the suicide of the Boy come as a complete surprise, and their fictional reality is left more in doubt. When the Director calls for lights, the house is immediately flooded with light, as if some supernatural

hand had suddently pulled the switch. This device is repeated when
he calls for the lights to be switched off: the action is immediate and
startling. When the Director finally calls for a little light to see his
way, a green flood immediately silhouettes *four* of the six Characters: the Girl and the Boy are missing as if they are truly dead.
The Characters advance downstage and stop at the footlights, but
the Stepdaughter bursts into strident laughter and runs up the aisle
through the auditorium. She turns at the door and screams with
laughter again, and finally runs laughing into the foyer and out
into the street, as if into the real world beyond. Only after this
frightening incident does Pirandello permit the curtain to fall and
the audience to leave the theatre.

In his book *Theatre of War*, Eric Bentley has bravely tried
to identify the kind of play Pirandello wrote in *Six Characters*. The
abstract, 'morality' qualities represented by the Characters —Re-
morse, Revenge, Disdain and Grief —seem to owe their conception
to the popularity of the new expressionist drama flourishing
elsewhere at the time, but the parts are too rich and alive to admit
the simplification of character which expressionism required.
Pirandello's obsession with his creatures, and their obsession with
their story, may even hint at Strindberg's form of dream play. But
the deliberate muddle of the narrative element, with one play
superimposed upon another, is a game in which the audience is
truly the victim — a symbolic theatre game. Inside the theatre,
characters can be more real than people, and live actors can be mere
impersonators, dealers in illusion. It is a game of paradoxes: a
character cannot die, but then it is never living. The place of the
play is the theatre itself, that is, illusion is reality. The name Pirandello is synonymous with such paradox.

That Pirandellian theatre should also imply some new
approach to acting was clear. As the reality of the human personality is illusory, so the actors must convey varying degrees of
reality in performance. Discarding Stanislavsky, they had to acquire
a more self-conscious flexibility, a quality of 'plasticity' in performance. To this end, and with the help of a state subsidy, in 1924
Pirandello, his son Stefano Landi, Orio Vergani and a few others
formed the Teatro degli Undici, their own tiny *Teatro d'Arte di
Roma*, seating only 300, rented in the Palazzo Odescalchi. With

Ruggero Ruggeri, later to be the first Henry IV, Lamberto Picasso and the talented Marta Abba, the Milanese actress who helped make the company famous, they toured Europe and South America, Picasso playing the Father and Marta Abba the Stepdaughter. The project lasted until 1928, when the minimal subsidy finally contributed to total financial failure. But only ensemble playing by a company working in repertory could fully succeed in making the subtle shifts in style that Pirandello's drama demanded.

Pirandello learned to direct his own plays at a fast, sprightly, even comic, pace, using the plainest of sets and emphasizing naturalistic acting: the plasticity came according to the intensity of the acting. Reinhardt directed *Six Characters* in 1924 as if the Characters were part of the vision of a compassionate Director, who was placed with his back to the audience in order to remain in the real world. In Pirandello's production, he kept the Characters central, making the Director a fussy professional man of the theatre. It is amusing to report that one criticism levelled at the play in its own time was that the Characters were more real and consistent than the Actors; this judgment, of course, represented a triumph for the author and the company, since the structure of the play and the shades of realistic acting were intended to tease the audience towards just such a conclusion. The performance signals to look for in the text are all stylistic, with one attitude contradicting and undercutting another until illusion itself evaporates. If, finally, our conviction of reality is undermined, then the imagination is free, and the stage acquires that impersonality we associate with the best symbolist drama and all great art.

---

12 *Symbolist drama in Spain: García Lorca*

The House of Bernarda Alba (1936)

In the twentieth century the Spanish theatre has largely been isolated from the sequence of European theatrical revolts which began with Ibsen. From the days of Spain's Golden Age in the late sixteenth and early seventeenth centuries, the time of Lope de Vega and Calderón, the Spanish theatre has always been somewhat independent of European influences. Even the Spanish romantic melodrama of the nineteenth century owed more to Spain's own drama of the seventeenth century than to Paris. Centred in Madrid, Spanish drama essentially reflected middle-class and escapist values, and the coming of Franco's republic in 1931, followed by the Civil War in 1936–9 and its repressive aftermath, prolonged its conservative tendencies.

The modern revival of Spanish drama began with the prolific output of Jacinto Benavente y Martínez (1866–1954), whose plays introduced a gentle social criticism into the theatre. The brothers Quintero, Serafín Álvarez (1871–1938) and Joaquín Álvarez (1873–1944), achieved a wider reputation with plays drawing upon their own Andalusia for local colour. But it was the playwright and producer Gregorio Martínez Sierrà (1881–1947) who most helped the revival of the Spanish theatre, and prepared the way for Spain's greatest modern playwright. In 1905, Martínez Sierrà had conceived his *Teatro de ensueño*, 'theatre of dreams', the name of his first play and a form for others to follow. His best-known play is *Canción de cuna* (*Song of the Cradle*, 1911). He also translated Shakespeare and Maeterlinck, who did not seem so incongruous a pair at the time, and ran the publishing house of Renacimiento, which introduced new European playwrights to Spain – Bernard Shaw, J. M. Barrie, Pirandello – and published outward-looking periodicals on the modern arts. Of great importance, he directed Spain's first art theatre, the Eslava Theatre in Madrid, from 1917 to 1928; his book is appropriately entitled *Un teatro de arte en España* (*An Art Theatre in Spain*, 1925).

The surrealist poet Federico García Lorca (1898–1936) arrived when the scene was set for the advent of a special talent in the theatre. He worked outside the mainstream of European symbolist drama, but his contribution to this genre is in many ways the most accomplished and exciting we have. Lorca wrote an outstanding trilogy of poetic folk-tragedies in the short years before his early death: *Bodas de sangre* (*Blood Wedding*, 1933), *Yerma* (1934) and *La casa de Bernardo Alba* (*The House of Bernardo Alba*, 1936). These plays brought to the Spanish theatre a unique quality of symbolism and ritual which could have sprung only from the rural community of southern Spain. They have the character of Andalusian folk-ballads, and just as Lorca had represented the spirit of Spanish life in his poetry, so he did in his drama.

Lorca was a gifted musician and painter, as well as a lyrical poet. It is as if he were the one playwright born to give theatrical life to the theories of Appia and Craig, those which held that all the arts should combine in the art of drama, and from the beginning his work was consciously experimental. In particular, his lyricism is inseparable from his playwriting. The form of his drama is conceived musically; songs and dances abound in his scenes so that at times they more resemble opera than drama, and in their visual features of setting, décor and lighting, the poetry of symbolist light and colour is made to speak. For example, *Blood Wedding* begins with a yellow room, the Groom's house, moves to a room painted rose, Leonardo's house, and then to the Bride's cave, which has a cross of large rose-coloured flowers with rose ties to hold the lace curtains. Outside the cave, the set is in white grey and cold blue tones with large cactus trees in shadowy silver. For the final scene of catastrophe, a simple dwelling with arches and thick walls is done all in white in order to convey 'the monumental feeling of a church'; and the instruction adds, 'There should not be a single grey nor any shadow, not even what is necessary for perspective.' The rich verbal and visual features of this play seem to propose a more valid poetic drama than any-thing conceived by Yeats or Eliot.

In his plays Lorca displays enormous sympathy with Spanish womanhood, and his poetry lends his female characters a primitive strength which makes them larger than life. Add to this an irresis-tibly melancholy and fateful element present in his heroines, without a shadow of hope for the future, no redeeming grace of heaven, and it is apparent that the standards of psychological realism are not to be strictly applied to them: they obey the laws of symbolism. It follows that those offstage characters whose presence is felt powerfully in all of Lorca's plays, assume even greater sym-bolic qualities. Pepe el Romano, the unseen male in the all-female *House of Bernarda Alba*, is the outstanding example of this practice.

In his short career, Lorca soon abandoned surrealism proper, although a few slight scenes written in 1929 and 1930 reflect his earlier interest in it. These are in the play *Así que pasen cinco años* (*If Five Years Pass*), together with some fragments from *El público* (*The Public*). They present figures of fantasy who are given incoherent lines of 'automatic writing' to speak, and the action is full of violent and bloodthirsty images. It is doubtful whether Lorca ever intended to produce this material, and he soon turned to the kind of play which had its roots more in reality without being altogether earth-bound.

Blood Wedding had its origin in a peasant incident which Lorca read of in a newspaper. The incident had occurred in the southern seaport of Almería, and had to do with family feuding, male jealousy and the abduction of a bride on her wedding day, with a tragic aftermath. But the play is in no way documentary; rather, it was influenced in tone by the poetically heightened and heavily ritualistic Irish peasant tragedy *Riders to the Sea* by J. M. Synge. *Blood Wedding* rises to the level of poetic fantasy, until in act III abstract personifications mingle freely with characters of flesh and blood. Thus, in the forest three fateful Wood-cutters meet the Moon in the form of a Young Wood-cutter, who appears washed in a blue radiance. Death enters in the form of an Old Woman dressed as a beggar in a dark cape:

> Two violins are heard. Suddenly two long, ear-splitting shrieks are heard, and the music of the two violins is cut short. At the second shriek the Beggar Woman appears and stands with her back to the audience. She opens her cape and stands in the centre of the stage like a great bird with immense wings.

The Beggar Woman leads the Bridegroom to his rival, and to his fate, as two girls in dark blue weave strands of red wool, symbolizing blood, death and grief. By such means nature itself becomes a character, no more impersonal than the central parts, which are designated simply as the Mother, the Bridegroom, the Bride and so on. Lorca directed the first production of this play himself at the Teatro Beatriz in Madrid with the company of Josefina Diaz de Artigas, and it was received with enthusiasm.

Yerma was first played in Madrid by Margarita Xirgu. The title means 'barren', and is the name of the wife of an impotent husband, Juan. After five years of marriage she has not had the child for which she longs, and she is increasingly attracted to the virile young shepherd, Victor. After a swaying fertility dance of her own devising, she strangles Juan. On the surface, the play might seem realistic in that it is concerned with Yerma's mind and spirit, and studies the psychology of her wish for motherhood and the misery of her frustration. Mistaken ideas about honour and fidelity are simultaneously subjected to criticism with a degree of comic irony, darkly mixed with the play's tragic view of social forces. But in fact the play is only a shade less poetic than *Blood Wedding*.

Lorca subtitled *Yerma* 'a tragic poem', and it is composed of a sequence of symbolic scenes. It begins with a mime, Yerma's dream of a Shepherd who brings her a Child dressed in white, thus introducing religious overtones from the start; when the Shepherd leaves, the stage is bathed in the light of a bright spring morning. Yerma's maternal instinct becomes the subject of the singing of a chorus of

16. Lorca, *Yerma*, 1934. Production by Luis Escobar at the Teatro Eslava, Madrid, 1960. Design by José Caballero.

village washer-women washing their clothes in a mountain stream. Her dance is performed as night falls before a shrine high in the mountains, and this scene is composed of women carrying lighted candles and girls running across the stage with long garlands in their hands. To a crescendo of harness bells, two figures enter to represent the male and female principles, each carrying a large mask 'of great beauty and with a feeling of pure earth'. This is the high point in an amazingly simple play which nevertheless makes a powerfully poetic statement about the fullness of life and the natural role of women.

Lorca deliberately attempted to suppress the lyrical element in his most famous play, *The House of Bernarda Alba*, written in prose just before his death in 1936. He called it 'a drama about women in the villages of Spain', and announced that it was intended as 'a photographic document'. But if it is rich in a realistic situation and in realistic nervous tension, it is far from being a realistic drama. Five repressed daughters are ruled by a tyrannical mother, a widow who represents the most narrow values of Spanish rural society. The girls are to mourn the death of their father for eight years, 'grinding their hearts to dust'. They are locked up in the house, and human nature fights back as each girl feel sexual desire for the unseen Pepe el Romano. Disaster follows when the youngest, Adela, spends a night with Pepe, and, believing that her mother has consequently shot him, hangs herself. With grim irony, Bernarda orders that Adela be dressed like a virgin for her burial.

Adolfo Salazar, a friend of Lorca's, heard him read the play aloud, and reported that everytime he finished a scene he cried out, 'Not a drop of poetry! Reality! Realism!' Lorca believed he had achieved cold, objective tragedy. However, although it is true that of all his tragedies *Bernarda Alba* has the most realistically individualized characters, the signs of poetic drama are everywhere. From the start, the play's bleak mood of chastity reflecting the family name Alba, is visually established by the bare prison of a setting, 'a very white room in Bernarda Alba's house', and the curtain rises to an empty stage filled with 'a great brooding silence', with only the tolling of bells heard in the distance. The icy, virginal whiteness of the set is contrasted with the black shawls and mourning clothes worn by the women as they sew white linen sheets. The atmosphere of sexual violence is suggested by the sounds of a stallion kicking restlessly in his stall, until Bernarda orders that he be allowed to run free — but only after the mares have been shut in the corral. Maria Josefa, the ancient grandmother of eighty, is mad from years of unrequited love, and is the ever-present image of what Bernarda and any of her daughters could become. The play is thus replete with symbolic elements intrinsic to the drama, each of which points relentlessly to the heightened theme of the play, the character of Spanish womanhood and Spanish domestic life. For political reasons, *The House of Bernarda Alba* had to wait until 1945 for its first production, and then not in Spain but at the Teatro Avenida in Buenos Aires, with Margarita Xirgu and her company.

From his childhood García Lorca was interested in the theatre, and in 1931 he had the good fortune to be offered a government subsidy to found his own travelling company of students in Madrid, the Teatro Universitario, affectionately named 'La Barraca' ('The Hut') because the theatre was set up on a converted truck. It was one of two such ventures planned to bring good theatre to rural areas in Spain and South America. Lorca was the right man to write for this company as well as to direct it. He had his roots in rural Spain, and his ideals were high. He would shake off ancient tradition, and adapt each show to its audience. In an address delivered after the opening of *Yerma*, he insisted that

> the theatre which does not feel the social pulse, the
> historical pulse, the drama of its people, and catch the
> genuine colour of its landscape and of its spirit, with
> laughter or with tears, has no right to call itself a theatre.

In the usual reaction against the commercial theatre, he also believed that the stage had a duty to lead: 'The theatre must impose itself on the public, not the public on the theatre.' Needless to say, in his plays Lorca set a standard few could begin to follow.

The quality of Lorca's dramatic writing, the unmistakable brilliance of his imagination, tempted directors everywhere in Europe, and in America even the Becks and their Living Theatre have tried to stage his work long after the original symbolist impulse had died. But the concern of these plays with the rigidity and intolerance of the Spanish code of behaviour, its unique mixture of honour and pride with pious bigotry, has proved difficult to recreate outside Spain and South America. It may be that this subject matter, infused with Lorca's spirit of intense sensuality and poetic ritualism, can be satisfactorily handled only by Spanish actors working with Spanish audiences.

13 *Stylization in France: Copeau and after*

Noah (1931), *The Trojan War Will Not Take Place* (1935)

It is a widely accepted idea that the French theatre lives for the word and not the spectacle, for the author and not the agent, but according to Jean Vilar, the first half of the twentieth century in Paris was an age of great directors rather than great dramatists. It was a time when the French director proved himself to be an interpreter of the text who could surpass the critic himself. The trend-setting theatre after the Théâtre-Libre of Antoine was not the Oeuvre of Lugné-Poe, but the small left-bank theatre in the Rue du Vieux Colombier. It seated less than 400, and it was opened in 1913 for a mere seven months by Jacques Copeau (1879–1949). Copeau was a disciple of Appia, who had written inspiring words to him of his 'cathedral of the future'. It was Copeau who reintroduced to the French stage its former 'classical' discipline of style in performance, in opposition to the artlessness of naturalism and the novelty of symbolism. Where other young rebels would set before the public the latest tricks of one or other mode, Copeau chose to open his theatre with a lesser-known Elizabethan play, Thomas Heywood's *A Woman Killed with Kindness*, which he followed with the Shakespeare classics, *Twelfth Night, The Winter's Tale, As You Like It* and *Much Ado about Nothing*. When it came to French plays, Copeau founded his repertory solidly on Molière, particularly those plays written in the high style of classical French farce, *La Jalousie du Barbouille, L'Amour médecin, Les Fourberies de Scapin, L'Avare* and *Le Misanthrope*; and he followed Molière with Marivaux, Musset and Mérimée. The meticulous study and rehearsal of the classics were the basis for all of Copeau's work, and he expected his company to share his devotion and enthusiasm.

By such means Copeau showed subsequent theatre artists an ideal of service to the drama. Moreover, two seasons (1917–19) in New York at the Garrick Theatre during the First World War, at the request of the French government, did much to spread Copeau's ideas beyond Paris.

While in New York, Copeau had tried out a stage in the shape of an Elizabethan platform, the so-called 'thrust' stage, and on his return to the Vieux Colombier in 1920, he rebuilt its stage, not as an Elizabethan replica, but as a modern equivalent designed to serve as a multipurpose medium of many acting areas. It was an open stage, having no proscenium arch, footlights or front curtain to restrict its depth. The audience was to feel that it was in the same room with the actors, not seated in front of a picture. Behind this forestage, in the centre, was built a small austere platform, backed by a gallery, an inner stage and steps. This platform was the famous 'tréteau nu' of the Vieux Colombier, its 'bare platform', for at the conclusion of his 1913 manifesto, Copeau had written like a call to arms, 'Pour l'oeuvre nouvelle qu'on nous laisse un tréteau nu!' ('For the new production let us have a bare platform!'). With its bare wall for lighting effects, the new stage was made up entirely of architectural features, and when Copeau had the floor painted with geometrical lines, the effect was to run counter to any naturalistic impression. This theatre has been called the first presentational playhouse of the modern world, and although Copeau later removed the architectural unit of gallery and steps as being too inflexible, the Vieux Colombier led inevitably to striking new developments in the art of the theatre.

Copeau was a cultured man and a sensitive artist, one of the founders of *La Nouvelle Revue Française*. His wish to return to the classics and his need to work on a bare stage stem from the same source: both reflect the kind of discipline he thought essential for the modern theatre. To his productions he brought an unaccustomed, healthy respect for the text, to the point where he was even accused of being literary. The object of his attack was the commercial drama of the boulevards, and for the usual decorative spectacle he substituted an extreme simplicity and purity of staging, aiming not at a photographic image, but at a functional suggestion — 'a tree to stand for a forest, a pillar for a temple'. In voice, movement and gesture, Copeau also sought the precisely correct rhythm and style appropriate to each play he handled. In this way he was careful to avoid being associated with any particular school of playwriting, or adopting as a formula any single style of playing, a policy which might have put at risk the life of the company as soon as the novelty wore off.

Copeau has written extensively about the proper treatment of Molière on the stage. He attacked the policy of the Comédie-Française, which he believed had made the great comedies unpopular by playing them with intonations and gestures based so much on encrusted tradition that they had lost all vitality. Listen to Molière's own voice, 'cette simple harmonie', Copeau advised, and avoid the accumulations of stage business which are not in the spirit of the words. He believed that the sense of a play's choreography should be developed only from the text. Copeau did, indeed, reinstate a more authentic Molière at the Vieux Colombier, and eventually at the Comédie-Française itself, but the argument that the playwright should be the strongest force in the theatre was a little ironic when the final effect of Copeau's work has been to lend more muscle to the director.

From 1920 to 1924 Copeau provided a home for the classics and a number of new French playwrights without uncovering any outstanding name. Then, at the height of his success, he gave up the Vieux Colombier and took his company off to Pernand-Vergelesses, a village in Burgundy, in order to start a school for actors. Every day 'Les Copiaux', as they were nicknamed, would exercise with fencing, dancing and gymnastics, and then improvise some mime on a chosen theme. At one point they rehearsed a *Noh* play and a farce from the *commedia dell'arte*. By such methods Copeau expected to dispense with the star system and create a true ensemble. He would train the actors' bodies as well as their minds, and emphasize the essential skills of acting based on movement and gesture. His ideal was to build a performance by discovering the underlying rhythm and shape of a play. In 1927, the village of Nuits St Georges asked Copeau to celebrate its wine harvest in mime and song, and he obliged by improvising upon the real life of the local *vignerons*, the vine-growers.

In a now legendary performance, the company demonstrated the life of the vineyards before a delighted assembly of villagers, and it is possible to think that on that special occasion a new mode of theatre was born.

The experiment lasted until 1929. The company finally broke up because Copeau preferred the exercise to the production; today, the English director Peter Brook may be in similar danger of losing sight of his audience. Nevertheless, Copeau's dedicated work was carried on by many who trained under him, and even by those who did not, as when George Devine of the English Stage Company felt the power of Copeau's discipline through his friendship with a disciple, Michel Saint-Denis. Copeau's particular followers were the great actor–directors who formed the 'Cartel des quatre', Dullin, Jouvet, Pitoëff and Baty, and these four between them determined to a large extent the direction of the French theatre between the wars.

In 1921, Charles Dullin (1885-1949) went off to form an experimental group of his own, the Atelier, which worked on the small circular stage of the Théâtre Montmartre. Dogged by poverty and ill-health, Dullin succeeded against odds in running his theatre until 1938, when it was taken over by André Barsacq (1909–73). Dullin presented plays which rejected realism as being wholly unnatural to the medium of theatre, but which exulted in its element of gay make-believe and colourful satire, plays like Calderón's *Life Is a Dream*, Ben Jonson's *Volpone* and Pirandello's *Each in His Own Way* and *The Pleasure of Honesty*, which Dullin first introduced to Paris. In later years he was the first to offer much of Salacrou, Achard, Anouilh and Sartre to the public, all playwrights who rebelled against naturalism to some degree, and it is significant that Artaud was one of his students. 'The theatre is not a place for contemplation, but for faëry', Dullin wrote, and the kind of training he gave his actors was intended to release them from the mud of the realistic convention by having them improvise in the manner of the *commedia dell'arte*. It is curious with what frequency in these years that rascal Harlequin reasserts his fundamental right to return to the stage.

Although Armand Salacrou (1899–   ) was first produced by Lugné-Poe, he worked with Dullin over a long period. Salacrou wrote prolifically in a surrealistic vein, introducing existentialist themes with Pirandellian twists. His best-known play is *L'Inconnue d'Arras* (*The Unknown Woman of Arras*, 1935). This enacts the life of a man at the moment of his suicide, and covers the story of his past in three acts made up of flashbacks in the manner of expressionistic cinema, mixing on stage the dead with the living. Salacrou enjoyed devising theatre games, juxtaposing styles, illogically manipulating place and time, introducing elements of parody and burlesque. He was altogether a director's playwright, calling for uncomplicated staging and bold effects, and Dullin was his man.

Like Dullin, Louis Jouvet (1887–1951) continued the Copeau tradition on his own, and after 1922 alternated productions with Pitoëff at the Comédie des Champs-Élysées. Jouvet also sought ways to free the stage from realism, and in 1953 the English critic Harold Hobson could report that his contempt for realism was so widely

17. Molière, *The School for Wives*, 1937. Production by Louis Jouvet and design by Christian Bérard at the Théâtre de l'Athénée.

shared on the French stage that characters in modern comedies everywhere pressed bells that were not there, and made speeches to the audience instead of to each other.

Jouvet scored an early success with Jules Romains's popular farce *Knock ou le triomphe de la médecine* (*Dr Knock*, 1923), for which he directed and played the title part. The play tells the story of how to intimidate a whole town with the threat of disease, and it was directed in the stylized manner of Molière. The actors were set against a simple backcloth painted in such a way as to remove any suggestion of realism, and Jouvet continued to play the charlatan Knock with a fine comic flair for twenty-five years. The performance of Molière became his special strength, and he achieved notable productions of *L'École des femmes* (1936) and *Dom Juan* (1948). The former had a modern stylized set by Christian Bérard, but the stage was hung with five magnificent Louis XIV chandeliers reminiscent of the *grand salon* in which the play was first performed in the seventeenth century. In 1934, Jouvet moved to the Théâtre Athenée, where he produced and acted in all but one of Giraudoux's plays as they were written, starting with *Amphitryon 38*. Director and playwright were perfect collaborators who together perfected a characteristic style. Like Copeau, Jouvet believed that a good play contained within itself the secret to its own staging, and that therefore a good director should accept his author's text almost as it was written. The art of the director, said Jouvet, was not a profession but a condition, always ready to adjust to new demands.

In *L'Impromptu de Paris*, Jean Giraudoux (1882–1944) wrote, 'Le théâtre est un acte d'amour —tout n'est que besoin de communication et de communion.' ('The theatre is an act of love —a need of communication and communion.') Diplomat, journalist, novelist and playwright, Giraudoux was possibly France's leading dramatist between the wars, cementing his reputation with *Amphitryon 38* (1929), *La Guerre de Troie n'aura pas lieu* (*The Trojan War Will Not Take Place*, or *Tiger at the Gates*, 1935), *Électre* (*Electra*, 1937) and *Ondine* (1939). His widely-acclaimed social satire *La Folle de Chaillot* (*The Madwoman of Chaillot*), in which the Madwoman defends the poor against the rich, was produced posthumously in 1945. Giraudoux's distinctive dramatic wit, spare and graceful, developed with the kind of playing practised by Jouvet and his troupe. In drawing so frequently upon Greek legend, and finding ironic parallels with modern subjects, he developed a theatrical mode akin to fantasy, whereby realism was never quite expected, and a simple impressionism in the staging and the acting gained strength and point for the play.

For *La Guerre de Troie n'aura pas lieu*, Giraudoux chose the moment from the Homeric story just after the rape of Helen and before the declaration of war. In spite of everything that Hector can do to avoid the conflict by persuading Paris, Helen and Priam to be reasonable, even allowing himself to be insulted by the Greeks and offering himself in single combat with Ulysses, the action moves inevitably to catastrophe, when an absurdly trivial chance event finally touches off Hector's anger and destiny takes its course. Giraudoux uses the myth to shape his story, with any modification of the original and any modern anachronism automatically lending the play its emphasis. The myth also adds aesthetic distance to the subject and suggests an appropriate stylization in its presentation, like a theatrical convention. In this practice, Giraudoux, with Cocteau, could have set something of an example in method and style to O'Neill, Eliot, Anouilh and Sartre, and others who made use of Greek myth on the modern stage.

The Russian-born Georges Pitoëff (1886—1939) left the Théâtre des Champs-Élysées with his actress wife Ludmilla (1896—1951) to pursue a strikingly abstract style of production at the Théâtre des Arts after 1924. The two then went to the Théâtre aux Mathurins in 1934, and there found a home for a few last years. For a production of Wilde's *Salomé*, Pitoëff resurrected some of the original ideas of a symbolist production of the play. He hung the walls and laid the floor of the stage with black velvet. The characters were dressed in colours to symbolize their feelings, violent desire in hot reds and yellows, reason and contemplation in cooler tones. The locations in Henri-René Lenormand's morbid dream play *Le Mangeur de rêves* (*The Eater of Dreams*, 1922) were suggested by coloured ribbons, green for the sea, a shell of pink for a boudoir, red for a desert. Pitoëff matched the theme of Pirandello's *Henry IV* by staging it with a thin cardboard set, which began to collapse as Henry's mind gave way, until, in a panic, he tried to prop it up himself. Pitoëff also directed the first production of Cocteau's *Orphée* (*Orpheus*) in 1926 and Gide's *Oedipe* (*Oedipus*) in 1932. The first plays of Jean Anouilh, *Le Voyageur sans bagages* (*Traveller without Luggage*, 1937) and *La Sauvage* (*The Savage*, 1938), also owe their first productions to the Pitoëffs. With stylized presentation, the aesthetic connections between these masters of the surreal were immediately apparent.

Gaston Baty (1885–1952) organized his own company, Les Compagnons de la Chimère, in 1921, and in 1930 took over his own theatre, the Théâtre Montparnasse. But Baty proved less of a disciple of Copeau than his contemporaries, for, fearing to be stamped as too literary, he freely added mime, colour, light and noise to his productions, which were in the more decorative and spectacular tradition of the nineteenth century, and paid less attention to the written word of the text.

Strong testimony to the stylistic importance of the French movement has come from Michel Saint-Denis (1897–1971). Copeau was Saint-Denis's uncle, and they worked together at the Vieux Colombier after 1919. From 1931 to 1935, Saint-Denis directed his own group, La Compagnie des Quinze, using a lyrical style with a near-Oriental element of pantomime. With André Barsacq, he rebuilt his stage after the manner of the Vieux Colombier in a studio theatre at Sèvres. Again, the idea was to eliminate any possibility of realistic illusion, in the belief that the *tréteau nu* would ensure that the play would seem to take place in the same room with its audience, and that, exposed in this way, the actors would be compelled to give simple and honest performances. The ceiling and walls of the stage were now fully visible, showing the lighting apparatus, ropes and other unmentionables of backstage, and columns formed a permanent architectural background. On one occasion, Saint-Denis even considered taking the final step and performing in La Salle Wagram, a boxing-ring.

When Saint-Denis produced Obey's *La Bataille de la Marne* (*The Battle of the Marne*, 1931) on a virtually bare stage, the London critic James Agate described how well a few players could prompt the imagination of the audience at the beginning of the play:

> On the stage nothing save a few dun hangings veiling
> the bare theatre walls, and the floor artificially raked to
> to enable the actors to move on different planes. Off the

stage an immense distance away a military band is playing, and in the wings the armies of France go by. We see them through the eyes of five or six peasant women clothed in black and grouped as you may see them in the fields of France or the canvases of Millet . . . On a bare stage the actors recreated not the passion of one or two, but the agony of a nation.

It was in good part because the medium of performance was so simple that Saint-Denis's company achieved so fresh and intense a

18. Obey, *Noah*, 1931. Production by Jerome Mayer, New York, with costumes by Remo Bufano. Pierre Fresnay as Noah.

style of playing, although, like Copeau and Jouvet, he recognized that each country and each age had its appropriate style, which he called its 'reality'. To complete the history: the success of Saint-Denis in London encouraged him to found the London Theatre Studio, which survived as a training school for actors until the early 1950s, and boasted Michael Redgrave and Peter Ustinov among its first students.

The plays of André Obey (1892—1975) owed much of their vitality in performance to Saint-Denis's production methods. Obey had joined the Vieux Colombier in 1929, and wrote his plays with known actors in mind, so that his play of Noah and his ark, *Noé* (1931), was well suited to the skills of the company. It was designed by Barsacq, with the costumes by Marie-Hélène Dasté. Pierre Fresnay played the lead, and Saint-Denis appeared as the Elephant. The fact that this play has simple charm, but questionable depth, testifies to the strength and weakness of the Copeau policy. Obey tells the Bible story in five impressionistic scenes, enlivening the material with a contemporary French idiom, much as the mystery plays did with their medieval vernacular. Thus Noah builds the ark trustingly, and seems to chat easily with God.

> Seigneur!... Oui, Seigneur, lui-même. Désolé de vous déranger encore, mais ... dois-je faire un gouvernail?
>
> (Lord!... Yes, Lord, it's me. Very sorry to trouble You again ... Should I make a rudder?)

More sympathy with the project comes from the chorus of animals than from Noah's wife and children, who desert him as soon as they reach land. But in spite of the mystery of God's commandments and the apparent failure of the flood to contain the selfishness of mankind, Noah remains faithful. The play thus makes a plain statement about the recurrent cycle of life, and shows how simple people behave under stress.

Obey claimed that the play was composed as theatre, not literature, as drama designed to capture a 'stage' life and rhythm before any words were spoken. Against a simplified setting — a platform for the ark, a ladder to the ground — the two choruses of animals and children gave Saint-Denis's company opportunities to demonstrate their ensemble work, especially in the group miming of falling raindrops, the rolling of the boat in the storm and the descent of the dove through the air. There was a clean-cut simplicity about this kind of theatre which was immensely pleasing, even if it was not destined to lead anywhere.

Jean-Louis Barrault (1910–   ) began his work in the theatre under Dullin at the Atelier in 1931, and so was in direct line of succession from Copeau. He played in Corneille's *Le Cid* at the Comédie-Française in 1940, and his name was made. With his wife Madeleine Renaud, he directed the Théâtre Marigny for the ten years from 1946 to 1956, and became director of the Théâtre de France at the Odéon from 1959 to 1968. As we saw, Barrault was responsible for the extraordinary revival of several neglected plays by Claudel before the playwright died in 1955. Barrault himself played Rodrigue in *Le Soulier de satin* in 1943, in a production which lasted for longer than four hours. He managed to speak the long, involved speeches of *Partage de midi* in 1948, and also produced *Christophe Colombe* in 1953. Writing in that year, Harold Hobson placed Barrault at the head of the theatrical talent in Paris, and, with its designer Christian Bérard and players like Edwige Feuillère, Pierre Brasseur, Pierre Blanchar, Jean Desailly and Jacques Dacqmine, ventured to name the Marigny as the world's leading theatre.

Barrault is a dedicated artist for whom the theatre is, as the saying goes, a way of life. He made the art of mime and the language of gesture his special forte, taking as his master the mime Étienne Decroux, who had also trained under Copeau, and as his inspiration the lively tradition of the *commedia dell'arte*. In his *Réflexions sur le théâtre*, Barrault tells how, when he was making a mimetic version of Faulkner's *As I Lay Dying*, he spent many days rehearsing the mime of taming a wild horse, using nothing to indicate the presence of the imaginary animal; suddenly he noticed that a cleaner was leaning on her broom and staring at him. Then she said, 'I've been trying to guess what you've been doing all this time on that horse of yours.' Barrault told this story as if she had given him a prize: 'What a victory! What joy!' The lengthy discipline of his training was rewarded. For Barrault followed Craig in believing that the role of the actor was that of a superpuppet, a creature of superbly controlled rhythms which could be applied to any non-realistic drama.

Copeau, Dullin and Barrault, all three, believed in training in the ways of the *commedia dell'arte* as a preparation for the performance of Molière, and both Copeau and Barrault played Molière's Scapin — with Barrault more like the *commedia* clown Scapino. Eric Bentley reported that this performance was remarkable in striking the fine balance between convention and life. Playing on an angular set by Bérard, with steps on either side of the stage, a bridge between them and houses artificially painted on the wings, Barrault wore a black skullcap in the 1950 production of *Les Fourberies de Scapin*, and the skullcap had the effect of making Scapin more like a robot and putting Barrault's lithe acrobatic body to full use, 'dashing up and down steps and stepladders, sliding down bannisters, mimicking men of war, dancing a jig'.

When Barrault produced Racine's *Phèdre* in 1943, he discovered the play to be like a 'hidden treasure' whose resources were inexhaustible once 'so many layers of varnish', the encrustations of tradition, had been removed. We may be grateful that he wrote a unique book, *Commentaries sur Phèdre* for *Éditions de Seuil* in 1946, which is unlike any description of a classical production ever written. The book consists of detailed notes on the setting and lighting, as well as the acting; it discusses the 'recitative', the use of voice, articulation, gesture, so that they may match the poet's power and subtlety. Barrault shows himself as intensely sensitive to the inner feeling of the play.

Barrault was not tied to any formula, and seemed equally at home with Feydeau as Racine — he is to be credited with the rediscovery of Georges Feydeau through his production of *Occupe-toi d'Amélie* (*Keep and Eye on Emily*, or, in another version by Noël Coward, *Look after Lulu*). Nevertheless, while founding his work on both grave and gay excursions into the great drama of the past, Barrault, like his contemporaries, believed that the primary duty of the theatre was to serve modern authors, and to bring every resource of the modern stage, including music, dance and film, to their aid. Barrault's company offered outstanding productions of Salacrou's *Les Nuits de la colère* (*Nights of Anger*), Montherlant's *Malatesta* and Anouilh's *La Répétition* (*The Rehearsal*). The production of André Gide's version of Kafka's *Le Procès* (*The Trial*) in 1947 tested Barrault's ability to stylize the stage and its movement sufficient to recreate the nightmare the surrealism of the novel demanded.

Bentley thought the décor for the play 'a perpetual transformation scene':

> From the first opening of the curtain, walls rise and fall. There are many broad, dark arches, many dark little rooms and eery perspectives. The acting is stylized. The actors drink from empty cups, and hammer away at imaginary typewriters. The telephone on Joseph K's desk is about eighteen inches long.

19. Kafka, *The Trial*, 1947. Production by Barrault and design by Félix Labisse at the Théâtre Marigny, Paris, with Barrault (left) and Madeleine Renaud (right of centre).

> The art of pantomime is brought in to reinforce these impressions. At one point Barrault performs the mime's slow-motion walk. At another he seems to be running but is actually treading air while two men hold him up. At another he holds his hat rigidly out before him during a long transition from one scene to the next (*In Search of Theater*, p. 197).

Barrault, who was a friend and disciple of Antonin Artaud, with his ideal of a physical theatre, claimed that the theatre of cruelty was in this production, and also in his version of *Gargantua and Panta-gruel*, performed as a three-act play entitled *Rabelais* in a boxing-ring in 1969.

The notable line of great French directors in the twentieth century is not ended. Firmin Gémier (1869–1933) had founded the Théâtre National Populaire in 1920 as an attempt to bring popular audiences back to the theatre in France. In 1951, Jean Vilar (1912–71) became the director of the Théâtre National Populaire at the Palais de Chaillot, and until his resignation in 1963 aimed to bring great drama, Shakespeare, Corneille, Aristophanes and Brecht, to the largest possible number, including working-class people. This was also the policy behind his summer festivals at Avignon, which opened with Corneille's *Le Cid* in 1951, with Gérard Philipe as Rodrigue. The famous battle speech of act iv had Philipe standing gloriously with a spotlight picking out his black and gold armour, backed by its red cloak and blue scarf, resembling some heroic figure in bas-relief on the Arc de Triomphe. Vilar was a crusader who believed that the theatre could not shrug off its obligations to society.

Vilar worked for an austere, simple staging, and declared himself against all theatrical pretension, 'symbolic' acting and other manifestations of art for art's sake. It was Vilar who, in a notable essay in 1949, 'The Director and the Play', concluded that the modern French director was more creative than the French playwright, and dared to argue that Racine had done great harm to the French theatre by suggesting that the source of drama lay in the ink-bottle, and that a play could be given life merely by good dialogue and strong 'sermonizing'. Vilar turned instead to Artaud's theory of theatrical creativity, that drama lay in magic, incantation and music working upon the emotions, and that it should make use of the stage as a physical medium with its own language of dance and mime independent of speech. Like Artaud, Vilar wanted a 'poetry of the senses', based on the work of Copeau's school of improvisation and the plastic arts of movement and gesture. This approach, thought Vilar, would have the advantage of restoring to popular appeal the spectacular element in drama without repeating the false values of the past. It seems that the modern French movement, which began with the intricate devices of symbolism, may have come full circle in its search for artlessness.

14 *Theatre of cruelty: Artaud and Peter Brook*

The Marat/Sade (1965)

It is difficult as yet to assess the force exerted on the modern theatre by the poet, actor and director Antonin Artaud (1896–1948). He has become a cult figure, and has been named as one of the strongest influences on new avant-garde production. But Artaud himself may be simply a symptom of the impulse towards a ritual theatre which would have existed without him. The fact that his pioneering was recognized so belatedly, as many as thirty or forty years after his own inadequate attempts at a surrealistic theatre, and then understood only in the vaguest terms as those of a mystic and a visionary, must give us further pause. Here may be a case of theory obscuring practice, aggravated because the very obscurity of Artaud's writing left his theory open to every kind of misinterpretation in practice.

Artaud acted for Lugné-Poe, Dullin and Pitoëff, and while he was not in the line of Copeau, he was particularly attracted to Dullin's improvisatory methods of training. From the beginning Artaud broke so decisively with realism that he managed to alarm his teacher. In his *Réflexions sur le théâtre*, Barrault tells the story of the time when Artaud was playing the Emperor Charlemagne, and was observed to be approaching the throne on all fours. Dullin, a little desperate, suggested in a tentative way that the performance was perhaps too stylized. At this, Artaud reared up and cried, 'Oh, if it's realism you're after! Well then!!' In 1924 he joined the official group of surrealists, until in 1926 it declared itself for communism. But Artaud continued to hold to the surrealist concept of theatre, and that year founded the Théâtre Alfred Jarry with the dadaist Roger Vitrac (1899–1952). In this way Artaud acknowledged, as it were, that Jarry was his true beginning. This theatre had no regular home, but various stages were hired as necessary for the presentation of surrealistic pieces of the founders' own devising.

Even as surrealism, the first plays must have seemed primitive. Artaud's *Le Jet de sang* (*The Spurt of Blood*, 1927) included human limbs and pieces of masonry falling from the flies to represent the collapse of civilization. The rebellion of mankind was conveyed by having a whore bite the wrist of God, which incident was followed by a great spurt of 'blood' shooting across the stage. Vitrac's *Les Mystères de l'amour* (*The Mysteries of Love*) was in the same programme, and is more verbal. It also attempts audience participation by starting its performance in a stage box, using extra-dramatic address to the house and, at the curtain, firing a gun into the audience. Pirandello's *Six Characters* had aimed at a comparable effect when it was produced by Pitoëff in Paris in 1923. For his next production in the following year, Artaud found Strindberg's *Dream Play* to be rich in the kind of subjective images he and his actors could develop, but the performance was broken up by a noisy party of his former surrealist-friends. Vitrac's shocker, *Victor, ou Les Enfants au pouvoir* (*Victor, or The Children Take Power*, 1928) was the last production of this questionable venture. This was the play in which the leading lady was expected at once to be beautiful and to give a belch on every line.

In 1935 Artaud founded his short-lived Théâtre de la Cruauté, working with the young Jean-Louis Barrault and Roger Blin as his assistants on *Les Cenci*, based on Shelley's play and Stendhal's *Chroniques italiennes*. It was played in the round and stacked with theatrical devices and flashing lights; music came from every corner of the house, and Artaud played the Count with a frantic passion. This production was an example of Artaud's asserting his freedom to take great plays or themes from the past and transform them completely. This he did in common with others of the symbolist persuasion, especially those who put ancient myth to use in the modern theatre. Nevertheless, partly because Artaud was compelled to use an inappropriate theatre, the Théâtre des Folies-Wagram, a vast music hall, and partly because his leading actress was quite inaudible, the *Cenci* experiment failed. Indeed, Artaud's actual practice was scanty — three full-length and four one-act plays produced in ten years, with some film scripts — a remarkably thin record for an artist of his subsequent reputation. Then in 1937 he was confined for almost ten years in a mental hospital, suffering from schizophrenia and opium addiction. He died from cancer shortly after his release.

Two or three theatrical experiences were of particular importance in his development as a theatre artist. In 1922 he saw a group of Cambodian dancers at the Colonial Exhibition in Marseilles, and in 1931 he saw the Balinese Theatre perform at the Colonial Exhibition in Paris. He was beguiled by those qualities of Oriental ritual which induced states of trance and frenzy in its dancers. Communication was by movement and gesture rather than words, and the performers used a vocabulary of hieroglyphs, whereby the turning of the eyes or the raising of a finger could magically evoke a music, a 'poetry', of its own, with sound and motion flowing rhythmically into one another. Artaud saw at once the contrast with the basic realism of western drama, which seemed to him excessively word-bound and basely moralistic. He believed that the re-creation of an Oriental mysticism and impersonality in performance would provide the rejuvenation that the French theatre needed. In 1936, Artaud also spent six months among the Mexican Indians, observing their occult rites and sun dances, and even joining in the ritual himself. He planned a play about Montezuma, but it was too late. Artaud's reputation therefore rests largely upon his theoretical writing, especially the two manifestoes of 1932 and 1933, collected in *Le Théâtre et son double* (*The Theatre and Its Double*, 1938).

In his recent book on Artaud, Martin Esslin discusses the possibility that Artaud's dream of a non-verbal theatre actually derived from an altercation he had in 1923 with Jacques Rivière, then editor of the *Nouvelle Revue Française*, over the rejection by that journal of some of Artaud's poetry. His letters to Rivière describe his mental anguish and addiction to opium, but they also suggest that the difficulties he had in expressing his deepest thoughts and feelings made him distrust language as a satisfactory medium of expression for profound emotion. Emotion may be evoked by words, but is not itself verbal, and words cannot communicate the full-ness of human experience, especially in the theatre. Moreover, those who can use words easily may be accused of a glib intellectual laziness and a lack of personal integrity. If the theatre was to trans-mit Artaud's physical suffering and exaltation to other human beings, words would not be enough. He wanted his theatre to

> swoop down upon a crowd of spectators with all the awe-some horror of the plague, the Black Death of the Middle Ages, with all its shattering impact, creating a complete upheaval, physical, mental and moral, among the popula-tion it struck (translated Martin Esslin, *Antonin Artaud*, p. 76).

Artaud was here embodying his 'theatre of cruelty'.

In his theory Artaud advocated the use of the theatre as therapy. He called for a drama of savage shock-tactics, one which employed all the ancient arts of theatre magic to expose the audience to its own secret crimes and obsessions and hostilities. The intention was to cleanse the audience's guilt, as Artaud put it, and so to bring to the surface its vital and valuable energies. At the same time, the new theatre was to supply a surrogate for life, a 'double', representing a more true, more intense experience of reality. It was Artaud's wish to revolutionize the over-civilized theatre of psycho-logical realism, which was always miserably analysing and dis-secting and cerebrating. This tune had been heard many times before from Artaud's predecessors, but he introduced his very un-French idea by insisting that it was 'the subjugation of the theatre to the text' that had been the worst result of this sophistication of the stage. In practice, of course, no director has ever been an absolute slave to words, but in Artaud's ideal theatre there would be no written play, only improvisation upon a theme. This would make each performance 'a kind of happening', Esslin's translation of 'une sorte d'évènement', and he wondered whether this was the first use of the term which was to become familiar in the 1960s. As it happened, Artaud was also a rigid disciplinarian who made a point of planning every detail of what was to seem like an improvisation.

Artaud's programme for a new theatre may be conveniently summarized:

1. The playhouse shall be nothing more than four plain walls (Artaud mentions a hangar or a barn) with the audience in the middle so that the action can flow around it. With the addition of galleries and catwalks, the actors can perform on all levels as well as on all sides, and light and sound will fall as much on the audience as on the performers. In this way there will be no 'set' in the usual sense; rather, space itself will be made to speak. It is of interest that Artaud's ideas about space in the theatre echoed the plans of Walter Gropius for the Bauhaus in Germany, and thirty years later have been fairly tested in major centres everywhere.

2. The dramatic images of the new theatre will not be a slavish copy of real life. It will have a code of its own, a concrete language devised to affect the sensibility of the spectators. It will be a theatre of great activity, and of direct experience 'pushed beyond all limits'. It will work hypnotically on the senses, using spectacle and sensation, with its actors performing like giant effigies in huge masks. It will be a theatre designed to induce a ritualism that crowds can share.

3. The stage will engulf the audience, not with words, but with physical and concrete sounds and images, music and dance, testing the nerves of the spectators by their conjunction and mixture. Colour and light and costume, everything theatrical, will be added to the effect. If words are used, the actors will make special use of their sounds, their intonations and incantations, to go with the new music and the new instruments.

4. The actor must 'use his emotions as a wrestler uses his muscles', developing them for their power over his audience by the exercise of his body and his breath. The director will be the new magician, the new priest, the 'maker of myth'.

5. The subjects of the new drama will be based on old and new gods and heroes and monsters, on natural forces, great cosmic conflicts, on 'famous people, atrocious crimes, superhuman devotions'. These the new theatre will transform into a poetry of its own, stamped with the terror, the cruelty and the eroticism appropriate to 'the agitation and unrest characteristic of our age' (quotations translated by Mary Caroline Richards).

While any part of this programme may seem in some respect silly, Artaud's anti-realistic position was sound enough. The drama can never reproduce real life, and probably, therefore, should not try. Paradoxically, only by seeking the 'inner reality' in the theatre's own basically unreal terms can drama begin to touch the real life, the 'outer reality' of its audience's world. This rather metaphysical thinking may explain Artaud's innovations in visual imagery on the stage, his search for a visual idiom. Balletic patterns of movement by groups of actors in *Les Cenci*, for example, patterns which assumed a kind of mystical significance, were intended to draw the audience into the magic circle. Symbolic images of the circle were reproduced throughout the play, ending with the wheel on which Beatrice is tortured. Artaud also aimed at effects of slow motion in the acting, and had dummies mingle with the live actors in order to suggest a bizarre society. Huge masks and stylized facial expressions and intense and frenzied gestures of the hands were evidently borrowed from the German expressionist theatre of the 1910s and 1920s. The arrangement of electronic notes, the reduction of words to sounds, mechanical amplification, a surrealist distortion of set design, the use of spotlights to pick out symbolic effects – everything was brought together. But even so, it is questionable whether Artaud could ever have realized his theories. The self-indulgent emotionality, the relentless imposition of feeling on the audience, which resulted from such generalizing techniques tended to reduce any subtlety of play or performance, and to dull the perception of the spectator. The programme note to *Les Cenci* offered to grip the audience with true tragic emotion, but in the event the sophisticated Parisian audience chose instead to protest as noisily as it knew how.

The debate over the final importance of Artaud and his

theatre of cruelty is nevertheless in full swing. The American critic and avant-garde playwright Paul Goodman (1911–72) tried to refute Artaud's theories in a notable article in *The Nation* of 29 November 1958. Goodman pointed out that western theatre must always be at some remove from primitive ritual, in which the magic is taken for real. Our theatrical 'illusion' is no substitute for this. For a true catharsis such as a genuinely ritualistic occasion may have produced, Artaud supplied only a temporary escape from a world to which modern audiences must return less able to cope with reality. Goodman also found Artaud's attack on the verbal drama too sweeping. Speech is itself a physical act, he argued, and it is impossible to ignore the strong 'inter-personal' effect demonstrable in the purely syntactical relationships of words.

In support of Artaud, the American critic and director Charles Marowitz declared in the *Tulane Drama Review* of winter 1966 that even the Method actor, trained for the intense realism of his performance by the Stanislavsky system, could seem superficial and fraudulent by comparison with his fellow in the theatre of cruelty.

> The Method actor's test for truthfulness is the intensity and authenticity of his personal feeling. The Artaudian actor knows that unless that feeling has been shaped into a communicative image, it is a passionate letter without postage.

The difference is that the Method actor is 'chained to rational motivation', whereas the Artaudian actor realizes that 'the highest artistic truth is unprovable'. From a playwright's point of view, Artaudian drama at least lacks cliché, because each time it has to be discovered anew. Marowitz believed that the methods of the theatre of cruelty could refresh the jaded senses of the audience, and force it to reconsider the value of its aesthetic experience.

Out of his time in the 1930s, Artaud struck the right note for the anti-realistic mood of the 1960s. Playwrights as different as Jean Genêt and Peter Weiss are indebted to him. His ideas have attracted directors from many countries, and some have been able to train a company of actors in Artaud's radically new methods of performance: in France itself, Jean-Louis Barrault; in Poland, Jerzy Grotowski (although he does not acknowledge Artaud); in Britain,

Peter Brook (1925–) and Charles Marowitz (1934–); in America, Julian Beck and Judith Malina with their Living Theatre, Richard Schechner and his Performance Group, and Joseph Chaikin and the Open Theatre. Of these, and other 'Environmentalists', more later.

In 1963 Brook and Marowitz developed an experimental group of actors affiliated with the Royal Shakespeare Company (RSC), but not subject to the pressure of public performance. Glenda Jackson, then an unknown actress, was selected to join them. For twelve weeks the group experimented with improvisations chosen to explore the inner feelings, the 'rhythms', of the actors. They finally mounted a workshop demonstration of what they had learned. The show was hopefully entitled 'The Theatre of Cruelty' and presented briefly at the London Academy of Music and Dramatic Art Theatre Club in London. The event was distinguished by a first tentative version of Artaud's *Le Jet de sang*, Marowitz's first and shorter collage of *Hamlet* (the beginning of his revealing excursions into the craft of restructuring Shakespeare), and scenes from Genêt's as yet unproduced *Les Paravents* (*The Screens*, 1961). The Artaud sketch was played with writhing actors on a simple plat-form and a flight of steps, and a huge 'hand of God' descended from above and gushed blood. Taken by surprise, the audience found that a foreshortened *Hamlet* with dislocated speeches and a Prince of Denmark swinging on a rope above its head meant very little. The fragments of the Genêt made a mystifying play the more mysterious. But it was a stroke of luck for Brook and the theatre of cruelty that at this time Peter Weiss (1916–) sent Brook a copy of his play of *The Persecution and Assassination of Jean-Paul Marat as Performed by the Inmates of the Asylum of Charenton under the Direction of the Marquis de Sade*, which had been first produced by Konrad Swinarski at the Schiller Theater in Berlin in 1964.

Brook's production of the *Marat/Sade*, as the play came to be known, was done by the RSC at the Aldwych Theatre, London, in 1965, and since he used the actors he had trained, the occasion was possibly the first full test of Artaud's theories in practice. Yet it is difficult to reach a firm critical conclusion, for although the pro-duction was certainly devised to shock the senses, the techniques of both the play and the production were as much Brechtian as Artaudian; there is even a strong shadow of Pirandello lurking there. Weiss is reported to have said that he wanted to combine in his play the two apparently contradictory forces of Brecht and Artaud. Just as the subject of the play is half fact and half fiction, and the script half prepared debate and half improvisation, Weiss was trying, he said, to write a 'thinking' play to be performed in a 'feeling' way.

The setting was designed by Sally Jacobs to keep the stage as empty as possible, and it is lit with a Brechtian cold white light. The scene represents the bathhouse of the asylum of Charenton where the Marquis de Sade was in fact confined in 1808. The director of the asylum, M. Coulmier, encouraged amateur theatricals among the inmates, and for the present occasion de Sade has written a play about the death of Jean-Paul Marat, the French revolutionary leader. It is this ritualistic play-within-a-play, complete with a Brechtian chorus in the figure of the Herald, which constitutes the focal action. The real audience watches a stage audience, Coulmier, his wife and daughter, as they smugly watch the antics of the insane. In this way the inner action of the play is from the start distanced in the best Brechtian manner.

The Artaudian sensory contribution lies largely in the inner theatricality. A quintet of musicians plays Richard Peaslee's sour music after the manner of Kurt Weill, and a choric quartet of singers, clownishly dressed as for the French Revolution, comment in ironic song upon the bad acting of the lunatics. The patients themselves are in white hospital suits, and the unsettling business of representing insanity is constant throughout the performance. With grotesque and insulting gestures, the wretched inmates hop and crouch, mutter and scream. At one point they enact an execution by guillotine and pour red, white and blue blood into the gulleys of the bathhouse – an extension of the idea in Brook's earlier production of *Titus Andronicus*, in which red ribbon was used to symbolize the spilling of blood. And, representing the poor at their most ugly and bestial, the inmates also play the revolutionary mob shouting their political slogans for freedom, mixed with their own howls of frustration and despair as prisoners in Charenton.

The characterization of the figures in the inner play cleverly reflects the pathological diseases of the inmates. Marat sits writhing in a bathtub, swathed in wet bandages to ease the pain of his skin disease, when he is not also on fire with revolutionary fervour. Charlotte Corday, destined to kill Marat, is played by a somnambulist; in Brook's revision of the text, she whips de Sade erotically with her long hair while the other inmates make the sound of whipping with their lips. Duperret the deputy is an erotomaniac who makes

20. Weiss, the *Marat/Sade*, 1964. Production by Peter Brook at the Aldwych Theatre, London, 1965, with Patrick Magee as De Sade and Glenda Jackson as Charlotte Corday.

obscene gestures at a passive Corday until he is strait-jacketed. De Sade himself is pale and fat and asthmatic, yet also tense and obsessed with the success of his play. At the end, the whole cast of lunatics rebels and attacks its guards before it advances menacingly downstage upon both the on-stage and the real audiences. It is a frightening moment. Suddenly a whistle is blown and the actors stop short, signifying that the play is over. When, however, the audience applauds in the conventional way, the actors applaud also, mockingly, threateningly, as if the on-stage and the real audiences have become one.

The critics in both London and New York were either shocked or thrilled. Those who disliked the play found fault with its political history. In *Against Interpretation* (1965), Susan Sontag reported that her admiration for Brook's production was virtually unqualified, but made the point that, although the play had strong intellectual content in its running argument about the human failure of the French Revolution, all this was secondary to the use of these ideas merely as 'sensory stimulants' for the theatre. The content of the inner play was not treated moralistically, but as an aesthetic experience. In Sontag's view, this was the cause of misunderstanding among those critics who were dissatisfied with the play's intellectual content. Since everyone on the stage was either a lunatic or an actor playing a part, the two frequently being the same, the realistic basis of the story was rendered irrelevant by the distancing devices.

Brook himself would not allow that the play's Brechtian qualities were in conflict with Artaud's immediacy. 'I believe', he wrote in his 1964 preface to the English edition of the *Marat/Sade*, 'that theatre, like life, is made up of the unbroken conflict between impressions and judgments — illusion and disillusion cohabit painfully and are inseparable.' He believed that Weiss's assimilation of both the didactic and the sensuous was complete, and the power of his production was directly related to the combination of these contradictory techniques. In this, of course, Brook also identifies the kind of clash of styles and change of levels characteristic of the best Elizabethan drama. The *Marat/Sade* can release the imagination through its sheer theatricality, using this word in its best sense of making full use of the physical theatre, and, to choose Brook's own words to the *New York Times* in January 1966, smash

through the 'intellectual barriers' of its audience. By the device
of a theatre-within-a-theatre, and by having the mad represent the
sane, the dramatic images of the play succeed in passing us from
reality to nightmare.

Brook's theatre of cruelty experiments probably never sur-
passed the *Marat/Sade* production, but they continued with *US*
at the Aldwych in 1966 and Seneca's *Oedipus* at the Old Vic in
1968. Then, with the help of the Ford Foundation, Brook was able
to set up the International Centre for Theatre Research in Paris in
1970. Exercises developed from Shakespeare's *The Tempest* were
presented at the Round House in London, and in the derelict
Théâtre des Bouffes du Nord in Paris he offered an experimental
Timon of Athens. Brook has continued to test the possibilities of
non-verbal theatre, notably in 1971 in the Festival at Persepolis,
for which the poet Ted Hughes created *Orghast* in a language made
up only of sounds. The quest for a universal language of theatre
was pursued in Brook's subsequent tour of West Africa, where it
was soon apparent that African expectations were different from
the European. Conventions mutually shared by actor and spectator
are still essential to the effectiveness of any kind of dramatic
performance.

Artaudian theatre may have been partly discovered in
1976, when Brook combined what Michael Billington of *The
Guardian* considered to be 'a subject of global importance with a
simple, concentrated imagery'. This was the production at the
Round House of *The Ik*, a true story of a displaced Ugandan tribe,
dramatized by Denis Cannan and Colin Higgins from Colin Turn-
bull's *The Mountain People*. The breakdown of our humanity, of
family bonds and human love, in the face of extinction was conveyed
by overwhelming understatement, not only because the actors had
spent time in Africa absorbing the rhythms of tribal life, but also
because Brook's own tact ensured a vividly spare presentation of
the harrowing details of famine, all played out on an undecorated
stage merely covered in sand. The production of Jarry's *Ubu*,
mentioned above (p. 48), followed in 1977, and the next international project planned is the great Hindu epic, the *Mahabharata*.

It may not be necessary to add that, while such experiments in
non-verbal theatre would have had Artaud's full approval, Peter

Brook's frequent return to the RSC and Shakespeare (especially with *A Midsummer Night's Dream* in 1970 and *Antony and Cleopatra* in 1978) must remind him and us that words long ago proved themselves to be capable of making an irreplaceable contribution to the use of the stage, theatrical communication, shared experience and ritual drama.

---

15 *The existentialist play: Sartre and Camus*

The Flies (1943), *Caligula* (1945)

Intellectual leaders in France have traditionally turned to the theatre to promulgate their views, and so it was during the Second World War and just after. During the German occupation in Paris, a uniquely French series of plays reflected the moral dilemma of an audience suspicious of the collaborator and shaken by the pent-up fear and hate of years of war, torture and execution. A people close to exhaustion found release in the drama, and for a short time a most uncommon theatre came about. The names of Jean-Paul Sartre (1905—80) and Albert Camus (1913—60) became a secret rallying cry, and attending their plays was like joining a conspiracy against the enemy right under their noses.

When the theatres were allowed to re-open after the fall of France in 1940, the unlikely *Saint Joan* by Bernard Shaw was permitted a production by the German censor because it appeared to be anti-British. Did it not, after all, show the English putting the French national heroine to the flames? As it turned out, the Paris audience automatically perceived the campaign to expel the English from France as analogous with their desire to be rid of the German forces of occupation. When Sartre came to write *Les Mouches* (*The Flies*, 1942), he took care to choose a mythological subject in order to conceal the subject of the play from the censor, and at the same time to bring to a beleaguered public a sense that the French situation was not new, but as old as the human race. Then in 1943, the

Antigone of Jean Anouilh (1910–   ) began a record run at the Atelier because his little heroine stubbornly refused all comfort and compromise. The French audience felt her stance to be its own. When Antigone declared that nothing would stop her burying her brother, the audience heard the voice of the Resistance and exulted. 'What is your reason for doing this?', she is asked. 'For myself', is her unabashed reply. A few spectators were troubled by the fact that the tyrant Creon, who was otherwise perceived as the Nazi oppressor, was given so eloquent a defence on the need for compromise, but it was in vain that the author denied the intention of introducing any political satire into his play. Anouilh was a dramatist before he was a politician, and it was a matter of pure chance that *Antigone* met the need for an anti-Nazi play. Such is the force of political circumstance that it can determine a success or a failure on the stage.

Sartre had been a prisoner of war in Germany in 1940, when he was released by a lucky mistake. In the prison camp, he had written and produced a Biblical play for his fellow prisoners. This was never published, but during the performance Sartre remarked the intense concern and concentration of his audience under the unnatural circumstances of their confinement. The occasion taught him, he said, the nature and virtue of a collective experience in the theatre, and justified his pursuit, in terms of drama, of the philosophy he had been formulating before the war. 'Existentialism' proposed that man was a lonely creature of anxiety and despair living in a meaningless world, and that he was merely existing until he made a decisive and critical choice about his own future course of action. By such a choice, a person would acquire an identity, a purpose and dignity as a human being. For preference, existential man should adopt some social or political cause in order to acquire this dignity and purpose, and in translating these ideas into dramatic form, Sartre's name became synonymous with the *théâtre engagée*, the theatre 'committed', that is, to positive social or political action. Each of his plays is representative of his philosophical concerns as an existentialist. *Huis clos* (*In Camera* in Britain, *No Exit* in America, 1944) is a carefully structured drama about the manoeuvring of three people forced to share a small room together in hell. *Morts sans sépulture* (*Men without Shadows*, 1946) is a play which explores the extreme predicament of men facing physical torture. *Les Mains sales* (*Crime Passionnel* in Britain, *Dirty Hands* or *The Assassins* in America, 1948) is a play which tests a man's true motives in committing a political assassination.

Like Anouilh, Camus also became an inadvertent spokesman for the spirit of the French Underground when he published a long philosophical essay, *Le Mythe de Sisyphe* (*The Myth of Sisyphus*) in 1942. For Camus, the legendary figure of Sisyphus was the prototype of an 'absurd' hero, condemned by the gods forever to roll a rock to the top of a mountain, only to have it roll back down again by its own weight. He represented the epitome of futile labour and pointless existence. Although Camus denied any connection with Sartre's existentialism, the book became a manifesto for the new existentialist drama, and later for the theatre of the absurd. In it, Camus asserted that it was legitimate and necessary to wonder whether life had any meaning. He described how man felt himself to be a stranger in an alien world, and believed that this divorce between man and life was properly *'le sentiment de l'absurdité'*, the feeling of absurdity. Was suicide the way to end this feeling? No. In the confrontation with the irrational, it was possible to proceed beyond nihilism, for there was a 'wild longing for clarity' in the human heart: 'If the world were clear, art would not exist.' In both his novels and his plays, Camus protested on behalf of the war-torn generation against man's fear of death and his helplessness in the face of a meaningless universe.

The plays which pleased Parisian audiences during the war have in common a classical austerity and a fierce moral purpose, both of which proved less attractive after the tension of the war had eased. When, for example, *Antigone* was produced in New York by Katherine Cornell under very different circumstances in 1946, the public found the return to Greek myth unaccountable and the play deficient in realistic characterization, a quality it had come to expect on the American stage. Sartre came to the play's defence in *Theatre Arts*, and followed up his arguments in *Qu'est-ce que la littérature?* (*What is Literature?*, 1948). The common quality that Sartre recognized as existentialist in the French plays of this period may be regarded in the context of this history as yet another variant of symbolism in the modern theatre. The new philosophical drama, Sartre maintained, had knowingly turned away from psychological realism, and rejected the kind of theatre for which a dramatic situation was chosen and developed only to exhibit characters. Anouilh's *Antigone*, for example, was not a study of 'human nature' in the usual sense, and not 'naturalistic' by the nineteenth-century definition. The character Antigone was not in the play to demonstrate the concerns of her society, or display the symptoms of a particular heredity and environment. The play was essentially one of 'situation', and Antigone represented 'a naked will' in a universal situation selected to throw light on *'la condition humaine'*, not the condition of society but the state of mankind. The dramatic interest was not in the person or personality of a young Greek princess, but rather in the choice she makes and why she makes it. Any directorial emphasis, therefore, on the characters of Antigone or Creon would be wholly misplaced.

This account of Anouilh's *Antigone* emerged rather blatantly as a formula for an existentialist play after Sartre's own heart. It is true, however, as Sartre contended, that his was a scheme for a 'theatre of situation', one dealing in general experience, collective human rights, universal conflicts, inevitable passions and final values. It was a return to the elements of classicism in the Corneillean tradition. Like Greek or French classical tragedy, existentialist drama quickly precipitates its central character into the symbolic conflict. In its brevity and its focus on a single event, its form approximates to the classical unities. And at its best its dialogue is simple and economical, even to the point of being dry and terse. Such a drama had no need to use visual or verbal symbols *per se*, but it emerged as a symbolic theatre of the ideal, intent on defining a kind of modern mythology. If its characters appeared to be of flesh and blood, this was only to lead the audience towards a conviction of their reality before the play went on to assert or imply their universality.

Luckily for all parties, author, actor and audience, the strong conflict of interests implicit in an existentialist choice lends itself wonderfully well to a dramatic expression that is full of challenge and suspense, and while Sartre's plots are symbolic of his personal philosophy, his plays are otherwise naturalistic in treatment. Their existentialist content did not alter one whit the fact that the actors had to play by the principles of Stanislavsky like those in any realistic drama. Indeed, some playgoers have been attracted to the existentialist play merely as a philosophical thriller, and the thread of violence running through many of Sartre's plays has supported this claim to their popularity.

The Flies is a specially interesting example of what was done. The play loosely modernizes Aeschylus's *Oresteia* to provide Parisians with a story of resistance against the German occupation and the Vichy government. It was first produced by Dullin at the Théâtre Sarah-Bernhardt in 1943, with sets, masks and statues designed by Henri-Georges Adam. In disguise, Orestes has returned home to Argos where his father Agamemnon was murdered by his wife, Orestes's mother, Clytemnestra, fifteen years before. He comes upon a spine-chilling scene. The city is afflicted with a plague of avenging flies, because the people have been cleverly persuaded by Zeus

21. Anouilh, *Antigone*, 1943. Production by André Barsacq at the Théâtre de l'Atelier, Paris. Antigone (Elisabeth Hardy) and the Guards.

(played by Dullin himself) that they are responsible for the murder: in this way the gods have enslaved them. The mask of Zeus was designed to have a vacant stare and a bloody head, and the movements of the insect-like old women of Argos may be suggested by Sartre's description of the old woman of Bouville in his novel *La Nausée* (*Nausea*, 1938):

> Suddenly she grows bolder, she scuttles across the courtyard as fast as her legs will move, stops for an instant before the statue, her mandibles quivering. Then she scurries off, black against the pink pavement, and disappears into a crack in the wall.

Orestes also witnesses the degradation of his sister Electra, who has been living at home in an atmosphere of hate with her mother and her stepfather Aegisthus. Act II depicts the Argives' grand festival of guilt and penitence, at which Electra must dance in an attempt to dispel the people's self-indulgent misery. This is the moment when Orestes chooses to reveal his identity and kill Clytemnestra and Aegisthus for the sake of the city. However, urged on by Zeus, the loathsome flies remain and flourish, a little like the plague in Camus's novel, and then as Furies they pursue Orestes and Electra to the shrine of Apollo. Electra is the weak one, and she succumbs to repentance and returns to Zeus's power, but the strong Orestes defies Zeus and declares that he is free. He has committed matricide without regret, and has chosen to stand alone. The play ends with a triumphant Orestes leaving the city with the swarm of flies and Furies at his heels.

This exit of Orestes is not far short of comic, and was characteristic of the risks taken by so theatrical and spectacular a conception. The play also sagged under an abundance of ponderous polemical speeches, in which Sartre's ideas resisted full dramatization and simply had to be mouthed. But the play's story, and therefore the symbolism in its situation, were simple and strong, making a plain moral statement in allegorical terms. If *The Flies* does not persuade an audience of the validity of existentialism, it is nearly acceptable as a modern drama of individual heroism in the face of the enemy and of social disapproval. But none of this detracts from the urgency and importance of the play's first production in 1943, the integrity of the dramatic event in its historical context. Sartre himself has commented upon Dullin's courage in putting the play on in occupied Paris:

> It was 1943 and Vichy wanted to drive us into repentance and shame. In writing *The Flies* I tried to contribute as best I could to the extirpation of this sickness of repentance, this abandonment to shame that Vichy was soliciting from us. The collaborators made no mistake about it. Violent press campaigns rapidly forced the Sarah Bernhardt theatre to withdraw the play, and the remarkable work of the man who was our greatest director was not rewarded (in *La Croix*, 20 January 1951, translated Dorothy McCall).

A philosophical approach to playwriting also inhibited the complete success of the plays of Camus in the theatre, although he was a great admirer of Copeau and, unlike Sartre, had gathered experience as an actor and a director. He had established the communist Théâtre du Travail in 1936–7, and when he broke with the party he created the Théâtre de l'Équipe, which lasted from 1937 to 1939. *Caligula*, which was also produced during the war years, was directed by Paul Oettly at the Théâtre Hébertot in 1945. This play had been written in 1939, and Camus evidently intended the title part for himself. With Gérard Philipe in the lead in 1945, it ran for nearly a year, and it will possibly be Camus's most enduring play. Certainly it is one of his more successful plays in dramatizing his philosophy of existential absurdity.

Camus called *Caligula* 'a tragedy of the intelligence', and made of it a very free treatment of Roman history. In Caligula's grief over the death of his sister, with whom he had enjoyed an incestuous love, the young emperor decreed that Rome should be ruled by the ugly logic of a purposeless universe. All patricians had to leave their wealth to the state and be prepared to die. At first a man of gentle disposition, Caligula now becomes a cruel despot in order to show others what a monstrous world they live in. He starves the poor and decimates the rich, and even strangles his mistress. But for all the illogic of absurdity, he achieves no happiness, and before he is stabbed to death, the only logical thing that happens in the play, he screams at his own image in the mirror and flings a stool at it.

The play was acceptable to the Paris audience because it readily identified Caligula's philosophical absolutism with the hated Nazism and Fascism, and his megalomania with Hitler's and Mussolini's. Nevertheless, as drama, the play reproduces a series of horrors, and for all its philosophical underpinning, it fails to dramatize any moral conflict in Caligula himself. But then, did not the existential dramatist wish to avoid the narrow limitations of psychological realism? Perhaps the one redeeming feature of the play might have been some probing of the human mind. But just as Sisyphus loved life and was absurdly punished, so Caligula dies without hope for the future, and the statement of the play is wholly negative.

Intractable ideas, and the unsatisfying message they conveyed, must account for the short life of the existentialist drama, and for its failure to be exported far from Paris. It is as unwise to enter the theatre as a writer with a philosophical theory as it is to act in a tragedy with a theory of tragedy in mind. It may be significant that from the strange phenomenon of French wartime theatre, only Jean Anouilh went on to write more and better plays — nearly forty of them — with each one in its own way an accomplished piece of ironic theatre having a wide appeal. They range from the near-farcical *La Valse des toréadors* (*The Waltz of the Toreadors*, 1952) to the near-tragic *Becket* (1959), possibly the best dramatic treatment to date of the relationship between the archbishop and his king. Anouilh finally has no philosophical position. At any rate, it comes no closer to definition than naming the tone and style of his plays: they are *pièces noires* ('black plays'), *pièces roses* ('rosy plays'), *pièces brillantes* ('sparkling plays') and *pièces grinçantes* ('grinding plays').

16 *Theatre of the absurd: Beckett and Pinter*

Waiting for Godot (1952)

Immediately after the Second World War, Paris again became the capital of dramatic art in the west, and French theatre was soon associated with a short-lived eruption of surrealistic drama which came to be known as 'theatre of the absurd'. It belonged to the feverish decade spanned by Beckett's *En attendant Godot* (*Waiting for Godot*, 1952) and Ionesco's *Le Roi se meurt* (*Exit the King*, 1962). It was the decade of the 'cold war' and the extreme tension between the nations of the east and the west. Those playwrights working in Paris and thought of as absurdists during that time, however, were never a school sharing a common cause or a common philosophy. Beckett, Ionesco, Adamov and Arrabal came from widely different backgrounds: they were born in Ireland, Rumania, Russia and Spain, respectively. Jean Genêt, the only Frenchman who might have been linked with this group, was not, it was soon apparent, writing in the same vein of theatre, and he will be discussed in a separate section (see ch. 18). Nor were Beckett and company wild young rebels, since in 1952 only Arrabal was under the age of forty. Nor were these writers associated with any particular development in stage practice, although his work with Beckett and Genêt brought into prominence the director Roger Blin (1907–). Like the Irish Dramatic Movement, the theatre of the absurd was a writer's theatre, not a director's.

The sudden outburst of French absurdism may in part be explained as a nihilistic reaction to the recent atrocities, the gas-chambers and the nuclear bombs of the war. Theatre of the absurd revealed the negative side of Sartre's existentialism, and expressed the helplessness and futility of a world which seemed to have no purpose. Beckett's bleak images of life in *Godot* and *Fin de partie* (*Endgame*, 1957) conjure up a human existence which, in Richard Coe's well-chosen words in his *Beckett*, is like an 'intolerable imprisonment' spent 'between the compulsion of birth [and] the worse compulsion of death' (p. 19). Our life has its temporary freedom, but it is 'the freedom of the slave to crawl east along the deck of a boat travelling west' (p. 58). In *Exit the King*, Ionesco's characteristic subject is death, together with, in this play, the actual dissolution of the mind and the body. In such drama, every signal from the stage is a representation of irrationality designed to surprise and shock. Its grim vision of life reflects Kierkegaard's spiritless man, wholly negative and atheistic — unless one is willing to believe that what is negative may also embody some inducement to take positive action, as if to say, 'When things are as bad as this, why not do something about them?' Camus's existentialist use of the term 'absurd' in *The Myth of Sisyphus* was ten years later vastly narrowed to connote man trapped in a hostile universe that was totally subjective, and made to describe the nightmare that could follow when purposelessness, solitude and silence were taken to the ultimate degree.

Absurdist plays fall within the symbolist tradition, and they have no logical plot or characterization in any conventional sense. Their characters lack the motivation found in realistic drama, and so emphasize their purposelessness. The absence of plot serves to reinforce the monotony and repetitiveness of time in human affairs. The dialogue is commonly no more than a series of inconsequential clichés which reduce those who speak them to talking machines. As plays, they do not discuss the human condition, but simply portray it at its worst in outrageous images chosen to undeceive the innocent and shock the complacent.

As a result of this singular content, absurdism presented a special set of practical problems to the writer who wished to make his way in the theatre. Purposelessness is inconsistent with everything dramatic art has achieved in the past, and, in addition, extremes of the absurdist vision are too repelling to stage in their own terms. Playwrights in this vein therefore adopted stylistic methods to hold the attention of the audience, to erect a kind of screen through which the statement of the play could be filtered, and at the same time to reduce the resistance of the spectator. Almost universally, the methods adopted were those of farce, and laughter was found to be the most successful device in disarming a wary audience.

The early plays of Samuel Beckett (1906–) particularly drew upon the content and techniques of mime, the music hall, the circus and the *commedia dell'arte* to represent the business of everyday living. All the characters of *Godot* and *Endgame*, Vladimir and Estragon, Pozzo and Lucky, Hamm and Clov, Nagg and Nell, are essentially pairs of comics or clowns who divert themselves, and so their auditors, with double-acts of cross-talk, tumbling and the *lazzi* of falling asleep, switching hats ('three hats for two heads') and so on. The tramps who wait for Godot quarrel, eat, try to sleep, even attempt suicide, all in the fashion of such performers, and the loss of dignity implicit in their antics itself becomes an absurdist image of life. In the first American *Godot*, Estragon was even played by a professional vaudeville comedian, Bert Lahr. The activity of these characters is not 'action' in the sense that it works to develop a story; it is merely 'performance', the visible presence of an entertaining character. In Beckett's novels, existence is nothing and only in the imagination; on the stage, it is not so easy for such a concept to be represented by live actors. His clowns are therefore abstractions standing more for the nature of existence than for people. Didi and Gogo wait endlessly, Hamm and Clov wait for the end that does not come, like figures carved in time, but they do so with a pathetic animation. And it turns out to be very funny to watch them.

As in farce, cause and effect are discounted, time is speeded up or slowed down, fate is unpredictable and anything can happen. This must seem as it is in an irrational universe. In *Godot*, a Boy suddenly appears in order to report that Godot will keep his appointment 'tomorrow'; when tomorrow comes, the Boy appears again with the very same information. But is it tomorrow, and is it the same boy? Yet our eyes tell us that time has passed, since the withered tree on the empty stage has grown a leaf or two. Under circumstances of appalling repetition and similarity, any little difference stands out vividly, and so it is with the appearance of a few miserable leaves on the tree. What then of the impact of Pozzo's unexpected blindness? In *Endgame*, Ham sits paralysed, blind and helpless in a chair as he contemplates his legless parents, Nagg and Nell, grotesquely confined in ashcans; only Hamm's servant Clov is free to move, although, because he cannot leave, he is as much a prisoner as they. Thus each is ridiculously dependent on the other, but the laughter is without mirth.

At its best, such drama achieves a kind of poetry and rhythm in comic form and farcical style peculiar to itself, and it is this comic method which has made theatre of the absurd more widely acceptable than the private and surrealist plays of Apollinaire and Cocteau. In Britain, several of the early plays of Harold Pinter were presented on the mass medium of television, and yet survived the demands of the popular audience amazingly well. *Godot* has now been presented before many prison communities, and has seemed immediately recognizable and understandable. After the initial strangeness of absurdist methods, it is now apparent that the style of

Beckett or Ionesco or Pinter has become generally familiar, just as the two-dimensional drawing of Picasso quickly became eminently suitable for poster advertising.

Because of Roger Blin's friendship with Artaud and his association with the production of *Les Cenci* in 1935, it has been suggested that the theatre of the absurd owes a debt to the theatre of cruelty. However, there is the twisted logic of unreason, an essential intellectuality, in the plays of Beckett and Ionesco which sets them apart from the extravagant emotionalism of Artaud's theatre. In the best plays of the absurd, all that is left of Artaud's theory of cruelty is the general notion of exposing the audience to horror. As will appear, each playwright has responded to his sense of the absurd in his individual way, some more constructively than others, but always with wit.

Godot was written in French between 1947 and 1949; it was published in 1952. Beckett said he wrote it in French in order to

22. Beckett, *Waiting for Godot*, 1953. Production by Roger Blin and design by Matias at the Théâtre de Babylone, Paris, with Pierre Latour, Jean Martin, Lucien Raimbourg and Blin.

make sure his words were simple. He had seen Blin's production of *The Ghost Sonata* in 1949, and for his consideration sent him both *Godot* and *Eleuthéria*, written in 1947, but as yet unpublished. Blin was impressed, but three years passed before he could find the money for a production of either. When the time came, he chose *Godot* because, with only five characters, it was cheaper and simpler to stage. So it was that in 1953 the play achieved a short run at the tiny Théâtre de Babylone on the Boulevard Raspail, a theatre now defunct, and Roger Blin became Beckett's first and most important link with the professional theatre. Matias was the designer, Blin himself played Pozzo, Jean Martin was Lucky, Pierre Latour Estragon and Lucien Raimbourg Vladimir. Distinguished critics like Jean-Jacques Gautier of *Le Figaro* and Thierry Maulnier of *Revue de Paris* virtually dismissed the production, and of the reviewers only Sylvain Zegel in *La Libération* saw any merit in it at all. But fortunately several prominent French writers had also seen the play, and their praises in *Arts* and *Critique* during those crucial months of January and February 1953, probably altered the course of dramatic history a little. Jacques Audiberti considered *Godot* to be 'a perfect work' and Armand Salacrou spoke of it as the 'play of our time' they had been waiting for. Above all, Anouilh testified that he thought the evening to be 'as important as the première of Pirandello put on in Paris by Pitoëff in 1923' (*Arts*, 27 January). The play was soon translated into many languages and staged all over the world, provoking endless discussion. Melvin Friedman has conveniently abstracted all the different interpretations in 'Crritic!' (*Modern Drama*, December 1966), and John Fletcher and John Spurling have assembled all the conflicting comments on the productions in their book *Beckett: A Study of His Plays* (1972). It was this play which threw the new absurdist drama into immediate prominence, and spurred lesser playwrights everywhere to try their hand.

Beckett's stage is always one of simple, almost empty, space, and his text dictates exactly what must be done, and how it must be done. Nevertheless, the treatment of Vladimir (Didi) and Estragon (Gogo) as tramps originated with Blin's production – indeed, at first he wanted Lucky to be dressed as a station porter. Alain Robbe-Grillet has somewhat questionably credited Blin's production with the circus effects in the play, but the evidence of cuts in the English version of 1954 better suggests the practical extent of Blin's influence. (The lines censored by the British Lord Chamberlain's office were restored in the edition of 1965.) Beckett has subsequently demonstrated his faith in Blin as his director by encouraging him to revive his production of *Godot* at the Théâtre Hébertot in 1956, and at the Odéon in 1961. The playwright also dedicated *Endgame* to Blin in 1957.

In Britain, *Godot*'s progress was less sure. Ralph Richardson declined to play the part of Estragon to Alec Guinness's Vladimir because the author could not or would not explain the play to him, just as John Gielgud on a later occasion rejected *Endgame* because he was unwilling to act in a play he did not fully understand. Eventually, Peter Hall directed an uncensored text of *Godot* in English at a club production at the Arts Theatre, London, in 1955, and this production was transferred with the censor's cuts to the Criterion Theatre. Hall brought out little of the clown in the tramps, and Alan Schneider, who was with Beckett watching this production, has reported that the author did not much like what he saw, particularly the realistic clutter of rubbish-dump debris on the stage, which destroyed the impression that the action was taking place in an empty space, and that Didi and Gogo were isolated from other human beings. Both the director and his cast have since confessed that they were uncertain what they were doing and what effects they were achieving. The play worked almost in spite of them. In his autobiography, Peter Bull, the actor who played Pozzo, tells of one remarkable occasion when the production was on tour and it was discovered that they had only a short time to catch their last train. They speeded up the pace of the second act, which partly echoes the first, and much to their astonishment, the effect was hilarious and in no way diminished the power or the point of the play.

Except for the reviews of Harold Hobson and Kenneth Tynan, reception by the London press was unfavourable. Nevertheless, interest in so unusual a play transcended the critics, and the play was produced successfully by students and amateurs all over the country, with the circus element growing more prominent. By the time of Anthony Page's revival for George Devine's English

Stage Company at the Royal Court in 1964, with Jocelyn Herbert as designer, Nicol Williamson as a Vladimir with 'sad, distressed eyes' and Jack MacGowran as brilliantly at ease in the part of Lucky as Jean Martin had been in Paris, the actors had got it right and few continued to find the play obscure. According to Ronald Bryden in the *New Statesman* for 8 January 1965, MacGowran in particular 'acted himself so far into Beckett's mind he almost seems part of its imagery'. This actor continued to give a number of outstanding performances and readings in Beckett until his death in 1973.

The American première of *Godot* had to wait until 1956, when Alan Schneider, a personal friend of the author, had the misfortune of opening the play to a disastrous beginning at the Coconut Grove Playhouse in Miami, Florida. Advance publicity had claimed the play to be 'the laugh sensation of two continents', and even with Tom Ewell and Bert Lahr as Didi and Gogo, the vacationers on the Florida coast had a rude shock. With his vaudeville training behind him, Lahr expected Ewell to play the straight man to his clowning, and he could not be restrained from improvising comic business during Lucky's long speech. Schneider reported the production to be a fiasco.

Most unusually, Beckett began to take a hand in his own productions. In Paris, he 'supervised' the 1961 production of *Godot* at the Odéon, personally approving the strong lighting, the thin, delicate tree designed by Giacometti, and a stone for Estragon to sit on. It seems that no one had thought to ask the author's opinion before. Since then, Beckett has himself directed *Endgame*, *Krapp's Last Tape*, *Happy Days* and *Godot*, this last on the main stage of the Schiller Theater in West Berlin, a production which was to visit the Royal Court Theatre in London. This activity has afforded a unique opportunity for observers to study Beckett's intentions, especially since he kept detailed promptbooks. As one might have guessed from his lines, he is totally professional as a director, precise and meticulous in controlling every gesture, move and intonation, and for all his plays insisting on a pace that is light and quick. George Devine was not alone in finding that Beckett's text was like a musical score, a limpid notation prompting its own rhythms in every word and phrase. Eyewitness accounts of his work as a director may be read in Walter D. Asmus in *Theatre Quarterly*, 19,

Pierre Chabert in *Gambit*, no. 28, and Ruby Cohn and James Knowlson in the first issue of their *Journal of Beckett Studies*.

At the Schiller Theater Beckett again had Matias as his designer for *Godot*, and a notable plan was devised for the costumes. Beckett cast Stefan Wigger, a tall, thin actor, as Didi, and Horst Bollman, a short, plump actor, as Gogo. Then he required that Didi wear trousers that were a tight fit and striped, while he also wore Gogo's black jacket which was to be too small for him. As for Gogo, he was to wear black trousers that fitted him, as well as Didi's striped jacket, which was too big for him. The effect was to reinforce the idea that these two characters were complementary parts of one man. On one occasion Beckett even arranged Didi and Gogo in a pose so that the striped jacket appeared to have the correct trousers. He repeated the same sort of idea for Pozzo and Lucky: Lucky wore shoes the colour of Pozzo's hat, and while Lucky's checked waistcoat matched Pozzo's checked trousers, Pozzo's grey jacket matched the grey trousers worn by Lucky.

Other details are also of interest. Gogo's pink undershirt was so long that when his trousers fell to the ground, it could be seen that the shirt reached all the way below his knees. For the dance of 'the tree', Beckett had Gogo take up the basic Yoga posture with his hands above his head as in prayer. Beckett's thinking about the stage composition appeared to have a certain metaphysical meaning for him: Ruby Cohn saw a pleasing symmetry on the stage, in that the squat stone was like Gogo and the thin, spare tree like Didi, and Walter Asmus reported that Beckett said, 'Estragon is on the ground; he belongs to the stone. Vladimir is light; he is oriented towards the sky. He belongs to the tree.'

Endgame was also first written in French, and was first staged by Blin in French at the Royal Court Theatre, London, in 1957, with Blin as Hamm and Jean Martin as Clov. The production was afterwards performed at the Studio des Champs Élysées, and received the customarily doubtful notices. The setting of the play was, if anything, even more bleak than that for *Godot*, which after all has some sense of an airy exterior landscape with its tree. *Endgame* is confined in a room, which Blin intended to look like a womb. Then two high windows upstage like eye-sockets suggested that the stage might also represent the inside of a skull, and mystification was multiplied. On the same bill at the Royal Court, Blin included Beckett's first metaphysical mime, *Acte sans paroles* (*Act without Words*, 1957), a balletic depiction of a man alone in a hot white desert, and controlled like an automaton by the shrill, impersonal blasts of a supernatural whistle.

Beckett has seemed bent on restricting his more recent plays to the minimum of dramatic elements, and his stagecraft after *Godot* and *Endgame* has almost eliminated the interchange of one

23. Beckett, *Play*, 1964. Production by George Devine at the Old Vic, London, with Rosemary Harris, Robert Stephens and Billie Whitelaw.

character with another. *La Dernière bande* (*Krapp's Last Tape*) was first
produced in Paris in 1958 with Jean Martin as Krapp (and subsequently in London with Patrick Magee and in Berlin with Martin
Held), and consists of a monologue by an old man responding to a
tape recording he made thirty years before. *Oh les beaux jours*
(*Happy Days*) was produced in 1961 with Madeleine Renaud as a
rather miscast Winnie (and subsequently in London with Peggy
Ashcroft), and is virtually a monologue by a middle-aged woman
sitting in a heap of sand as it appears steadily to engulf her. These
plays and others which have confined actors in burial urns or have
reduced them physically to a pair of lips moving in the dark, begin
to deny the need for the actor, or even the theatre itself. The
operation of symbolism may in this way have sharply simplified
the work of the stage, but one suspects that such anti-theatre is
cold comfort for the future development of dramatic art.

It is perhaps fortunate therefore that Beckett has proved
to be inimitable. In Britain, the actor and director Harold Pinter
(1930–   ) has acknowledged his debt to him: for Pinter, Beckett
is 'the greatest writer of our time'. The debt has shown itself
in Pinter's bleak settings and in the occasional patterning of
spare dialogue in some of his early plays. In one or two more recent
compositions, *Landscape* and *Silence* in 1968 and 1969, he has
inclined towards Beckettian monologue. But for the most part
Pinter's extraordinary talent for suggestive obliquity in his dialogue
is distinctively his own; if it has an ancestry at all, it may be that
uniquely understated game, the English drawing-room comedy.
Relevant to this, many of Pinter's plays, beginning with *The Collection* (1962), have had as their British director another Englishman,
Peter Hall, director first of the Royal Shakespeare Company and
then the National Theatre, who has adopted a dry, measured style of
production rich in comic overtones. This has proved itself the best
way with Pinter, and helped his plays to reveal their basis in
psychological realism more and more. Speaking of his script for the
film *Accident* in *Sight and Sound*, autumn 1966, Pinter said,

> Life is much more mysterious than plays make it out to be.
> And it is this mystery which fascinates me: what happens
> between words, what happens when no words are spoken.

Here the author puts his finger on his greatest strength as a dramatist, but there is more than a touch of self-indulgence in those words,
and some have wondered whether the mystification, particularly
in his recent plays, *Old Times* (1970) and *No Man's Land* (1974), has
been employed, not as a means, but an end.

At least, it is now clear that Pinter is no longer to be regarded
as a reductive absurdist. Part of his achievement has been to find a
dramatic way of revealing the threat behind the evasive exchanges
of everyday life, and to convey the tension between people who
think they know each other. This is obvious in his most recent play,
Betrayal (1978), and was even more obvious in those earlier plays
into which needless mystery and violence were introduced, suggesting the playwright's uncertain confidence in his method. In
the one-act play *The Room* (1957), a woman learns with alarm that
a stranger has been waiting outside the house for several days to see
her. When this person is eventually seen, it comes as a completely
unexplained surprise to find that he is a black man, and when
without motivation the woman's husband kills him, it comes as an
even greater surprise to learn that she goes blind. *The Birthday Party*
(1958) was Pinter's first play to sustain this kind of teasing of his
audience for three acts. Nevertheless, the conception behind each of
his plays is redeemed by a unique sense of comedy, an ironic humour
founded in a highly idiomatic use of English. This has not always
been easy to translate into productions outside Britain. In particular,
the idea that the commonplace props in his plays are in some way
symbolic — which the playwright has repeatedly denied — has
frequently resulted in a leaden treatment of his text.

Pinter's typical props, a kettle, a bucket, an electric fire,
may not be symbolic, but his dramatic treatment of reality is
certainly symbolist. He does not build his drama on any current
philosophy of the absurd, but he is concerned to show people
engulfed in trivia, whether of persons or things or talk. He achieves
a comic response by representing these trivia with meticulous
accuracy, which may obscure any symbolist intent, but the trivia
themselves are hugely representative of our lives. After *A Night Out*
(1960), and especially in *The Collection, The Lover* (1963) and *The
Homecoming* (1965), Pinter has added a powerful ingredient to his
concoctions, that of sexuality. When relationships between the sexes

are under his microscope, each little fear of rejection and loneliness, each hint of a threat to security and identity, is as amusing as before, but also much more painful. Pinter's perception of human behaviour is acute, and his ability to convey objectively what he sees through character and dialogue has made him the best comic dramatist writing in English since Shaw.

One theme has become increasingly prominent in Pinter's work of the last ten years, particularly in *Landscape* and *Silence*, *Old Times* and *Betrayal*. This is the elusive nature of time as it chases round inside the head, together with our ability to manipulate memory. Pinter has celebrated his growing interest by devoting a year to writing a screenplay for Proust's novel *À la Recherche du temps perdu*, although the film projected by Joseph Losey has not been made. *Betrayal* notably experiments with our sense of time in an unusually open manner, by dividing the action of the play into nine scenes and then, as it were, playing them in reverse order, so that the audience is enabled to track an adulterous relationship back over a period of nine or ten years. Beginning with a deadly reunion between the couple involved after the affair is all over, and ending with its passionate beginning, the technique has the effect of allowing each scene to explain a little of the previous one. In this way Pinter has removed much of the mystery of motives, and we are but a step from the kind of retrospective drama Ibsen learned to write a hundred years ago.

Also leaning on Beckett, *Rosencrantz and Guildenstern Are Dead* (1967) by Tom Stoppard (1937–   ) was originally a one-act farce presented at the Edinburgh Festival of 1966, for which the National Theatre requested a second act. The play borrowed the idea of a pair of interchangeable fools from *Waiting for Godot*, and had them act out the scenes which Shakespeare did not write for the courtiers in *Hamlet*. Just as Didi and Gogo are utterly dependent on Godot, so Ros and Guil have no freedom without the Prince. Beckett had prepared the way for this kind of comic symbolism, and the play was immediately popular everywhere. The critics, however, have been unwilling to commit themselves to a judgment. Robert Brustein considered Stoppard to be 'a clever author manipulating rather than exploring', and John Russell Brown was one of many who thought the play was a parody of theatre of the absurd, merely anthologizing its features. Nevertheless, Stoppard has since proved himself to be, not only a fine verbal wit, but also an accomplished theatre gamesman in the manner of Pirandello. Now something more than those of a 'university wit' and an 'intellectual mounte-bank', his purposes have seemed more substantial in his most recent plays, *Jumpers*, with Michael Hordern and Diana Rigg at the Old Vic for the National Theatre in 1972, *Travesties*, with John Wood, John Hurt and Tom Bell at the Aldwych for the Royal Shakespeare Company in 1974, and *Night and Day*, with Diana Rigg at the Phoenix Theatre in 1978.

---

17 *Theatre of the absurd: Ionesco and others*

The Bald Prima Donna (1950)

In some ways Eugène Ionesco (1912–) is a better theorist than playwright. Like Beckett, Ionesco saw the world as an object of simultaneous ridicule and pain. His earliest plays explored this contradiction through the spate of illogical words he put in the mouths of stereotyped characters, and if his jokes were overlong and his dialogue overwritten, the results were always hilarious and achieved quick popularity. But unlike Beckett, Ionesco has never hesitated to speak and write of his intentions, and these were often more profound and better thought out than his plays.

It was apparent that Ionesco had built up a considered philo-sophy of the absurd when in 1958 he bothered to respond to the charge of a British journalist, Kenneth Tynan, who wrote in the London *Observer* that the playwright had no message, no commit-ment. Tynan was a narrow advocate for social realism in the theatre, holding Sartre and Brecht as his exemplars of dramatic purposefulness, and encouraging the work of new British realists like John Osborne and Arnold Wesker. Ionesco's reply, published in the *Observer* and reprinted in 1962 in *Notes and Counter Notes*, was the time-honoured one that 'a work of art has nothing to do with doctrine', but adopts 'its own means of directly apprehending the real'. Social realism was only one level at which to apprehend reality, and itself an inadequate one. Ionesco's concern is to express the absence of meaning in life, and in his plays he has made frequent use of his typically innocent, but sensitive, anti-hero figure, Bérenger, in order to show man's brave but hopeless attempt to bear some responsibility, even inspire some compassion, for the pointless position in which he finds himself.

To Ionesco must go the distinction of having had the first transparently absurdist play produced after the war. *La Cantatrice chauve* (*The Bald Prima Donna*, or, in America, *The Bald Soprano*) was written in 1948 and produced in 1950 by Nicolas Bataille at the Théâtre des Noctambules. The married couples in this play merely sit and talk in near-meaningless clichés. This, according to the author, is 'the tragedy of language', symbolically representing the

24. Ionesco, *The Bald Prima Donna*, 1950. Production at the Théâtre de la Huchette, Paris, 1955.

grotesque banality of their unlovely marriages. The characters convey the spirit of automata without brains, 'characters without character'. Ionesco has explained with some satisfaction how he took the idea for this play from reading the random lists of words and phrases in a teach-yourself-English book. 'The surreal is there', he said, 'within our reach, in our daily conversation.'

His first full-length play was *Amédée ou Comment s'en débarrasser (Amédée or How to Get Rid of It)*, directed by Jean-Marie Serreau in 1954. This also depicted a marriage in which love had died, but even more preposterously. Love was literally dead, and remained as an embarrassing corpse in the adjoining bedroom. As mushrooms sprout from the walls, the corpse actually begins to grow and fill the stage. The atmosphere is one of ludicrous insanity. However, *Amédée* and the others in this vein have achieved their fullest response from the audience when the characters retained their dignity through thick and thin, and caught a solemn but quick rhythm in the patter of the nonsense dialogue. In performance, Ionesco's plays best obey the laws of farce and the discipline of the straight face.

In his later plays, Ionesco's plots have grown stronger and his

25. Ionesco, *Amédée*, 1954. Production by Jean-Marie Serreau at the Théâtre d'Aujourd'hui.

characters more three-dimensional — even, dare one say, a little
more socially realistic? His subjects have increasingly turned upon
the incontrovertible fact of death, the one fact that overrides all
dreams and illusions. *Tueur sans gages* (*The Killer*, 1958) presents on
stage the 'radiant city', an urban development in which everything is beautiful — or so the audience is told, for it sees only an
empty space in dim, grey lighting. Further, it emerges that this city is
plagued by a deathly figure who will not go away, but relentlessly
persists in taking the lives of its citizens. Ionesco's Bérenger here
appears as a Charlie Chaplin character who is determined to resist
the killer, especially when he sees that he is only a dwarf. However,
in answer to Bérenger's reasoning, the dwarf merely chuckles
and draws his knife from its sheath. For all his idealism, Bérenger
becomes just another victim like all the others.

   Rhinocéros (1959) has been Ionesco's most widely successful
play, perhaps, we may observe, because it seemed to embody a more

26. Ionesco, *Rhinoceros*, 1959. Production by Jean-Louis Barrault
at the Théâtre de France, Paris, 1960.

purposeful moral allegory that could be readily applied to a variety of social and political situations. It was his most 'relevant' play to date. In it the people of a French provincial town turn into rhinoceroses, willingly conforming to the behaviour of the majority as the collective hysteria of a dehumanizing 'rhinoceritis' spreads through the community. To the end, Bérenger clings ridiculously to his individuality in the face of social pressures, even when such idiosyncratic behaviour seems doomed. In this play, the unforgettable sound of rhinoceroses' hooves thundering down the street outside must be the funniest offstage effect in all the plays of the absurd. In Paris in 1960, Jean-Louis Barrault directed the play as a terrifying farce, but in other productions the style and tone have ranged from the heavily tragic in Germany to a frothy burlesque in America.

Beginning as a highly subjective surrealistic poet, and influenced by an indigestible mixture of works by Strindberg, Kafka and Artaud, Arthur Adamov (1908–70) presented the unusual case of an absurdist playwright whose perspectives noticeably widened as his plays reached a bigger public. Adamov's early plays dramatized his personal despair, but before he committed suicide, he was writing in the more positive manner of Brechtian epic theatre, and was fully committed to the social realist cause. His first play, *La Parodie* (*The Parody*) was another early absurdist piece written in a surrealistic style before *Waiting for Godot* was known. Written in 1947, it was not produced until 1952. It was intended as a 'parody' of life, in which one man, a nameless optimist, keeps a pointless rendezvous with a girl, Lili, who never meets him; meanwhile, another man, a pessimist, merely waits in despair for her to pass by, although she never does. As a result of their behaviour, the first man is sentenced to a term in prison, and the second is run over in the street and swept up in an ashcan. As in some Strindbergian dream play, the same characters appear in different guises, all to emphasize man's loneliness and the world's meaninglessness. *Le Professeur Taranne* (*Professor Taranne*), directed by Roger Planchon in 1953, was based upon an actual nightmare Adamov had had. In this play an elderly scholar and gentleman is accused, among other things, of the unlikely crime of indecent exposure. However, in the manner of Kafka's *The Trial*, the more poor Taranne denies the charges and defies his accusers, the more he appears to convict himself.

With *Le Ping-pong* (*Ping Pong*, 1955), it is possible to recognize Adamov's new interest in the stage as a medium for social criticism. This is a play of great wit, in which two young students devote their lives to the study and worship of pinball machines, which are presumably to symbolize the mechanical emptiness of modern society. They are still obsessed with the trivial intricacies of the machine when they are old men on the point of death. Social realism is even more explicit in Adamov's *Paolo Paoli*, directed by Planchon in 1957. This is a Marxist satire on capitalism in France just before the outbreak of the First World War. The play uses the informative and distancing device of news headlines projected on screens, a technique borrowed from the theatre of Piscator and Brecht, but its cleverest alienating effect is built into the subject itself. The chief objects of trade between Algeria and metropolitan France at that time, and the source of heated interest to the characters of the play, are nothing more than butterflies and ostrich feathers. However, implicit in such satire must be the desire to correct what is wrong with society, and once it is accepted that the wrongs of the world can be put right, then an absurdism that preaches the total irrationality of life is no more.

In America, Edward Albee (1928–) was initially influenced enough by Ionesco to write surrealistic one-act plays in the absurdist manner. His brief allegory of modern society, *The Zoo Story*, was first produced in the Werkstatt of the Schiller Theater in Berlin in 1959, directed by Walter Henn. It was afterwards produced at the Provincetown Playhouse in New York by Milton Katselas in 1960, and then at the Arts Theatre, London, by Henry Kaplan. The play presents two men who meet on a bench in Central Park, New York. Peter is an older man and comes from the middle-classes; Jerry is a young working-class rebel. Speaking in quasi-realistic dialogue, they are unable to understand each other: in the jargon of the day, they fail to communicate. Not only this, but violence is the only medium they have in common. So it is that Jerry provokes Peter to fight him, with Jerry finally impaling himself on the knife he had tossed to Peter.

Albee's *The Sandbox*, written in 1959 and directed by Lawrence Arrick at the Jazz Gallery, New York, in 1960 and *The American Dream*, written in 1960 and directed by Alan Schneider at the

York Playhouse, New York, in 1961, are twin one-act plays, amusing but caustic, intended to satirize the hollow social values of contemporary America. In the latter play, American aspirations towards the good life are symbolized by the arrival of a handsome, but vacuous, young man. He is joyfully adopted by a stereotyped American family, with a domineering Mommy and an emasculated Daddy. Only Grandma, every moment expecting to be taken away by the removal van, speaks the truth. These sketches are strongly derivative from Ionesco, but were simple to stage, made their point immediately and were immensely popular on college campuses during the rebellious sixties. With their emblematic, two-dimensional, cardboard characters, they also seemed refreshing after so long a period of realism on the American stage.

In 1961, Albee's gift for fluent and incisive dialogue helped his first long play, *Who's Afraid of Virginia Woolf*, to immediate and international fame. It was directed by Alan Schneider with Uta Hagen and Arthur Hill in the leading parts at the Billy Rose Theatre, New York, and at the Piccadilly Theatre, London, in 1964. An idealistic and newly married couple are entertained by a disillusioned, older couple, and the conjunction of the two groups has the effect of throwing up a variety of ghosts and skeletons. In spite of its absurdist title, the play constituted a retreat to a naturalistic mode of accentuated, Strindbergian, psychological realism, with a liberal addition of symbolic suggestions about the futility of human illusions. Harold Clurman found Albee's next play, *A Delicate Balance* (1966), to be superior, but if it was more subtle, it was less popular, more absurdist and less verbally sensational. It was directed by Alan Schneider with Jessica Tandy and Hume Cronyn at the Martin Beck Theatre, New York, and afterwards by Peter Hall with Peggy Ashcroft and Michael Hordern at the Aldwych Theatre, London, in 1969. In this play, another family is catalysed, this time by a visit from friends who are trying to escape from a mysterious terror, and who insist on staying the night when they are not wanted. It is the task of the quiet but downtrodden head of the family, Tobias, to maintain a 'balance' between family and friends. *All Over* (1971) has a famous man dying in his bed on the stage throughout the play while his wife and mistress, his family and friends, talk about him and each other. The play was not so well received as its predecessors, but in its experiments with forms of speech selected to lend a ritual tone to the scene, it was an interesting advance in absurdist technique. Nevertheless, Albee's strength lies in his cynical and seemingly realistic observation of people under stress, and 'theatre of the absurd' is a term that can no longer be readily applied to his work.

Back in Paris, the Spanish Moroccan Fernando Arrabal (1932–   ), writing strongly subjective and pitch-black comedies, has taken his departure from absurdism in less sophisticated ways. His first play, *Pique-nique en campagne* (*Picnic on the Battlefield*, 1958) contained many of Arrabal's now familiar ingredients of violence and the ridiculous. Its scene is set pointedly in the front line in the middle of a war. There on the battlefield a soldier and his prisoner receive a visit from the soldier's family one Sunday afternoon. The weather is fine, and they have come in all innocence to enjoy a picnic with him all together. Unfortunately, they are oblivious to the fighting raging all about them, until suddenly they are destroyed by machine-gun fire.

Violence to the point of sadism became a recurring theme in Arrabal's plays, often at the expense of some Chaplinesque figure presented as the victim of a hostile society. In the nightmarish play *Le Cimetière des voitures* (*The Car Cemetery*, 1959), this figure is the kindly, Christ-like Emanou — the religious overtones in the play are intended. With a variety of other types of people, he lives contentedly in his junk-yard of old cars. Then he is obscenely murdered by those he lives with — beaten to death while tied to a bicycle like a figure on a crucifix. *L'Architecte et l'empereur d'Assyrie* (*The Architect and the Emperor of Assyria*), which was brilliantly produced by Jorge Lavelli in 1967, had been worked up from an idea in Artaud's manifesto for a theatre of cruelty. The two characters of the title are marooned together on what passes for a desert island, and between them they enact such complementary roles as mother and son, husband and wife, tyrant and subject, judge and prisoner — all relationships which are essentially interdependent. Even the two characters themselves are interchangeable, and in a final gesture of mutuality, the Emperor urges the Architect to consume him, to eat him up. Which he does.

These plays have contributed little or nothing to the techniques of the stage. Pure absurdism was like private poetry: even when it had expressed itself as fully as it could, it had little future. In any case, Joseph Chiari asked tellingly in his *Landmarks of Contemporary Drama*, if there is no communication possible between people in an absurdist world, why try to write an absurdist play in the first place?

---

18 *Ritual theatre and Jean Genêt*

The Balcony (1957), *The Blacks* (1959)

Ritual is an act of solemn ceremonial. It is usually an organized expression of prescribed customs of religious belief or social behaviour, but it can also have a use on a solely secular stage. A playwright can exploit the conventions of the regular theatre to induce in an audience a special response which the performers share. A whole play like Shakespeare's tragedy *Richard III* can be made up of ritual scenes of funeral and execution, of coronation and deposition, of mourning and supernatural visitation. Whether this is done with irony or not, the ritual devices used formalize the theme of the play — here the work of providence in the affairs of state. Moreover, the ritual scenes make of Richard himself something of a role-player and master of ceremonies. In his fundamental essay, *The Idea of a Theater*, Francis Fergusson found that Shakespeare's drama generally was built upon rituals which marked out the action, the device showing the characters each time in a clearer light. In a ritual drama, the actor becomes a stage manager, and the play is as intensely concerned with form as with content, for it is form itself which induces the participation of the audience, and grants it special insights into the mystery of the occasion.

The last stage of development in symbolist drama would seem to be ritualistic. By means of ritual, the symbols are transcended, the metaphoric meaning of the stage action is assimilated without question, and communion between stage and audience is complete.

In this way the action on the stage retains a mystery which is of another order of reality, and which can be felt only through its experience as ritual. Just as in the ancient religious theatres, the ritual elements are perceived in common, taken on trust and remain sacred, so in a secular ritual theatre, parallel assumptions of mutual faith are necessary. However, where the ritual is not rooted in common custom, there is a terrible risk of ridicule.

The risk is even greater in the unique case of Jean Genêt (1910–   ), because he does not try to mollify society, but to attack it. His plays are without comfort, and his ritual forms are built upon scorn and hate. So negative is his view of people, that his plays can be said to succeed only when they are themselves disliked. However, Genêt has no doubt calculated that, since he knows his audiences must share some part of a common guilt, his drama always has the possibility of biting home. Even with the 'inverted' ritual to be discussed in this section, Genêt's plays achieve an aesthetic beauty born of his single-mindedness and his genius for devising an irreducible form.

Genêt's work was at first associated with existentialism by those who knew only his early plays. He created ugly images of people who rejected, and were rejected by, society in his first two plays, the one-acters *Haute Surveillance* (*Deathwatch*) and *Les Bonnes* (*The Maids*), and Jean-Paul Sartre was mostly responsible for the assumption that their purpose was existentialist. Discussing at length Genêt's early years in reformatory and prison, Sartre's 600-page half-psychological, half-philosophical biography of the playwright, *Saint-Genêt, comédien et martyr* (*Saint Genêt, Actor and Martyr*, 1952), held its subject to be the prototype of modern existential man, although, since the world still had meaning for him, Genêt was no absurdist. Sartre believed that, excluded from society, Genêt created his characters as rebels and outcasts like himself, and explained that he gloried in degradation. Genêt had created a philosophy of inverted values, asserting evil as an ideal of beauty, and the appropriate avenue by which to affirm any positive values in life. All of this may be true, and there is more than a touch of absurdity in finding the positive in such a negative, but Sartre's argument does not go very far towards accounting for Genêt's unparalleled form of theatre.

Some, like Robert Brustein, believe Genêt to be a true successor to Artaud, and Brustein claims that in Genêt, Artaud 'would unquestionably have seen his most promising heir'. The theorists who believed with Artaud that the violent immediacy of dream could be presented as an image of life seemed justified by Genêt's practice. Peter Brook, using extensive improvisation as part of his rehearsal technique, produced *Le Balcon* (*The Balcony*) in Paris in 1960, and with Charles Marowitz produced, as we saw, twelve of the seventeen scenes of *Les Paravents* (*The Screens*) as part of his experiment with Artaudian 'cruelty' in 1964. The Living Theatre of Judith Malina and Julian Beck attempted a production of *The Maids* in pursuit of their form of theatre of cruelty. It is the interest of such Artaudian practitioners in Genêt's plays that has lent support to the idea that his work derived from Artaud. It is true that Genêt's theatre is emotionally disturbing in its symbolism of evil, its rites enacted by criminals, prostitutes and outcasts, and its re-creation of the secret needs of the audience. But for all its sensational results, there is a sharp intellectual edge, a shocking clear-headedness, present in the outline and structure of a play by Genêt that links him more with Pirandello than with Artaud.

From the start, Genêt's ritual arrangements are a form of Pirandellian theatre-game. Genêt's devices for involving the audience in the illusory action of the play set him well apart from his contemporaries. He found that the conventions of the theatre suited his fantastic vision of society, for in the theatre social roles can be enlarged, interchanged and mocked. Where theatrical illusion is usually received passively, Genêt explored ways of reflecting and implicating his audience by using the stage as a mirror of its secret impulsions. Genêt's theatricality does not use the stage to imitate life, but to show that life is as fake as the theatre itself.

His earliest play, *Deathwatch*, was produced after *The Maids*, and directed by Genêt himself at the Théâtre des Mathurins in 1949; it also had a production at the Royal Court, London, in 1961. The play's structure is almost conventional, and it relies for any ritual impact upon the uncertain effects of stylizing. The play is set in a French prison cell, and depicts three criminals, with the presence of a fourth implied offstage. The four represent a heirarchy of criminality. The three on the stage worship almost as a god an unseen black murderer named Snowball, who killed purely for gain. By contrast, the murderer Green Eyes, lying on the stage in chains, killed in a fit of temper, an act of lesser evil; he is jealous of Snowball's superiority. The petty thief Lefranc aspires to the superior glory of Snowball and Green Eyes by committing a sacrificial act of murder — he strangles the juvenile delinquent Maurice to whom he is homosexually attracted. The play is a black rite to evil, with Lefranc the priest and Green Eyes the godhead.

It has proved hard for audiences to accept the subjective scheme in *Deathwatch*, although the play is full of hints of what was to come in Genêt's later work. The performance is conceived as a ritual which is to 'unfold as in a dream', but with none of the direct appeal to the audience found in the other dreamlike play, *The Balcony*. *Deathwatch* manipulates merely the externals of the theatre: the set and costumes are in violently clashing black and white, the make-up is deliberately heavy, the lighting very bright. On top of this, the gestures are stylized, and the movements are either slow or 'incomprehensibly rapid, like flashing of lightning'. Certainly the play is meaningless if it is played in any degree realistically as a psychological prison drama, but even with the stylizing the author calls for, it fails to spark the imagination of the audience.

The other one-act play, *The Maids*, was commissioned by Louis Jouvet in 1947, but at the Athénée was a disaster. Its first successful performance in French was directed by Peter Zadek at London's Mercury Theatre in 1952, and this production was transferred to the Royal Court. Genêt revised the play in 1954, and since then it has attracted widespread interest among amateur avant-garde groups. In *The Maids*, the Pirandellian trickery makes a first appearance in Genêt's work, and the opening itself is a *coup de théâtre*. When the curtain goes up, the audience is deceived into believing it sees an elegant lady in a Louis XV boudoir insulting her maid Claire as she dresses her mistress. When an alarm-clock rings, pretence ceases and it is revealed that the lady is actually the maid Claire, play-acting with another maid, Solange, who is herself playing Claire.

It emerges that Claire and Solange have created their own ritual of hate, playing these roles every night in the absence of their mistress. So we watch two players playing lesbian sisters who play mistress and maid, or, since their roles are interchangeable, maid and mistress. By playing and exchanging these roles, they mirror each other, and express at once their mutual loathing and self-loathing. In his first conception of the piece, Genêt wanted the two to be played by male actors, still further to ritualize the roles, but Jouvet considered that the spectators would have enough mirrors to worry them without this complication, and men did not play the parts until a production in Berlin in 1965. In 1967, the Malina and Beck production, on tour in Europe, not only played Claire and Solange in 'drag', but increased the impact of the play and its ambiguities by presenting Madame herself as a hairy male, with muscles bulging beneath her gold *lamé*. The author was delighted. By such means he tried, he said, to abolish characters in favour of signs: 'My characters are all masks. How do you expect me to tell you whether they are true or false? I no longer know myself.' The ritualism worked. The device of the play-within-the-play ensured an objective treatment of class rebellion, and, as the device has always done, it accentuated the realistic frame in which it was set, reinforcing the hatred for the real mistress and all she stood for.

The Balcony, written in 1956, had a first production at the Arts Theatre Club in London in 1957 which was the cause of a remarkable backstage scandal. The production was directed by Peter Zadek, with Selma Vaz Dias as Mme Irma and Hazel Penwarden as Chantel. (Subsequently revised, the play was produced in Paris by Peter Brook in 1960). This play was Genêt's first outright success, with its audacious ritual elements working effectively inside the frame of Mme Irma's so-called 'house of illusions' (the traditional French name for a brothel). At the beginning, the play seems to be a series of comic burlesques designed to relax the audience, until what is idiosyncratic and preposterous in the brothel merges astonishingly with the pattern of society itself. Even if the play's parts are not perfectly integrated, Genêt's plan is ingenious and devilish, and owes something to Brecht's ironic methods of alienation. From criminal pathology and a study of the evil demon, Genêt has advanced to the more political examination of how man chooses his role in society.

The setting itself places the play on a self-conscious stage, that of the brothel, where performances of a sort are to be enacted. A mirror on the right wall reflects a bed, which therefore seems to be in the auditorium: 'The playgoer does not enter into *The Balcony* with impunity — once the curtain is up, he *is in* a bawdy house', writes David Grossvogel in *The Blasphemers*. This illusion is recalled at the end of the play, when Mme Irma speaks to the members of the audience as if they are clients who must slip out furtively, through a side alley. But the room of the brothel we see is itself an illusion, representing a sacristy, where some priest might robe himself. The three blood-red screens which create the sacristy tenuously suggest the impermanence of the make-believe. Behind it all hangs a huge Spanish crucifix.

The Balcony, like *The Maids*, opens with a *coup*, for we see an actor playing a bishop who is himself an actor: 'He has the mitre and cope of the first, and the unmistakable cothurni of the second.' He is a giant figure in garish make-up, dominating his pretty whore, a penitent in lace gown, who in turn will dominate *him* as soon as she chooses to stop playing her role of sinner. When that happens, the

27. Genêt, *The Balcony*, 1956. Production by Peter Brook at the Théâtre Gymnase, Paris, 1959. Stage design by André Acquart, with Jean Babilée, William Sabatier and Roger Blin.

Bishop is undressed and reduced to normal size – he turns out to be the gas company man. So the scene passes to reveal another salon and another pretence, and we learn that this house of illusions has no less than thirty-eight such salons for sexual fantasizing. The spectator has himself been cast as a voyeur, incriminating himself by his very presence in the theatre.

Genêt has still another surprise for the audience. Outside the illusory world of the brothel, a social revolution has taken place in the real world. Already the revolutionaries have adopted Chantel, one of Mme Irma's girls, as their symbolic figure of liberation, and when the palace is destroyed, an envoy demands that Mme Irma herself stand in for the queen. Further, the men we saw in the brothel, the Bishop, the Judge and the General, are to assume in real life the characters they play in private. The power structure of society is seen to be based upon fantasies as outrageous as those in the brothel itself. Writing in the avant-garde theatre magazine *Encore*, Charles Marowitz found this development in the play's action to be

> one of the most shocking hypotheses ever put forward in
> the drama ... the sexual pervert lives his fantasies in private
> and is therefore harmless; whereas the social personages
> play out their roles in public, which on the one hand makes
> them hypocritical and on the other dangerous.

The social reference of the play, hardly felt in the opening scenes, becomes explicit and ugly when the creatures of the brothel become images of familiar social institutions, and society itself is seen as just another house of illusions. By its nature, stage ritual tends to be static and repetitive, but in *The Balcony* Genêt found a way of having it burgeon in the mind and penetrate the frontier between illusion and reality.

It should be said that the second half of the play did not work for everyone. David Watt in *The Spectator* reported that 'a fog of symbolic rhetoric descends with appalling suddenness', and T. C. Worsley in *The New Statesman and Nation* found that the second act 'fumbles and falters', so that 'the play becomes a huge steaming muddle'. Worsley concluded, 'A plunge into the visionary comedy of the first act is warmly recommended. But at the interval you may well reach for your respectable hat and coat.'

The production at the Arts Theatre not only scandalized the audience, but also angered Genêt. He harangued the actors and the stage staff from the stage during rehearsals, and had to be barred from the first performance. He expected five months of rehearsal, not the four weeks Zadek had allowed: 'No actor can learn to walk beautifully on 10-inch lifts in four weeks.' Genêt also claimed that the play called for 'a Grock in every role', and demanded that it 'be performed with the solemnity of a mass in a cathedral' and at the same time be 'vulgar, violent and in bad taste'. The director afterwards wrote in *The New Statesman* that he had been told by the translator, 'If you want Genêt's genius, you'll have to take his violence.' The whole event was one of violence:

> The violence of castration, rebellion, flagellation on the stage; the violence of the collision between author and director, between author and management; the violence of popular revulsion, of the sensation surrounding the opening night — all were subordinated to the violent clash, in real life, between fantasy and reality, both in the author's mind and, during every performance of the play, in the minds of the audience (4 May 1957).

Zadek recognized that Genêt was disillusioned by the distance separating his text from its realization, which is a problem in staging any symbolist drama. The difficulty was increased in the case of Genêt, who was unable to compromise with his own vision, whereas in practice performance has always to accommodate the written fantasy.

Possibly Genêt's most satisfying achievement, and his most ingenious, was *Les Nègres* (*The Blacks*, written in 1957). This play was first produced by Roger Blin at the Théâtre de Lutèce, Paris, in 1959. London saw it in English at the Royal Court in 1961, in a production flawed by the difficulty of assembling a cast of black actors. Although in this play Genêt was not championing an exploited social minority, but merely using an obvious rebel group, the choice of Blacks as performers introduced a clearly partisan viewpoint. In addition, the ceremonial in the play was wholly explicit, with the stage being used for performance which was frankly play-acting. The curtain was seen to be drawn by hand. The Whites who play the Court (Queen,

Judge, Bishop and General again) were very obviously black actors in masks: 'The mask is worn in such a way that the audience sees a wide black band all around it, and even the actor's kinky hair.' Those who watch the Court are an on-stage audience composed of both spectators and actors, spectators who become actors especially when they witness a ritual killing of a white woman by a black man. The implication is that the real audience will be spectators and actors also, while remaining aware that the Whites it sees are merely the stereotypes of Whites seen through the eyes of Blacks, and the Blacks it sees are merely the stereotypes of Blacks seen through the eyes of Whites. And in case the audience should forget that the action is only play-acting, Genêt supplies a master of ceremonies, Archibald, who is on stage throughout like a chorus to explain everything, if sarcastically.

As in *The Balcony*, Genêt again has an ace up his sleeve. At the height of the ritual murder, the action is interrupted by the news of an event offstage, one happening in the apparent world of reality outside the theatre. There it is reported that an actual racial uprising is taking place — indeed, such an event was not uncommon to the experience of the audience in the years after the Second World War. Again, our perception of the ugly ritual on stage is emphasized by its parallel with what could be happening offstage, at the same time as it is distanced by the new development.

The Blacks is made up of an elaborate framework of ritualistic elements in every department of theatre. Calling his play a '*clownerie*', a clown show, Genêt insisted that it be performed specifically before a white audience. If it had to be performed before a black audience, then

> a white person, male or female, should be invited every
> evening. The organizer of the show should welcome him
> formally, dress him in ceremonial costume and lead him to
> his seat, preferably in the front row of the stalls. The actors
> will play for him. A spotlight should be focused upon this
> symbolic white throughout the evening.

If no white person wished to undergo this ordeal — as might not seem entirely unlikely — then Genêt suggested that 'white masks be distributed to the black spectators as they enter the theatre'. This move would of course reproduce the concept of the masked Court in the auditorium itself, and carry the play from the stage into the house, which is precisely the intention of the ritual. In Blin's production, the Court entered from the auditorium.

So the action on the stage constitutes a play-within-a-play-within-a-play: black actors impersonating black actors impersonating both black and white. This pattern is echoed and reinforced by the separate levels on the stage, upper and lower, with the Court playing on a gallery which runs all round the stage. The whole is backed by black curtains that set off a catafalque placed downstage and draped in white cloth. Tension will exist between the two levels of the stage, representing and ridiculing the tension between the white audience and the black actors.

The effect of having some of the characters wear masks further distances, and deliberately distorts, any quality of realism in the action, and this is helped by unrealistic exaggerations of speech and gesture. Thus when the Court laughs, it 'bursts into very shrill, but very well-orchestrated laughter', and this is echoed by 'even shriller laughter' from the Blacks. It is symbolic laughter, we could say. When the Court weeps, it wipes away its tears with 'a very theatrical gesture and heaves a long sob of grief'. The Blacks are to dance 'a kind of minuet' round the catafalque to an air by Mozart, 'which they whistle and hum', plucking flowers from their bodices and lapels to lay on the catafalque. Archibald speaks and bows with mock ceremonial, and at one point 'saws the air with his hands like an orchestra leader' as if directing one of the speakers. The Blacks are dressed in evening clothes, but the men wear tan shoes with their dark suits and white ties, and the women wear 'heavily spangled evening gowns' to suggest fake elegance, all in 'the very height of bad taste'. In this way the subject of the black rebellion and the ritual murder involves and disturbs the white audience, while the manner of playing makes it temporarily acceptable. Finally, the action actually seems to be more real as a result of obscuring the reality, and the spirit of an uncertain voodoo alarmingly infects the whole production. This careful indirection in the play was reflected in the reaction of the critics, some of whom considered the subject infantile and the treatment wordy, while others, like the American director, Harold Clurman, thought it 'one of the most original theatre pieces of our day'.

The Screens is a dramatic treatment of the misery of life in Algeria when it was under French military rule. The play's production in Paris was therefore delayed by the years of the Algerian civil war, from 1954 to 1962, and it received its first production at the Schlosspark State Theatre, West Berlin, in 1961. It had to wait for a production in France until 1966, when Roger Blin directed it at the Théâtre de France, and Genêt's *Lettres à Roger Blin*, saying how he wanted the play to be presented, were published soon after. *The Screens* was named after its principal scenic elements, folding screens carried on stage by the characters, and sometimes painted with symbolic objects and designs by the actors in front of the audience. Thus on a symbolic and unlocalized stage of varying levels yet further symbols were to be placed, silently moved by the actors. By having each actor double several parts, each masked or heavily made up, realism is again reduced. The same actors also make the sound effects of animals, wind and rain. The extraordinary arena of *The Screens* in this way achieves a mystery which is part of the theatrical show itself, a grand deceit in which the audience cannot help but acquiesce.

Nevertheless, the production in Paris was received angrily. The doll-like cartoon characters, the masks and the screens provided no defensive barrier against the ugly reality of the recent French experience in Algeria and the atrocities of the civil war. Genêt's letters to Blin suggested that the tone of the production assume a quality of lyricism in order to combat the commonplace realism inherent in the subject. As in the theatre of the absurd, the solution to communicating a repellent subject lay in hitting an appropriate tone and style for performance. Style and level of performance presented a special challenge in Genêt's later plays, in which an increasingly uncompromising criticism is showered on society. Some commentators believe that Brecht's influence is recognizable in *The Screens*, not only because of the play's episodic nature, but because of its relentless political content.

In attacking what he considered to be the trivial realism of the modern theatre, Genêt used the apparatus of the theatre itself more fully than his symbolist predecessors. In his book *The Imagination of Jean Genêt*, Joseph McMahon reminded us that 'once the theatre is unbridled it is liable to go anywhere'. With an unusual eye for the frontiers of dramatic form, Genêt explored this exciting tendency in the art of the theatre. He was concerned that his stage should mirror the true reality, and tried to dissolve the aesthetic barrier which separates play and audience by shaking the very supports that make it work, its conventions. Genêt recognized that deception was at the heart of all theatre, but after deception was complete, his plan was then to undeceive. *The Blacks*, for example, advertised as a 'clown show' or 'minstrel show', would seem to offer only a harmless experience, but before the evening is over, all the comfortable assumptions of the audience are destroyed.

More than this, Genêt's demand for stylization, his deliberate staginess, was part of his design for having the stage reflect the pretences of his audience. He set ritual and ceremony on the stage so that the audience might witness, recognize and be suitably shocked and contrite. Writing in the *Tulane Drama Review*, the American director Herbert Blau claimed that 'Genêt gives us the most direct *sensation* of the experience modern drama has been defining since the more rationalistic dualities of Pirandello: that of the rationality of illusion.' From his first attempts, Genêt's constant effort has been to objectify what was at first subjective, using the theatre to penetrate reality and our consciousness at the same time.

19 *After Artaud: avant-garde theatre in Poland and America*

Frankenstein (1965)

The line of 'irrational' theatre in this century is recognizably from symbolist to surrealist, from dada to the absurd, and from the theatre of cruelty to the 'alternative theatre' of the 1960s. The many non-commercial groups which sprang into being, albeit briefly, in the last ten or so years were believed to be, in the jargon of our time, a 'counter-culture', serving the art of drama outside the established theatre. These companies usually worked as collectives, often bringing a play into existence by group improvisation. The narrative logic of cause and effect, therefore, was often absent, and in its place the actors substituted complex theatrical images, visual compositions or tableaux intended to symbolize social or spiritual conditions. Group play-making also had the effect of de-emphasizing words, the actors mixing elements of mime and dance, popular music and film (the current term for this is 'mixed media'), rather than working from a preconceived text. In the programme for the American Living Theatre's *Mysteries and Smaller Pieces* (1964), it was claimed that the 'radical theatre' companies were

> in the vanguard of a new phenomenon in theatrical and social history — the spontaneous generation of communal playing troupes, sharing voluntary poverty, making experimental collective creations, and utilizing space, time, minds and bodies in manifold new ways that meet the demands of our explosive period.

It is hard to deny the continuing evidence of this new phenomenon. Certainly, Artaudian ideas about the aggressive purpose and style of drama have recently been discernible everywhere.

The actor-leader whose workshops have met with the widest enthusiasm on both sides of the Atlantic is Jerzy Grotowski (1933–). He founded his Laboratory Theatre in Opole, Poland, in 1959, and moved it to Wroclaw in 1965. The book of essays about his work, *Towards a Poor Theatre*, edited by his Italian associate, Eugenio Barba, was first published in Denmark in 1968 and translated into English in 1969. Although Grotowski acknowledges Stanislavsky's System as part of his training as an actor, the Polish technique is actually an attack on methods of emotional recall, and on the realistic theatre which is based on them. Following Artaud, Grotowski has returned to what he considers to be the archetypal roots of drama, when the theatre had a spiritual and religious role and the actor's task was ritualistic and priestlike. For Grotowski, this is also a return to Jung's concept of the 'collective unconscious'. He calls it the 'poor' theatre because, unlike the rich theatre which aims to synthesize all the arts, his theatre is stripped down to the essentials. To remove setting, costume, make-up, music, lighting effects and even the playhouse itself leaves only the actor to find his basic relationship with the audience.

Thus, for Grotowski, the actor is at the heart of the theatre experience. The actor is expected to give himself wholly to his art, and Grotowski's theatre has the reputation of requiring the most rigorous physical training. Only if the body is extended to the limit, as it is in the practice of the *Kathakali* actors of India, are 'pure impulses' released from the deepest levels of the unconscious. By such means theatre can become a personal discovery for the actor and the spectator, who must also be subjected to rigorous requirements. Like Vakhtangov, Grotowski mixes naturalistic and symbolist elements, and jumbles up the conventions of the west and the east, in order to expose his audiences to new theatrical experience.

Grotowski's Auschwitz play, *Akropolis* (1964), by Stanislaw Wyspianski, was brought to the Edinburgh Festival in 1968, and for many playgoers in Britain was a first taste of 'poor theatre'. The auditorium is a great black room, a box for exterminating the

28. Calderón, *The Constant Prince*, 1969. Production by Grotowski. The relationship between stage and audience.

victims of Nazi Germany. The actors are the inmates of the concentration camp, and they enact moments of Jewish history before they go down through a trapdoor to the gas chamber. The experience was intense and overwhelming. Calderón's *The Constant Prince*, in a version by Julius Slowacki (1969), impressed audiences in New York and throughout Europe. Played by Grotowski's leading actor and collaborator, Ryszard Cieslak, the Prince is shown to be a martyred hero, a victim of the Spanish Inquisition in the seventeenth century. Half-naked in a loin-cloth, he is placed on a slab for

29. Calderón, *The Constant Prince*, 1969. Production by Grotowski, with Ryszard Cieslak as the Prince.

torture and castration, with the spectators looking down on him as in an operating theatre or a cockpit. The production of Slowacki's *Kordian* (1962) takes place in a mental hospital, with the mentally defective 'patients' scattered among the spectators, so that everyone is treated like an inmate of the same asylum. Grotowski's images are all of violence and human suffering.

In America, the first radical expression of Artaudian theatre had been felt some years before. The Living Theatre was founded in New York in 1947 by Julian Beck (1925—   ) and his wife Judith Malina (1926—   ) when they were in their early twenties. Malina had previously studied in Piscator's Dramatic Workshop of 'The New School for Social Research' in New York, and Beck's training as an actor at Yale University had been based on Stanislavsky. For a year in 1951 they presented scenes from T. S. Eliot and Gertrude Stein in Cherry Lane, converting their verbal pieces into vastly imaginative, physically rhythmical action. Any dependence on words, however, soon diminished; *Mysteries and Smaller Pieces*, for example, involved an attack upon the audience with political clichés and physical ritualism which ended with a great heap of stiff bodies piled on the stage as an alarming image of death. From 1959, Beck and Malina worked off-Broadway on 14th Street in an attic playhouse of only 170 seats, until it was padlocked in 1963 by the federal authorities for non-payment of taxes. The Becks' scenery and costumes were sold off, and they even lost the set of *The Brig* in this way, little as it must have brought on the market. Yet in spite of such hazards, they managed to create a kinetic and poetic theatre of balletic movements and stage images caught in rich light and shadow, all intended to grant its audience an experience of great immediacy. Securing the greatest response was one of the company's important objectives, even to the point, in *Paradise Now* (1968, published in 1971), of challenging the spectator with provocative whispers into his ear and erotic gestures. Living Theatre productions were essentially Artaudian.

Two productions made the Becks' reputation in both America and Europe. *The Connection*, written by Jack Gelber (1932—   ) and directed by Malina in 1959, would have been a realistic treatment of heroin addicts waiting Godot-like for their 'connection', had it not been for the interpolations of a jazz group and the free improvisation of the junkies. Over all this is arranged a Pirandellian structure in which the characters are supposedly making a documentary film about *real* addicts, and to complete the deception, they also accost the audience in the interval. The symbolic suggestion is that we all live in a world without direction, all in need of our 'fix'. Even more sensational was *The Brig*, written by Kenneth H. Brown (1936–   ) and directed by Malina in 1963. The script of this play is simply a notation for the ritualistic punishment of US Marines during a single day in the penal Camp Fuji in Japan, where the author had himself been a prisoner. In witnessing the prisoners, indeed their guards, too, brutalized by the mechanical barking of orders, the clashing lids of garbage cans and the delivery of quick, sharp blows of the truncheon, the audience is itself assaulted by violent sounds and images. It was during this production that the Becks, following a three-day sit-in, were put in prison and had their theatre closed by their landlord, the police and the Internal Revenue Service.

In 1964 the Living Theatre exiled itself and toured Europe for four legendary years, becoming involved with left-wing movements as a 'guerrilla theatre' wherever they went – most noticeably in the Paris riots of May 1968. '*Le Living*' became synonymous with anarchist and pacificist politics. Then in 1968 they returned to America at the invitation of Yale University, and performed a series of their major productions in the style they had been evolving over the years, and for which they are now best known.

In their 1965 adaptation of Mary Shelley's *Frankenstein*, with Beck playing the Doctor, the rest of the company played the Monster. The Monster is made to symbolize the ego of modern man, and the 20-foot setting of tubular scaffolding built in three tiers changes from the laboratory in which the Monster is brought to life, to the inside of the Monster's head, where he is shown gaining knowledge of the world. This again changes to a prison which represents the world itself, in which the Monster's energy is passed to human prisoners who die in the fire which regenerates him. In act I, startlingly revealed by a slowly falling curtain, the spectators see that the Monster's limbs and torso are formed by the swaying bodies of some twenty actors clinging to the scaffolding; to this impression are added two red eyes. In act II, the spaces in the scaffolding cleverly represent the Monster's senses and other functions. The performance becomes particularly acrobatic when the actors playing inside the head are stimulated by ideas of modern civilization; these ideas are fed as words from Dr Frankenstein into the Monster's sensorium, which writhes in agonized response. So the creature is 'educated', and the stage represents a nerve-centre able to create Artaudian sensations intended to grip the spectator's imagination. In act III, when the head has become a prison, prisoners are caught in all parts of the auditorium and placed in the spaces formed by

30. The Living Theatre, *Frankenstein*, 1965. Production by Julian Beck and Judith Malina, 1968. © Fred W. McDarrah, 1980.

the scaffolding as if in cells. Needless to say, none of this would have worked if the production had not been a masterpiece of timing and coordination.

Paradise Now brought notoriety to the company everywhere they played it. The performance lasted about five hours, and was another spectacle with a minimum of plot. Its apparent purpose is to promote a non-violent revolution, and it conveys its anarchism by displaying degrees of nudity which the audience is invited to share. Stripping off clothing is intended to sharpen the spectator's perception by having him see or do what is forbidden. The action of the play consists of a series of ritual enactments of preconceived revolutionary phases, each of which is depicted on a large chart handed to members of the audience on entering the theatre. But in this play the innovative element is the physical contact required between the actors and the spectators. Throughout the play, the actors ridicule and intimidate the spectators at random, in order to make anger rid the audience of its emotions and tensions. The play ends in an erotic ritual, the creation of the now commonplace 'love pile' of bodies.

The Living Theatre began as a personal expression of the non-violence and anarchism of its founders, and their protest was demonstrated in largely naturalistic terms. Realistic images of poverty, suffering and death were enacted on the stage. But increasingly their style of performance became a visual and aural attack on the senses, until they acquired the reputation of being the foremost practitioners of Artaud's theories of cruelty. If it seems perverse that pacificists should use such violent techniques, it is fair to cite Artaud's belief that violence inside the theatre will surely subvert violence outside it:

> I defy any spectator to whom such violent scenes will have transferred their blood . . . to give himself up, once outside the theatre, to ideas of war, riot, and blatant murder (translated Margaret Reynolds).

At least it is encouraging to find anyone who today believes that art has such power.

In their incredulity, the New York critics have largely dismissed these productions, with only the *Village Voice* giving them any serious consideration. However, it is proper to ask whether these attempts at audience participation have only involved the spectator in a perfunctory way, or whether they have resulted in a truly therapeutic promotion of non-violence. In the late 1960s, an uncommon period of youthful and rebellious protest marked as much by antisocial violence as by the wearing of beards and beads, the spontaneity of Living Theatre productions had immense appeal. Nevertheless, seen against the actual bloodshed on the streets of Paris or Chicago, as well as in the tropical forests of Vietnam, guerrilla theatre must seem puny, and not too many years later also seems dated. Yet the Becks bravely persist in their search for a style and a theme, a 'meaningful dialogue', with which to reach, not the bourgeois 'liberal establishment', but those who have been repressed by society. Such a search will never end, and possibly never should.

20 *Happenings and other improvisation in America*

Dionysus in 69 (1968)

During the 1960s, a form of dramatic activity known as a 'Happening' had a vogue in several countries, particularly the USA, France and Japan. Happenings could be said to derive from the dada exhibitions of 1916—21, and the surrealist exhibitions which followed after that. Happenings have sometimes been referred to as 'neo-dada'. But the term was actually coined by accident for the title of an improvised performance in 1959 by the American painter, Allan Kaprow (1927—), and is now associated with all mixed media art. Kaprow was an action painter who tried to find ways of breaking out of the two-dimensional frame and providing a more direct and living experience for his viewers. Beginning with the collage exhibition 'Penny Arcade' in 1956, his art included complete pieces of furniture, and on occasion special rooms were needed to house it. Kaprow later joined the American avant-garde musician John Cage (1912–), who as early as 1952 had arranged a 'simultaneous' event at Black Mountain College, North Carolina, an event which has since become celebrated. In the course of performance, speech, dance, film, live and recorded music and a variety of sounds were projected from all parts of a large room, which also contained the audience. By this technique Cage created what he called an 'environment', and he has stated that 'theatre takes place all the time wherever one is, and art simply facilitates persuading us this is the case'.

Kaprow's first performance was *18 Happenings in 6 Parts*, staged in the Reuben Gallery in Greenwich Village, New York, in 1959. The walls were decorated with projected slides, coloured lights, paintings and nude photographs. Each member of the audience was given a card with instructions written on it, and at the sound of a bell everyone did as asked – lying down, dancing, lighting a match, undressing, and so on. This elementary performance contained the basic ingredients of the Happenings which followed in the next few years:

1. The audience constituted both spectators and participants.
2. Actions and events happened simultaneously, as they did in life.
3. The area of performance was virtually unlimited, with no separation of stage and auditorium.
4. The 'acting' was largely improvised.

The search got underway for a new aesthetic to account for this kind of improvisational drama. In France, Jean-Jacques Lebel, author of *Le Happening* (1966), used the form to propagate personal theories of social revolution and sexual liberation. In America, the designer Michael Kirby, author of *Happenings* (also 1966), talked of a Happening as a 'non-matrixed' performance, by which he meant that the performer ignored the traditional boundaries of time, place and characterization, and acted without trying to establish some fictional world. In *Assemblages, Environments, and Happenings* (1966 again), Kaprow made it clear that his intention was to close the gap between art and life, keeping time and space 'variable and discontinuous'. It is true that in their unpredictability Happenings brought the theatre closer to real life, but in *Lunatics, Lovers and Poets* (1974), Margaret Croyden pointed out that their performance depends so much on the commonplace and on popular culture that they tend to become mundane and repetitious. To be more generous, it could be suggested that the junk which made up a Happening was somehow symbolic of a 'junk society'. At all events, the ease with which a Happening could be set up encouraged a great number of painters, sculptors, dancers and composers to try their hand before the movement died its natural death. Now, possibly, only the questionable species 'pop art' survives, but it is significant that Happenings suggested one more impulse to bring the arts of drama, poetry, painting and music together, even if the tactics of 1916 in Zürich were not quite appropriate to 1966 in Paris and New York.

The story of the avant-garde in America is by no means concluded. The San Francisco Mime Troupe, founded by R. G. Davis in 1959, began by playing Molière and Goldoni in the style of the *commedia dell'arte*, until Davis took his productions out-of-doors as a form of street theatre. Peter Schumann brought his Bread and Puppet Theatre from Germany to New York in 1961, and was equally prepared to play anywhere. Schumann makes his performances something of a ritual by passing a loaf of bread that

31. The Bread and Puppet Theatre. An anti-war parade in Washington, 24 April 1971.

he has baked himself round those who have come to watch. But the outstanding element in his productions are the giant puppets, up to 15 feet high, created by actors standing on stilts and wearing huge masks. He works this way, he says, 'to make the world plain', and bases his plays on simple Biblical and folk-tales, with simple archetypes – or, if you will, stereotypes – for characters. The fortunes of New York's La Mama Experimental Theatre Club also began in 1961, when it was founded by Ellen Stewart and Paul Foster. La Mama specialized in rigorous, acrobatic training after the manner of Grotowski, and in providing an outlet for new play-wrights with something exciting to say.

The American group which particularly believed in working in collaboration with the writer was the Open Theatre of Joseph Chaikin (1935–). Chaikin had trained as an actor with the Stanis-lavsky System, and had served with the Living Theatre, acted in Brecht's epic theatre, assisted Brook with *US* at the Aldwych and worked with Viola Spolin. Spolin was the leading advocate of improvisational techniques and group games, author of a seminal book, *Improvisation for the Theatre* (1963), and founder of the Second City Theatre in Chicago. On the face of it, Chaikin was ready for anything. He and Peter Feldman had started the Open Theatre in a loft in 24th Street, New York, in 1963, naming it to contrast with what they considered to be the 'closed' theatre of Broadway. They continued in business for ten years, until they voluntarily disbanded for fear of becoming 'institutionalized'. It should happen more often – in all spheres of life. Chaikin has written of his work in *The Presence of an Actor* (1972), as has one of his actors, Robert Parolli, in *A Book on the Open Theatre* (1970).

Like Brecht, Chaikin thought of his theatre as a workshop where plays were always 'in progress', always growing and chang-ing. His method of acting owed something to Yoga meditation, and the group worked collaboratively through sounds and move-ments, rather than words, in order to explore 'zones of feelings' of fantasy and dream. Margaret Croyden quotes from Feldman's notes:

> Our object was to make visible onstage those levels of
> reality which usually are not expressed in situations:
> the elusive, irrational, fragile, mysterious or monstrous
> lives within our lives (p. 174).

The Open Theatre also practised 'transformation', a rare technique developed by the group by which an actor could change from one character to another in view of the audience.

In 1966, the Open Theatre assembled the show *America Hurrah*, three one-act plays by Jean-Claude van Itallie (1936—) for the Pocket Theatre on Third Avenue. It consisted of three highly

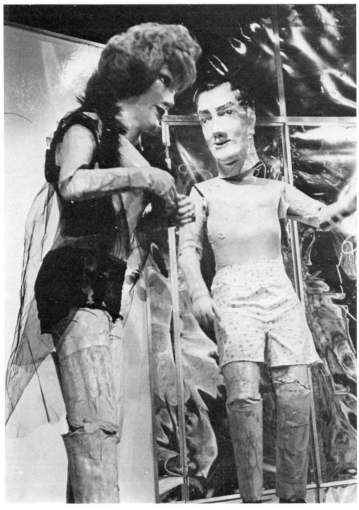

32. Jean-Claude van Itallie, *Motel*, 1966. Production by the Open Theatre, New York, 1968. © Fred W. McDarrah, 1980.

satirical images of modern American life, the most powerful being *Motel*, in which a grotesque doll describes the accommodation as two other dolls tear the room apart, a bizarre and terrifying picture of modern life and violence. *America Hurrah* was the first production to carry the work of the Open Theatre overseas, and *The Serpent* (1968) was van Itallie's first full-length play. It mixes stories of man's first disobedience and fall from the Book of Genesis with shocking contemporary images like the assassinations of President Kennedy and Martin Luther King, until the common guilt is assumed to be shaken off in an energetic chant and dance by the whole cast. Susan Yankowitz (1941–) contributed the words of *Terminal* (1969), a disturbing play about mortality. The living awaken the dead by a ritualistic chanting and the clacking of sticks painted white to resemble bones, and then the dead re-enact the manner of their former deaths. If there is a point here, it is that we must learn to face the reality of our end.

Unusually, the Open Theatre refused to allow itself to become a political vehicle, but promoted the statements of its individual playwrights. This policy resulted in its breaking up into several workshops, and perhaps was the cause of its final demise. Meanwhile, the Open Theatre was responsible for *Viet Rock*, a group improvisation by Megan Terry (1932–) performed at Café La Mama in 1966, one of the few stage treatments of the Vietnam War; others are Peter Brook's *US*, Armand Gatti's *V comme Vietnam (V for Vietnam)* and Victor Haïm's *L'Arme blanche (Side-arm)*. In 1973, *Nightwalk*, a play built like the levels of sleep, was actually the collaborative effort of three of its young playwrights, Terry, van Itallie and Sam Shepard (1943–). The American theatre has need of more companies prepared to nurture the new playwright.

Only slightly less productive has been the Performance Group, started in New York in 1967 by Richard Schechner, a former editor of the avant-garde quarterly, the *Tulane Drama Review* (now the *Drama Review*). Influenced by Grotowski, whom Schechner had met in 1966, by the Becks and by the environmentalists and their Happenings, the Performance Group set up an environmental theatre in a garage in Wooster Street, with Michael Kirby and Jerry Rojo as designers. It was here in 1968 that the group attracted national attention with *Dionysus in 69*, loosely based on the *Bacchae* of Euripides. The intention was to make Euripides's play pertinent to the 1960s by means of an extended experiment in audience participation, but since the performance placed excessive emphasis on a sexual interpretation of the original, the production became an outrageous exercise in self-consciousness. It was also, unfortunately, subject to frequent police action.

The 'environment' of the Wooster Street garage was carefully arranged with the intention of breaking down the space between the actor and his audience. Margaret Mead's thesis that modern civilization has disastrously separated art and the artist from the passive consumer was to be put to the test. Members of the audience were allowed to enter slowly, by small groups – a procedure lasting as long as an hour. While the audience waited, actors moved among it, on occasion picking up a spectator gently and carrying him or her to another place in the room. Sitting or standing anywhere it wished on a structure of scaffolding and platforms, the audience for *Dionysus in 69* was assumed to be part of the setting, involved physically as well as emotionally. The play itself

33. The Performance Group, *Dionysus in 69*, New York. Production by Richard Schechner. The birth ritual.

was deemed to be a ritual event, just as a church service or a game of football might be. With an almost naked Dionysus, the revels of the Bacchantes required people to take off their clothes and mimic sexual behaviour.

In the circumstances, it was hard for the audience to concentrate on the lines. Instead of using words from the play, the actors spoke for themselves in a free colloquial manner and at their own intellectual level, which by chance was not very high. Having heard the actors discuss their 'frustrations', Robert Brustein complained in his review,

> I hope these analyses prove therapeutic for the actors;
> I can testify that they do nothing for the observer, except
> to convince him that it's more fun to be on stage than in
> the audience.

Brustein went on to say that the actors revealed lives of considerably less significance than one has the right to demand in the theatre, and that it was a banal descent from ancient Greece to twentieth-century New York. As for those members of the audience who chose to participate in the ritual by joining in the unaccustomed sexual byplay, it is legitimate to wonder what kind of ritual it is if it has no genuine foundation in what people customarily do. However, one should also remember Jean-Louis Barrault's story about Georges Pitoëff — when the realist Antoine asked the symbolist Pitoëff where he had ever seen a room without a ceiling, the reply came pat: 'In the theatre, monsieur'.

21 *Recent fringe theatre in Britain*

Christie in Love (1969), *AC/DC* (1969)

From the sea and slime of the subculture of strikes and lockouts and *Monty Python*, tower blocks and vandalism and saccharine on the box, galloping inflation and Irish-American bombs, motorways and discos and racial rumblings, promiscuity and anal humour and a smug class-consciousness that is a wonder of the world, emerged the British fringe with an enormous sense of humour. It may be considered a kindness to include it in a book on symbolist manifestations of drama, but a free use of symbolic character and situation best describes the new direction.

The new American companies sprang up partly as a protest against the commercial theatre. In Britain in the late 1960s and 1970s, a wealth of similarly avant-garde, iconoclastic dramatic activity marked a new age of do-it-yourself drama. A dozen young playwrights ransacked the 'imaginary museum' of past styles and techniques of stage presentation, and added touches of their own culled from the circus and the comic strip. They mixed realism and symbolism in a happy disregard for academic proprieties and artistic restraint. Their companies received modest grants from the Arts Council of Great Britain, the government agency for disbursing public money to the arts, but were still compelled to cut costs and perform in every imaginable physical situation, from fields and pubs to city streets and, like Piscator, union halls. Audiences ranged, therefore, from young intellectuals to working people who had never been to a theatre in their lives. The subjects of the plays were always, at bottom, satirical. Peter Ansorge's book *Disrupting the Spectacle* (1975) has usefully traced some of the new British offerings.

The year of world-wide student rebellion, 1968, was the likely watershed in recent British theatrical history. It was in that year that an American director, Jim Haynes, started a short-lived 'Arts Lab' in Drury Lane, close to the centre of London's West End, but hardly a challenge to its prosperous theatres. Before the workshop closed in 1969, a surprising number of new writers and artists had begun to take underground groups round the country in a new kind of itinerant theatre. Using a minimum of scenery and props, 'Portable Theatre' was actually the name of one such company adopted by its founders David Hare and Tony Bicât. From 1968 to 1972, this group spawned others, until there were three companies of much the same kind performing at the Edinburgh Festival in 1971. As many as twenty groups came together at the Royal Court Theatre in 1969 for the unprecedented fringe festival they called 'Come Together'. By the time of the Edinburgh Festival of 1978, as many as fifty were at work there at the same time. An altogether remarkable phenomenon.

All the Portable plays were fiercely critical of society. Howard Brenton (1942–   ), Portable's leading writer, chose to depict criminals and murderers in such plays as *Christie in Love* (1969) and *Hitler Dances* (1972), as if to symbolize the rotten elements in a country of rapidly changing values. Brenton developed a personal, 'cabaret' style of clipped and fast-moving dialogue sprinkled with songs and wisecracks, as if the style itself epitomised the mood and mentality of the new society. *Christie in Love*, directed by David Hare first at the Ovalhouse and then at the Theatre Upstairs of the Royal Court, was based on the actual murders of John Reginald Halliday Christie in the 1950s. A pair of police officers behave like comic cut-out characters as they dig up Christie's victims from his garden. The garden is a set composed surrealistically of old news-

34. Howard Brenton, *Christie in Love*, 1969. Production by David Hare at the Royal Court Theatre Upstairs, 1979. William Hoyland as Christie. Throttling the doll-woman.

papers, and Brenton wrote a note which explains the originality of his approach to a sleazy subject:

> The 'Garden' is a pen, ten feet by six feet. Its sides are two
> and a half feet high, and made of chicken wire. It's brim
> full of torn and screwed up pages of a popular newspaper.
> The spectators sit all around, and very close — there's
> barely enough room for the actors to walk round the sides.
> The pen is a filthy sight. The chicken wire is rusty, the
> wood is stained, the paper is full of dust. It's used as
> Christie's garden, his front room, a room in a police station,
> an executioner's shed, a lime pit. But it's not a 'Setting'
> in a conventional sense. I don't want it to be *like* a garden,
> or a room. It's a theatrical machine, a thing you'd only see
> in a show. It's a trap, a flypaper for the attention of the
> spectators to stick on.

The comic policemen build up an impression that Christie is a monster. The production note suggests that he make his entrance like Dracula, rising from the grave luridly in a frightening mask: 'It looks as if a juicy evening's underway, all laughs, nice shivers, easy oohs and aahs.' However, when the real Christie emerges from behind the mask and 'the lights are slammed on', he is represented as a mild little man — as he might have been in real life, perfectly respectable: 'a feeble, ordinary man blinking through his pebble glasses'. He is a natural figure in contrast with the artificial buffoons who bring him to trial, and the change in the Christie image is the first of a series of incongruities, which Brenton describes as

> a kind of dislocation, tearing one style up for another, so
> the proceedings lurch and all interpretations are blocked,
> and the spectator hunting for an easy meaning wearies,
> and is left only with Christie and his act of love.

These dislocations are not achieved by the racy dialogue — and like many of the fringe playwrights Brenton takes liberties with slang and obscenities of speech unthinkable a few years before — so much as by pacing. The scenes are to be played slowly, so that sudden flashes of human behaviour are seen, 'as if a cardboard black-and-white cut-out suddenly reaches out a fully fleshed, real hand'. Brenton describes this technique as one of bathos — 'it is very cruel' — presumably because in Pirandellian fashion the reality is glimpsed through the pastiche.

The characters are not identified in the usual way in the text. Brenton writes of 'the Constable actor' and 'the Inspector actor', as if the players do not fully embody their parts, but merely represent them. So as the Constable 'digs' in the garden for bodies, he stops from time to time and addresses the audience with a bawdy limerick. He does this, not like some concerned chorus figure, but without a smile and in a flat voice. His is a puppet part which comments on the action by means of the contrast between the horror of what is going on and the irreverence of what is being said, even if murder and sex are related in the Christie case. The police are Brechtian presenters, challenging the audience by direct address:

> INSPECTOR. Ladies and Gents, John Reginald Christie did six women in.
> CONSTABLE. The manner in which they were done was not nice.
> INSPECTOR. So if anyone feels sick, go ahead. Throw up. We won't mind.
> CONSTABLE. If you want to spew, spew.

This is juxtaposed with a monologue on tape in which Christie discusses his hatred of women and his lust while the Christie actor simulates masturbation with a length of rubber tubing.

The murdered women are represented by a doll who is a little larger than life-size. But the doll's lines are spoken by the Constable in a falsetto voice as he moves her arms and legs from behind — an effect of distancing that makes the sexuality of the play's theme all the more grotesque. Christie finally makes use of this doll to demonstrate how he committed murder, a moment of ritual reminiscent of Genêt's *The Blacks*. After this, the climax of the play, the policemen hang Christie in his garden of newspaper, and tidy up the stage as if the world is temporarily returning to normal and the theatre to reality.

> INSPECTOR. That's that then.
> CONSTABLE. Yes Sir.

INSPECTOR. Another crime solved.
CONSTABLE. A blow struck for married life.

This could be any atrocity in the world, watched for sixty minutes by 'guilty creatures sitting at a play'. Evil is frighteningly common-place in Brenton's drama, and he does not hesitate to make his point by theatrical tricks: policemen as clowns in *Christie*, and the killer Hepple and the policeman, 'MacLeish of the Yard', actually doubled by the same actor in *Revenge* (1969), ensure that the audience cannot make a simple judgment about who the criminal is.

Brenton has increased his skills in presenting alarming images of contemporary social and political life, so juxtaposed as to prompt sharp critical reactions. *Weapons of Happiness*, for example, directed by David Hare at the National Theatre in 1976, carefully selected two ugly pictures of our time: one of irresponsible youth, callous about the elderly, mouthing easy left-wing slogans, dis-rupting the work of a small London factory; the other of an older man, a former Czech communist leader who had been tortured and brainwashed before escaping to the apparently placid shores of Britain. In Brenton's curious manner of symbolist poetry, a girl describes her idea of bliss:

> I want to be in the warm. I want to be under a hair drier,
> a bit too warm, you know? Trickle a sweat between the
> shoulder blades. And everything fuggy and safe (act II, scene 5).

This is set against the words of the older man, as he remembers the kind of treatment by freezing that he had suffered in the past:

> Look they put me in a cellar. There were icicles on the
> bricks. I had to walk in mud. I suffered frostbite. They
> were trying to make a new human being (act II, scene 4).

By its sequence of short scenes, this play indicates directly and vividly the immense differences of mood and attitude that have characterized our uncertain age.

Brenton followed Christopher Hampton, David Hare and E. A. Whitehead as 'resident dramatist' in William Gaskill's English Stage Company at the Royal Court Theatre, a position which has

come to represent a sort of accolade for playwriting. David Hare
(1948–) is possibly the most inventive dramatist of the new set.
He began his theatre work as a director for Portable Theatre,
but soon found himself writing material for the company to act.
How Brophy Made Good (1969) was a satire on television and the
mass media. *The Great Exhibition*, first presented at the Hampstead
Theatre Club in 1972, ingeniously satirized class differences by
inventing a Labour Member of Parliament whose work in the
political arena had been as much an exhibition as his sexual per-
version on Clapham Common. Then in 1973 Brenton and Hare
collaborated in writing the wittily vitriolic satire *Brassneck* for the
Nottingham Playhouse. In the midlands vernacular, the title means
'criminal nerve', 'political impudence', and the play creates the
fictitious but plausible town of 'Stanton' in the industrial midlands
in order to set up a picture of corruption. One Alfred Bagley is the
first of three wretched generations of Bagleys who trace the progress of capitalist self-interest over a period of thirty years in post-
war Britain. There is one overwhelming scene written to attack
freemasonry, whose rituals translate into first-rate absurdist theatre,
with Bagley like a Renaissance Borgia pope sitting on his throne as
master of his lodge, with Paul Dawkins as Bagley the image of
confident corruption. The scenes of the play are essentially non-
realistic, and its characteristic mode could be described as impres-
sionistic-symbolist – but there comes a point when the jargon of
dramatic theory can no longer contain so liberal a use of a metaphorical stage.

Michael Blakemore directed Hare's *Knuckle* at the Comedy in
1974, a play of London nightlife which was praised for having the
'pop format' of the 'hard-edged Mickey Spillane thriller'. Yet this
too was a satirical metaphor of modern life, as was *Teeth 'n' Smiles*,
directed by the author at the Royal Court in 1975, a play creating
the squalid world of a contemporary rock group. Hare has proved
himself adept at recapturing evocative periods and atmospheres
which are themselves symbolic of aspects of human behaviour. In
1978 he turned to themes of contemporary history: *Licking Hitler*
exhibits the dirty propaganda machinery of British Intelligence
during the Second World War, and *Plenty*, directed by the author
at the National Theatre with Kate Nelligan, contrasts the values of

working for the French Resistance with the corruption of post-war Britain. Episodic sequences of brief incidents contrast past with present in the manner of a flashback in the cinema, and place English society in a vividly critical perspective.

From the many new playwrights of the fringe, it would be right to select Snoo Wilson (1948–). Like others of his generation, he was attracted to Ionesco's early style of absurdist theatre, but Wilson was never an absurdist who doubted that life had a purpose. He was strongly committed to shocking his audiences with distasteful images of the Britain he knew. The one-act *Pignight* (1970) made use of 'pigmasks' and was made even more sinister by having the women played by men. *Vampire* (1972) was a longer play in which each of three acts represents a different example of psychological vampirism – sexual repression, excessive patriotism, racial prejudice. Wilson's acrobatic imagination developed irrepressibly with the three-act play, *The Pleasure Principle*, a preposterous treatment of modern sexual frustrations directed by David Hare at the Royal Court Theatre Upstairs in 1973. At the centre of this play is an act of adultery committed by a married man and a girl who dreams she is Leda to his swan. It takes place in a circus tent to the flashing of coloured lights, the whole place looking like 'a junkyard of the mind'. The comment is, 'What a rotten world for the baby Jesus to come into.' This play sports a pair of gorillas for a chorus, and it was characteristic that Wilson should have wheeled a replica of Leda's swan on stage for the big scene and given the audience funny noses to wear as they went home. Portable Theatre dramatists treat the theatre with a delightful irreverence as a glorious games-room, serving their symbolism to their audiences with a flourish.

During this period, American avant-garde theatre was filtering into London, and it is open to debate how far this prompted or guided the British. It was an American who started the Arts Lab, and from it sprang the British Portable Theatre, Freehold, Pip Simmons and the People Show. America brought to London the Open Theatre's *America Hurrah* and La Mama's *Tom Paine* in 1967, and the British writers and actors gratefully grasped the new underground styles they saw. Nancy Meckler, who founded Freehold, was American herself and owed a direct debt to the Open Theatre, as Pip Simmons did to Café La Mama.

Meckler adopted the gymnastic, balletic theatre she knew, using the actor's physical skills rather than words to express her ideas. In 1969 she tackled *Antigone* in a version by Peter Hulton, and her mode of free expression made good use of the chorus where modern productions usually find it an embarrassment. Antigone's dead brother remained a presence on the stage symbolizing death, and her protest against Creon's policies seemed a cry for peace to the American presidency. Peter Ansorge reported that at the end of the play the audience was ritualistically invited to scatter sawdust on the dead body, and this gesture, which might well have seemed strained, implied an authentic concurrence with the message of the play by those who witnessed it. Pip Simmons's volatile style of theatre lasted until 1973, and his group turned to American popular culture for general analogies to convey a world-wide insanity. Just as Chicago's gangsters had attracted Brecht as a pattern for his *Arturo Ui*, so the bloody encounters between protesters and police outside the Democratic Convention in Chicago in 1968 supplied Simmons with lively images for *Do It!* (1971), a dramatization of Jerry Rubin's book. *Superman* (1969), treating the Civil Rights movement in America, adopted a brilliant 'comic strip' mode of theatre, a joyous 'cartoon' style of cliché action, paper-thin characters and 'bubble' dialogue. This was a stylization in good fun and high spirits, with rock music lightly binding together the episodes in the play.

Pirandellian theatre games, in which the stage consciously acknowledges its conventional activity as symbolic of the world outside, and in which it suggests that the business of acting is not unlike the role-playing of real life, date back at least to Shakespeare's comedies. The Welfare State, a group formed in Leeds by John Fox in 1968, well exemplified this characteristic with *The Travels of Lancelot Quail* (1972). The actors toured the country with a tent show in which they mixed local history and legend with contemporary events in a constantly changing performance. Ansorge described this play as 'a 24-hour-a-day theatrical event, aimed at converting an entire landscape into an area of fantasy, a background for role-playing and actor-audience confrontations'. Max Stafford-Clark, director of Edinburgh's Traverse Theatre after 1966, encouraged abnormally collaborative plays: *Dracula* (1968) came into existence during rehearsal, with no fewer than eight writers working with the actors. *Lay By* (1971) was actually conceived at a meeting of directors at the Royal Court, when a casually selected news clipping about a sexual assault on a motorway provided the subject for seven writers to work on simultaneously.

All British fringe theatre has been more or less politically radical, and often adopted a music-hall style of performance to suggest a more ubiquitous target. The leading political group of the 1970s was a company calling itself the 7:84. It was formed in 1971 by John McGrath (1935–), and celebrated in its name the fact that in Britain 7 per cent of the people own 84 per cent of the wealth. Its productions were usually arranged for performance in the most informal way in pubs, so that playgoing was kept at a casual level. Nevertheless, one 7:84 playwright, the Marxist Trevor Griffiths (1935–), was recognized by having one play, *Occupations* (1970), produced by the Royal Shakespeare Company in 1971, and another, *The Party*, by John Dexter for the National Theatre in 1973. The latter is a debate play about socialism whose dialectical method of expecting the audience to weigh one value against another is agreeably sophisticated, but it did, however, betray a verbosity which did not sit well with the critics. *Comedians* (1975) appears to be a play about how to be a comedian by going to an improbable night class in Manchester, but its oblique method of presenting the sources of human response ('thinking of something deep, personal, serious ... then being funny about it') constituted a great advance on anything Griffiths had done before.

The British fringe is no doubt as evanescent as its makeshift stages, its uncertain finances and the fashionable banners it waves. Its concern has been to make an immediate appeal to the audience it finds. But in all this changeable activity, the rebel playwright will become part of the established order by a process of theatrical osmosis, and we look for something of permanence to shoot up. Has this happened in the case of a theatrical *tour de force, AC/DC,* by Heathcote Williams (1941–), directed by Nicholas Wright at the Royal Court Theatre Upstairs in 1969 and then in New York in 1971? This play takes five young people as representative of modern society, and reveals their attitudes in a flood tide of parodistic technical terms from the modern world and the media. This is mixed with the psychological cant of the drug set, with its own demonic delusions and demands. It is as if people were themselves electronic gadgets, subject to voltages and power failures. In the second part of the play ('Direct Current'), a bank of video-screens provides 'a surge of news bulletins' and a wall of photographs 'starts humming', until a character cries,

> They're altering my neural rhythms. They're pulling them
> into synch with their neural rhythms. They're coding all
> my cells. What are you doing about it? The whole atmos-
> phere needs cloning. What are you doing about it???

To say the least, it is hard to remain indifferent to this kind of speech, and indeed, one of the few reviewers, John Peter of *The Sunday Times*, found the play 'an electronic nightmare' in the worst sense; the play offered 'a monstrous vision of a monstrous world where passions rage but meaning is lost', and he added that although the production had a bleak air of sincerity about it, its method defeated itself by sheer blinding boredom. Yet the point of *AC/DC*, that individuality is being eliminated and that people are being turned into stereotypes, is fully dramatized, and the play's style, subjecting the audience to a ferocious barrage of fire, is irreplaceable for its content and theme.

The fact is that at bottom *AC/DC* is infuriatingly Artaudian, in some ways the extreme expression in the vein of symbolism we have so far seen in this story. As representative of the British underground theatre, it is typically undisciplined, idiosyncratic and aggressive. Some may see it as a symptom of the disintegration of the western theatrical aesthetic. In the long term, however, the full-blooded existence of so vigorous a fringe, attracting audiences where none existed before, will surely be seen as a sign that the live theatrical medium continues, as always, to be self-renewing.

22 *Symbolist theatre: retrospectively*

The American avant-garde and the British fringe — and comparable activities in other western countries might have been added — amply demonstrate the persistence and the freedom with which the symbolist mode of theatre has flourished in the twentieth century. Commanding no particular school or philosophy of drama, it has ranged and thrived virtually without restriction according to the needs of the time and the place. There has seemed to be no limit to the possibilities of symbolism on the stage as its purposes have increased, and our notion of what constitutes a symbolic stage has smoothly adjusted to fantasy, surrealism, cruelty or the absurd, so that the advances were made by artists as different in quality and achievement as Jarry and Craig, Yeats and Artaud. The only cry common to them all was against what they perceived as the commercial theatre of bourgeois realism. It is interesting that the history of symbolist theatre has recorded just as many riots as that of the realistic theatre: a *Ghosts* can be matched by an *Ubu*, a *Playboy of the Western World* by a *Six Characters in Search of an Author*.

The recurring need was for the theatre to regain its artistic licence, to create outrageous images whether of tragedy or farce, to penetrate to a truth and a reality by means of an essentially metaphorical use of the stage. In an interview with Kenneth Tynan for the London *Observer* on 25 June 1961, Jean-Paul Sartre made the point for all poetically inclined dramatists:

> At bottom, I am always looking for myths; in other words, for subjects so sublimated that they are recognizable to everyone, without recourse to minute psychological details. . . . The theatre is not concerned with reality; it is only concerned with truth.

We can see that while in this century Wagner's seminal thinking has ruggedly supported one theatrical experiment after another in the use of the arts, and both the surrealists and the environmentalists continue to attempt various forms of Wagnerian *Gesamtkunstwerk* and bring the arts together, the great originators in the symbolist vein — Pirandello, Artaud, Beckett, Genêt — are very few, and of these there are only one or two to whom the stage repeatedly returns for a basic design.

While we may think of the extravagant symbols of a Cocteau or an Ionesco, a *Bernarda Alba* or a *Marat/Sade*, as characteristic of our own irrepressible age, it is fair to remember that in the past the stage has created even more preposterous images. What more unthinkable than an Oedipus who must kill his father and marry his mother to enlighten his audience? What more outrageous than the demented worship of the Bacchantes, than a Faustus who sells his soul to the devil, than a black general who must murder the white wife he adores, than a Jew who can threaten to cut a pound of flesh from a Christian? The symbolist and ritual theatre is strong in our heritage, and doubtless it would be with us even without the exertions of an Artaud or a Peter Brook. Moreover, the loosely symbolist play that leaves its philosophical tails flapping may survive longer than the play which makes a preaching convenience of theatrical symbolism.

Table of events in the theatre

1 Realism and naturalism
2 **Symbolism, surrealism and the absurd**
3 Expressionism and epic theatre

[The entries in **bold type** are the subject of this volume]

Legend: w = written, p = produced, f = formed, d = died

World events	Writers, artists and events in the theatre	Plays and productions
1851		
Louis Napoleon president of France	**'Opera and Drama' w Wagner**	
Great Exhibition, London	Ibsen directing in Bergen and Christiana (to 1862)	
	limelight in use	
1859		
'Origin of Species' w Darwin		
1861		
Italy unified		
American Civil War (to 1865)		
1865		
Lincoln assassinated		**'Tristan und Isolde' w Wagner**
		'Society' w Robertson
1866		
	Saxe-Meiningen company f Georg II	
		'Brand' p Ibsen
1867		
Dominion of Canada		'Peer Gynt' p Ibsen
'Das Kapital' w Marx		'Caste' w Robertson
Baudelaire d		
1870		
Franco-Prussian War (to 1871)	Dumas père d	
Dickens d		

World events	Writers, artists and events in the theatre	Plays and productions
1871 Germany unified	**'Purpose of the Opera' w Wagner**	
1872	**'The Birth of Tragedy' w Nietzsche**	
1873		'Thérèse Raquin' p Zola
1874	Saxe-Meiningen company on tour	
1876 telephone invented	**Bayreuth theatre built**	**'The Ring cycle' p Wagner**
1877 gramophone invented		'Pillars of Society' w Ibsen
1879		'A Doll's House' w Ibsen Büchner's 'Woyzeck' published
1880 George Eliot, Flaubert d	'Naturalism in the Theatre' w Zola electric light in the theatre	'Pillars of Society' ['Quicksand'] in London
1881 Dostoevsky d		'Ghosts' w Ibsen
1883	Deutsches Theater, Berlin f **Wagner d**	'Ghosts' p Stockholm 'The Wild Duck' w Ibsen
1887	Théâtre-Libre, Paris f Antoine	'The Father' w Strindberg
1888	Dagmar Theatre, Copenhagen f Strindberg	'Power of Darkness' w Tolstoy 'Miss Julie' w Strindberg
1889 Browning d	Freie Bühne, Berlin f Brahm	'A Doll's House' p London and New York

World events	Writers, artists and events in the theatre	Plays and productions
1890		
Van Gogh d	Freie Volksbühne, Berlin f Wille	'Ghosts' p Paris
		'Hedda Gabler' w Ibsen
	Boucicault d	**'The Intruder', 'The Blind' w Maeterlinck**
1891		
Melville, Rimbaud d	Independent Theatre Company, London f Grein	'Ghosts' p London
		'Spring's Awakening' w Wedekind
	'Quintessence of Ibsenism' w Shaw	
1892		
Tennyson d		'The Weavers' w Hauptmann
		'Widowers' Houses' w Shaw
		'Countess Cathleen' w Yeats
1893		
Maupassant, Tchaikowsky d	**Théâtre de l'Oeuvre f Lugné-Poe**	'Mrs Warren's Profession' w Shaw
		'Pelléas et Mélisandé w Maeterlinck
1894		
	Brahm at Deutsches Theater	'Arms and the Man' w Shaw
		'Land of Heart's Desire' w Yeats
1895		
first films made	**'La Mise-en-scène du drame Wagnérian' w Appia**	'A Doll's House' in America
		'Earth Spirit' w Wedekind
1896		
Verlaine d	**'The Treasure of the Humble' w Maeterlinck**	**'Salomé' p Lugné-Poe**
		'Ubu roi' p Jarry
		'The Seagull' in St Petersburg

World events	Writers, artists and events in the theatre	Plays and productions
1897		
Brahms d	Moscow Art Theatre f Stanislavsky and Danchenko	
1898		
Mallarmé d		'The Seagull' p MAT
		'To Damascus' w Strindberg
1899		
Boer War (to 1902)	**'Die Musik und die Inszenierung' w Appia**	**'When We Dead Awaken' w Ibsen**
	Irish Literary Theatre f Yeats and Lady Gregory	'Uncle Vanya' w Chekhov
1900		
Nietzsche d	**Wilde d**	**'To Damascus' p Stockholm**
1901		
Commonwealth of Australia		**'Easter' w Strindberg**
Queen Victoria d		'Three Sisters' w Chekhov
Freud's 'Interpretation of Dreams'		
1902		
	Kleines Theater, Berlin f Reinhardt	**'A Dream Play' w Strindberg**
	Zola d	'The Lower Depths' w Gorky
		'Danton's Death' p Berlin
1903		
Wright brothers' flight		'Shadow of the Glen' w Synge
1904		
Entente Cordiale	**Abbey Theatre, Dublin f**	'The Cherry Orchard' w Chekhov
Russo-Japanese War (to 1905)	English Stage Society at Court Theatre (Vedrenne and Barker)	'Riders to the Sea' w Synge
	Chekhov d	**'On Baile's Strand' w Yeats**
1905		
	'The Art of the Theatre' w Craig	'Mrs Warren's Profession' p New York

World events	Writers, artists and events in the theatre	Plays and productions
	Reinhardt at Deutsches Theater	'Man and Superman' w Shaw
	Meyerhold at MAT Studio	Reinhardt's 'Midsummer Night's Dream', Berlin
1906		
Cézanne d	**Appia meets Dalcroze**	'Partage de midi' w Claudel
	Meyerhold in St Petersburg	
	Reinhardt f Kammer-spielhaus	'Spring's Awakening' p Reinhardt
	Ibsen d	**'Hedda Gabler' p Meyerhold**
1907		
Dominion of New Zealand	Intima Teatern, Stockholm f Strindberg	'Ghost Sonata' w Strindberg
	Jarry d	'Playboy of the Western World' w Synge
		'The Life of Man' w Andreyev
		'Murderer, the Hope of Women' w Kokoschka
1908		
	'L'umorismo' w Pirandello	**'The Blue Bird' w Maeterlinck**
1909		
Ballets Russes in Paris	**'The Mask' ed. Craig (to 1929)**	
	Synge d	
1910		
Union of South Africa	**'The Tragic Theatre' w Yeats**	'Oedipus Rex' p Reinhardt
King Edward VII d	Tolstoy d	'Dom Juan' p Meyerhold
1911		
first Post-Impressionist exhibition		'The Miracle' p Reinhardt
		Synge's 'Playboy' p New York
1912		
second Post-Impressionist exhibition	Debussy's 'L'Après-midi d'un faune' p Nijinsky	**'Hamlet' p Craig in Moscow**

World events	Writers, artists and events in the theatre	Plays and productions
Titanic disaster	Brahm d Strindberg d	**Shakespeare p** **Barker at the** **Savoy** 'Theatre of the Soul' w Evreinov 'The Beggar' w Sorge
1913 **Freud's 'Interpretation** **of Dreams' trans. into** **English** 'Sons and Lovers' w Law- rence	**Vieux Colombier** **f Copeau** Stravinsky's 'Le Sacre du printemps' p Nijinsky	**'The Mask and the** **Face' w Chiarelli** 'Danton's Death' and 'Woyzeck' p Munich 'Burghers of Calais' w Kaiser
1914 First World War (to 1918)	Kamerny Theatre, Moscow f Taïrov MAT Third Studio f Vakhtangov	**Barker's 'Midsummer** **Night's Dream'** **at the Savoy**
1915 Lusitania torpedoed	Provincetown Players, Washington Square Players f New York	'Patricide' w Bronnen
1916 Easter Rebellion, Dublin Henry James d	**Dada exhibition,** **Zürich** 'Theatre Arts' published New York	'Heartbreak House' w Shaw **'At the Hawk's Well'** **w Yeats** **'Right You Are'** **w Pirandello** 'From Morn to Midnight' w Kaiser
1917 America enters the War Russian Revolution **Jung's 'Psychology of** **the Unconscious'** **trans. into English** *1918* Armistice signed Debussy d	**Copeau in New York** **(to 1919)** Reinhardt's 'Das junge Deutschland' Wedekind d	**'The Breasts of** **Tiresias' w** **Apollinaire** **'Parade' w Cocteau** Kaiser's 'Gas' trilogy O'Neill's one-act plays of the sea 'Baal' w Brecht

World events	Writers, artists and events in the theatre	Plays and productions
1919		
'Cabinet of Dr Caligari' (film) made	Reinhardt f Grosses Schauspielhaus, Berlin	'The Transformation' w Toller
Renoir d	Theatre Guild, New York f	
	The Bauhaus, Weimar f Gropius	
1920		
League of Nations f	State Theatre, Moscow f Meyerhold	'The Dybbuk' p Vakhtangov
	Salzburg Festival f Reinhardt and Hofmannsthal	'The Emperor Jones' w O'Neill
	Théâtre National Populaire f	'Beggar's Opera' at the Lyric, Hammersmith
1921		
Irish Free State f	**Atelier f Dullin (to 1938)**	**'The Wedding on the Eiffel Tower' w Cocteau**
	Macgowan's 'Theatre of Tomorrow'	**'Six Characters in Search of an Author' w Pirandello**
		'R.U.R.' w Karel Čapek
		'Masses and Man' w Toller
1922		
Mussolini in power in Italy	MAT visits Paris and Berlin	**'Henry IV' w Pirandello**
Irish Civil War	American Laboratory Theatre f	'The Hairy Ape' w O'Neill
radio broadcasting begins	'Continental Stagecraft' w Macgowan and Jones	'The Magnanimous Cuckold' p Meyerhold
'Ulysses' w Joyce	Vakhtangov d	
'The Waste Land' w Eliot		'Turandot' p Vakhtangov
1923		
	Schlemmer's Bauhaus Theatre (to 1929)	Triadic Ballet p Schlemmer
	MAT visits New York	'The Adding Machine' w Rice
	Bernhardt d	**'Knock' p Jouvet**

World events	Writers, artists and events in the theatre	Plays and productions
1924		
Stalin in Power in Russia	'My Life in Art' w Stanis-	'Juno and the Paycock'
'The Magic Mountain' w	lavsky	w O'Casey
Mann	**Copeau's school in**	**'The Infernal**
Puccini d	**Burgundy**	**Machine' w Cocteau**
	first surrealist manifesto	'Desire under the Elms'
	Provincetown experimental	w O'Neill
	season, New York	Piscator's 'Rowdy Red
	Piscator at the Volksbühne	Revue'
1925		
	Pirandello f Teatro	Berg's opera 'Wozzeck'
	d'Arte, Rome	'Hamlet' in modern
		dress
1926		
British General Strike	**Théâtre Alfred Jarry f**	'Plough and the Stars'
'Metropolis' (film) made	**Artaud and Vitrac**	w O'Casey
		'Great God Brown' w
		O'Neill
		'A Man's a Man'
		w Brecht
		'Inspector General'
		p Meyerhold
1927		
Pavlov's 'Conditioned	Gropius designed Total-	**'The Spurt of Blood'**
Reflexes' trans. into	Theater	**w Artaud**
English	Isadora Duncan d	'Hurrah, We Live!'
		w Toller, p Piscator
1928		
Thomas Hardy d	O'Casey leaves Ireland	'Threepenny Opera'
	Appia d	w Brecht
		'The Silver Tassie'
		w O'Casey
		'The Good Soldier
		Schweik'
		p Piscator
1929		
Wall Street crash: world	Group Theatre, New York f	'Street Scene' w Rice
economic depression	**Religious Drama Society**	**'Amphitryon 38'**
first 'talkie'	**f**	**w Giraudoux**
	'The Political Theatre'	'The Bedbug' w
	w Piscator	Mayakovsky
	Diaghilev d	

World events	Writers, artists and events in the theatre	Plays and productions
1930		
D. H. Lawrence d	**Baty at Théâtre Montparnasse**	'Rise and Fall of the City of Mahagonny' w Brecht 'The Bathhouse' w Mayakovsky
1931	**Lorca's La Barraca f Madrid** **Saint-Denis f La Compagnie des Quinze (to 1935)** Piscator's Drama Workshop f New York	'Noah' w Obey **'Atlas-Hôtel' w Salacrou** 'Mourning Becomes Electra' w O'Neill
1932	**first manifesto of the Theatre of Cruelty** Okhlopkov at the Realistic Theatre, Moscow	
1933 Hitler in power in Germany Roosevelt president in America (to 1945)	**second manifesto of the Theatre of Cruelty**	**'Blood Wedding' w Lorca** 'Within the Gates' w O'Casey
1934	**Jouvet at Théâtre Athenée** **Pitoëff at the Théâtre aux Mathurins**	'The Children's Hour' w Hellman **'Yerma' w Lorca**
1935 Federal Theatre Project in America (to 1939)	**Theatre of Cruelty f Artaud**	'Waiting for Lefty' w w Odets **'The Trojan War Will Not Take Place' w Giraudoux** **'Murder in the Cathedral' w Eliot**
1936 Spanish Civil War first public television	Stanislavsky's 'An Actor Prepares' trans. into English	**'The House of Bernarda Alba' w Lorca**

World events	Writers, artists and events in the theatre	Plays and productions
	Pirandello, Lorca d	**'School for Wives' p Jouvet**
1937		
		'Golden Boy' w Odets
		'Electra' w Giraudoux
1938		
Germany annexes Austria	**Artaud's 'Theatre and**	**'Les Parents ter-**
Munich agreement	**Its Double'**	**ribles' w Cocteau**
	Brecht's 'Street Scene'	'Our Town' w Wilder
	Stanislavsky d	
1939		
Second World War	**Yeats,** Toller, **Pitoëff d**	'The Little Foxes'
(to 1945)		w Hellman
		'Galileo', 'Mother
		Couragé w Brecht
1940		
Paris occupied, Battle of	**Barrault at the Comédie-**	'Good Woman of Set-
Britain	**Française**	zuan w Brecht
Churchill prime minister	Meyerhold, **Lugné-Poe d**	'Purple Dust' w O'Casey
1941		
Germany and Russia at	Brecht in America	'Mother Courage p
war	(to 1947)	Zürich
Pearl Harbor: America		
enters the War		
Joyce d		
1942		
	'The Myth of Sisyphus'	**'The Flies' w Sartre**
	w Camus	'Skin of Our Teeth' w
		Wilder
		'Red Roses for Me'
		w O'Casey
1943		
	Antoine, Danchenko,	**'Antigone' w Anouilh**
	Reinhardt d	
1944		
D-Day landing in	German and Austrian	'Glass Menagerie' w
Normandy	theatres closed	Williams
	Giraudoux d	**'Caligula' w Camus**
		'Huis clos' w Sartre

World events	Writers, artists and events in the theatre	Plays and productions
1945		
first atomic bomb	Littlewood's Theatre	**Giraudoux's 'Mad-**
United Nations f	Workshop f	**woman of**
Labour in power in Britain	Kaiser, Jessner d	**Chaillot' p Jouvet**
		'Caucasian Chalk Circle' w Brecht
1946		
	Compagnie Renaud-	O'Neill's 'Iceman
	Barrault f (to 1956)	Cometh' p
	Hauptmann d	**Men without**
		Shadows w Sartre
1947		
	Actors' Studio f New York	'Streetcar Named
	The Living Theatre f	Desire' w Williams
	Beck and Malina	**Barrault p Kafka's**
		'The Trial'
		'The Maids' w Genêt
		p Jouvet
		'Galileo' p in America
1948		
Israel proclaimed	Brecht's 'Little Organon for	**'Les Mains sales'**
Czechoslovakia communist	the Theatre'	**w Sartre**
	Artaud d	**Barrault p Claudel's**
		'Partage de midi'
1949		
	Ionesco f Collège de	'Death of a Salesman'
	'Pataphysique	w Miller
	Brecht, Weigel f Berliner	**'The Cocktail Party'**
	Ensemble	**w Eliot**
	Maeterlinck, Copeau,	'Cock-a-Doodle Dandy'
	Dullin d	w O'Casey
1950		
Korean War (to 1953)	Piscator back in Germany	'Come Back, Little
McCarthy hearings in	Shaw, Taïrov d	Sheba' w Inge
America (to 1954)		**'The Bald Soprano'**
		w Ionesco
1951		
Festival of Britain	**Vilar at the Théâtre**	'The Rose Tattoo'
	National Populaire	w Williams
	(to 1963)	
	Jouvet d	

World events	Writers, artists and events in the theatre	Plays and productions
1952 H-bomb tested	**'Saint-Genêt' w Sartre** **Cage at Black Mountain** **College**	**'Waiting for Godot'** **w Beckett** 'The Parody' w Adamov
1953 East German uprising Stalin d	Shakespeare Festival of Canada O'Neill d	'The Crucible' w Miller **'Professor Taranne'** **w Adamov** 'Camino Real' w Williams
1954 Algerian Civil War (to 1962) Matisse d	'Theatre Problems' w Dürrenmatt Berlin Ensemble at first Paris festival	**'Amédée' w Ionesco**
1955	Littlewood at Stratford, East London **Claudel d**	'View from the Bridge' w Miller **'Ping-pong' w Adam-** **ov** 'War and Peace' p Piscator
1956 Hungarian uprising Suez Canal crisis	English Stage Company at Royal Court Theatre f Devine Berliner Ensemble in London Brecht d	O'Neill's 'Long Day's Journey' p 'Look Back in Anger' w Osborne 'The Visit' w Dür- renmatt **'The Balcony'** **w Genêt**
1957 Treaty of Rome establishes European Economic Com- munity first Russian space flight Sibelius d *1958* De Gaulle president of France (to 1969)		**'Endgame' w Beckett** **'The Blacks' w** **Genêt** 'The Entertainer' w Osborne **'Picnic on the Battle-** **field' w Arrabal**

World events	Writers, artists and events in the theatre	Plays and productions
Berlin airlift		**'The Birthday Party'** 'The Fire Raisers' w Frisch
1959	**Polish Lab. Theatre f Grotowski** **San Francisco Mime Troupe f Davis** **'18 Happenings' p Kaprow**	'Roots' w Wesker **'The Zoo Story' w Albee** 'Serjeant Musgrave's Dance' w Arden
1960	Peter Hall p Royal Shakespeare Company (to 1968) **Camus d**	**'The American Dream' w Albee** 'The Happy Haven' w Arden
1961 American forces in Vietnam Berlin Wall erected	**Bread & Puppet Theatre, New York** **La Mama Experimental Theatre Club, New York**	**'Happy Days' w Beckett** 'Andorra' w Frisch
1962 Cuban missile crisis Lincoln Center for the Performing Arts opened New York (completed 1969)	**Ionesco's 'Notes and Counter Notes'** **Esslin's 'Theatre of the Absurd'**	**'Exit the King' w Ionesco** **'Who's Afraid of Virginia Woolf?' w Albee** 'The Physicists' w Dürrenmatt **Brook's 'King Lear' for RSC**
1963 President Kennedy assassinated	National Theatre f London **Brook's Theatre of Cruelty season** **The Open Theatre f New York** **Tzara, Cocteau,** Odets d	**'The Brig' p Malina** 'The Workhouse Donkey' w Arden Littlewood's 'Oh, What a Lovely War!' Hochhuth's 'Representative' p Piscator

World events	Writers, artists and events in the theatre	Plays and productions
1964		
	Living Theatre in Europe	**'Marat/Sade' w Weiss**
		Grotowski's 'Akropo-
	O'Casey d	**lis'**
1965		
	second Berlin Ensemble visit to London	**'Marat/Sade' p Brook**
		'Saved' w Bond
	Eliot d	**'Frankenstein' p Beck**
1966		
	Kirby's 'Happenings'	**'A Delicate Balance'**
	Craig, Breton, Piscator d	**w Albee**
		'America Hurrah'
		w van Itallie
		p Chaikin
		'Insulting the Audience' w Handke
1967		
	The Performance Group	**'Rosencrantz and**
	f New York	**Guildenstern Are**
	Rice d	**Dead' w Stoppard**
		'The Architect and
		the Emperor of
		Assyria' w Arrabal
1968		
Paris riots	**'The Empty Space'**	**'Paradise Now'**
Stage censorship lifted in Britain	**w Brook**	**p Beck**
	'Towards a Poor Thea-	**'Dionysus in 69'**
	tre' w Grotowski	**p Schechner**
	'Notes towards a De-finition of Documentary Theatre' w Weiss	'Kaspar' w Handke
1969		
American moon landing		**Grotowski's 'The**
		Constant Prince'
		'Christie in Love'
		w Brenton
1970		
	International Centre	**Brook's 'Midsummer**
	for Theatre Research	**Night's Dream'**
	in Paris	

World events	Writers, artists and events in the theatre	Plays and productions
		'AC/DC' w Heathcote Williams
		'Home' w Storey
1971		
	Brook's Festival at Persepolis	**'Old Times' w Pinter**
	Vilar, Adamov d	'Lear' w Bond
1972		
	Weigel d	**'Jumpers' w Stoppard**
1973		
Britain joins the Common Market	Hall at National Theatre	**'Nightwalk' p Chaikin**
		'Bingo' w Bond
		'Brassneck' w Brenton and Hare
1974		
		'Travesties' w Stoppard
1975		
Watergate scandal in Washington	Wilder d	'Norman Conquests' w Ayckbourn
		'Comedians' w Griffiths
		'American Buffalo' w Mamet
1976		
Vietnam War ends	National Theatre opens on	**'The Ik' p Brook**
American Bicentennial	the South Bank	**'Weapons of Happiness' w Brenton**
1978		
		'The Woman' w Bond
1979		
		'Betrayal' w Pinter

Bibliography

This is a comprehensive list of works, chiefly in English, covering the subject of symbolism, surrealism and the absurd in modern drama.

SYMBOLISM AND THE SYMBOLIST MOVEMENT

Anderson, David L., *Symbolism: A Bibliography of Symbolism as an International and Multi-Disciplinary Movement*, 1975.

Balakian, Anna, *The Symbolist Movement: A Critical Appraisal*, 1967

Block, Haskell M., *Mallarmé and the Symbolist Drama*, 1963

Bowra, C. M., *The Heritage of Symbolism*, 1943

Burke, Kenneth, *Language as Symbolic Action: Essays on Life, Literature and Method*, 1966

— *The Philosophy of Literary Form: Studies in Symbolic Action*, 1941

Chiari, Joseph, *Symbolism from Poe to Mallarmé*, rev. edn 1970

Cornell, Kenneth, *The Symbolist Movement*, 1951

Dickinson, Hugh, *Myth on the Modern Stage*, 1969

Engelberg, Edward, *The Symbolist Poem*, 1967

Frye, Northrop, *Anatomy of Criticism*, 1957

Henderson, John A., *The First Avant-garde, 1887–1894*, 1971

Jullian Philippe, *The Symbolists*, 1973

Lehmann, Andrew G., *The Symbolist Aesthetic in France, 1885–1895*, 1950

Symons, Arthur, *The Symbolist Movement in Literature*, 1908

Wilson, Edmund, *Axel's Castle: A Study in the Imaginative Literature of 1870–1930*, 1931

Sigmund Freud

— *The Interpretation of Dreams*, 1932

— *On Creativity and the Unconscious*, 1958

— *Wit and Its Relation to the Unconscious*, 1922

Fromm, Erich, *The Forgotten Language: An Introduction to the Understanding of Dreams, Fairy Tales and Myths*, 1951

Marcuse, Herbert, *Eros and Civilization*, 1955

Philips, William, ed., *Art and Psychoanalysis*, 1957

Shumaker, Wayne, *Literature and the Irrational*, 1960

Richard Wagner
  — *Prose Works*, trans. William Ashton Ellis, 8 vols., 1892—9
  — *Essays*, trans. William Ashton Ellis, 1914
  — *Opera and Drama*, trans. Edwin Evans, 1913
  — *Wagner on Music and Drama*, ed. Albert Goldman and Evert
    Sprinchorn, 1964

Barzun, Jacques, *Darwin, Marx, Wagner*, 1941
Bekker, Paul, *Richard Wagner: His Life and Work*, 1931
Bentley, Eric R., *The Cult of the Superman*, 1944
Burlingame, Edward L, *The Art, Life and Theories of Richard Wagner*, 1875
Chamberlain, H. S., *Richard Wagner*, trans. G. Ainslie Hight, 1897
    — *The Wagnerian Drama*, 1915
Dahlhaus, Carl, *Richard Wagner's Music Dramas*, trans. Mary Whittall,
    1979
Evans, Edwin, *An Introduction to the Study of Wagner's Prose Works*, 1913
Finck, Henry T., *Wagner and His Works*, 1904
Garten, H. F., *Wagner the Dramatist*, 1978
Krehbiel, E. H., *Studies in the Wagnerian Drama*, 1898
Newman, Ernest, *A Study of Wagner*, 1899
    — *Wagner as Man and Artist*, 1914
    — *Wagner Nights*, 1949
Schmidt-Weiss, W., *Bayreuth / Interview, 1957—1958*, 1958
Shaw, George Bernard, *The Perfect Wagnerite*, 1898
Skelton, Geoffrey D., *Wagner at Bayreuth: Experiment and Tradition*, 1965
Stein, Jack M., *Richard Wagner and the Synthesis of the Arts*, 1960
Symons, Arthur, *Studies in the Seven Arts*, 1907

Friedrich Nietzsche
  — *Works*, trans. Oscar Levy, 18 vols., 1909—13
  — *The Birth of Tragedy* and *The Genealogy of Morals*, trans. Francis
    Golffing, 1956

Brandes, Georg, *Friedrich Nietzsche*, trans. A. G. Chater, 1914
Brinton, Crane, *Nietzsche*, 1941
Coplestone, F., *Friedrich Nietzsche, Philosopher of Culture*, 1942
Förster-Nietzsche, Elizabeth, ed., *The Nietzsche-Wagner Correspondence*,
    trans. Caroline V. Kerr, *et al.*, 1922
Kaufmann, Walter, *Nietzsche, Philosopher, Psychologist, Antichrist*, 1950
Knight, A. H. J., *Aspects of the Life and Work of Nietzsche*, 1933
Knight, G. Wilson, *Christ and Nietzsche*, 1958
Lavrin, Janko, *Nietzsche: An Approach*, 1949
Lea, F. A., *The Tragic Philosopher: A Study of Friedrich Nietzsche*, 1957
Ludovici, Anthony, *Nietzsche and Art*, 1912
Mann, Thomas, *Last Essays*, trans. Richard and Clara Winston and Tania
    and James Stern, 1959

Morgan, George A., Jr, *What Nietzsche Means*, 1941
Stern, J. P., *A Study of Nietzsche*, 1979

Adolphe Appia
- *Music and the Art of the Theatre* (1899), trans. Robert W. Corrigan and Mary Douglas Dirks, ed. Barnard Hewitt, 1962
- 'The Staging of Tristan and Isolde', trans. Lee Simonson, in *Theatre Workshop*, I, April — July 1937
- *The Work of Living Art: A Theory of Theatre* (1921), trans. H. Darkes Albright, 1960

'Adolphe Appia: A Memorial', *Theatre Arts Monthly*, XVI, August 1932
Albright, H. Darkes, 'Appia Fifty Years After', *Quarterly Journal of Speech*, XXXV, April 1949
Stadler, Edmund, *Adolphe Appia*, 1970
Volbach, Walther R., *Adolphe Appia, Prophet of the Modern Theatre: A Profile*, 1968

Edward Gordon Craig
- 'Hamlet in Moscow', *The Mask*, I, May 1915
- *Index to the Story of My Days*, 1957
- ed., *The Mask*, 15 vols., 1908–29
- *On the Art of the Theatre*, 1911
- *Scene*, 1923
- *The Theatre Advancing*, 1919
- *Towards a New Theatre: Forty Designs with Critical Notes*, 1913

Bablet, Denis, *Edward Gordon Craig*, trans. Daphne Woodward, 1966
Barshay, Bernard, 'Gordon Craig's Theories of Acting', *Theatre Annual*, 1947
Craig, Edward, *Gordon Craig: The Story of His Life*, 1969
Ilyin, Eugene, 'How Stanislavsky and Gordon Craig Produced *Hamlet*', *Plays and Players*, March 1957
Leeper, Janet, *Edward Gordon Craig: Designs for the Theatre*, 1948
Nash, George, *Edward Gordon Craig, 1872–1966*, 1967
Rose, Enid, *Gordon Craig and the Theatre*, 1931
Senelick, Laurence, 'The Craig-Stanislavsky *Hamlet* at the Moscow Art Theatre', *Theatre Quarterly*, 22, 1976

Maurice Maeterlinck
- Preface to the *Plays*, in *Pelleas and Melisanda*, trans. Laurence Alma Tadema, 1896
- *The Treasure of the Humble*, trans. Alfred Sutro, 1897

Bithell, Jethro, *Life and Writings of Maurice Maeterlinck*, 1913

Clark, Macdonald, *Maurice Maeterlinck, Poet and Philosopher*, 1916
Daniels, May, *The French Drama of the Unspoken*, 1953
Halls, W. D., *Maurice Maeterlinck: A Study of His Life and Thought*, 1960
Henderson, Archibald, *Interpreters of Life and the Modern Spirit*, 1905
Knapp, Bettina Liebowitz, *Maurice Maeterlinck*, 1975
Moses, Montrose J., *Maurice Maeterlinck: A Study*, 1911
Symons, Arthur, *Plays, Acting, and Music*, 1909
Taylor, Una, *Maurice Maeterlinck: A Critical Study*, 1915
Thomas, Edward, *Maurice Maeterlinck*, 1911

Aurélien-Marie Lugné-Poe
— *Sous les étoiles: souvenirs de théâtre, 1902–1912*, 1933

Jasper, Gertrude R., *Adventures in the Theatre of Lugné-Poe at the Théâtre de l'Oeuvre to 1899*, 1947

Paul Claudel
— *Break of Noon (Partage de midi)* and *The Tidings Brought to Mary (L'Annonce faite à Marie)*, trans. Wallace Fowlie, 1960
— *The City (La Ville)*, trans. John Strong Newberry, 1920
— *The Hostage (L'Otage)*, trans. Pierre Chavannes, 1917
— *The Satin Slipper; or, The Worst Is Not the Surest (Le Soulier de satin; ou, Le Pire n'est pas toujours sûr)*, trans. John O'Connor, 1931
— *Tête-d'or*, trans. John Strong Newberry, 1919
— *The Tidings Brought to Mary*, trans. Louise Morgan Sill, 1916

— *Claudel on the Theatre*, ed. Jacques Petit and Jean-Pierre Kempf, trans. Christine Trollope, 1972
— *The Correspondence, 1899–1926*, trans. John Russell, 1952
— *Letters to a Doubter* (to Jacques Rivière), trans. Henry Longan Stuart, 1929
— *Positions et Propositions*, 2 vols., 1928
— *Ways and Crossways* [essays], trans. John O'Connor, 1933

Beaumont, Ernest, *The Theme of Beatrice in the Plays of Claudel*, 1954
Chiari, Joseph, *The Poetic Drama of Paul Claudel*, 1954
Fowlie, Wallace, *Paul Claudel*, 1957
Watson, H., *Claudel's Immortal Heroes: A Choice of Deaths*, 1971

Oscar Wilde
— 'The Critic as Artist' in *Intentions*, 1891

Agate, James, *Oscar Wilde and the Theatre* in *The Masque*, no. 3, 1947
Bird, Alan, *The Plays of Oscar Wilde*, 1977
Ellmann, Richard, *Oscar Wilde: Twentieth Century Views*, 1969
Hyde, H. Montgomery, *Oscar Wilde*, 1976
Jullian, Philippe, *Oscar Wilde*, trans. Violet Wyndham, 1969

O'Sullivan, Vincent, *Aspects of Wilde*, 1936
Ransom, Arthur, *Oscar Wilde: A Critical Study*, 1912

Gerhart Hauptmann
See vol. I

Hugo von Hofmannsthal
 — *The Play of Everyman*, trans. G. Sterling and R. Ordynski, 1917
 — *Poems and Verse Plays*, trans. Christopher Middleton, 1961
 — *The Salzburg Everyman*, trans. M. E. Tafler, 1933
 — *Selected Plays*, trans. with introduction by Michael Hamburger, 1963
 — *The Theatre of the World*, trans. T. G. Jones, 1936

Bangerter, Lowell, A., *Hugo von Hofmannsthal*, 1977
Coghlan, Brian, *Hofmannsthal's Festival Dramas*, 1964
Hammelmann, H. A., *Hugo von Hofmannsthal*, 1957

DADA AND SURREALISM
Alquié, Ferdinand, *The Philosophy of Surrealism*, trans. Bernard Waldrop, 1965
Balakian, Anna E., *The Literary Origins of Surrealism*, 1947
 — *Surrealism*, 1959
Benedikt, Michael and Wellwarth, George E., eds., *Modern French Theatre: The Avant-Garde, Dada, and Surrealism*, 1966
Fowlie, Wallace, *The Age of Surrealism*, 1950
 — *A Guide to Contemporary French Literature*, 1957
Grossman, Manuel L., *Dada*, 1971
Lemaître, Georges, *From Cubism to Surrealism in French Literature*, 1941
Matthews, J. H., *Theatre in Dada and Surrealism*, 1974
 — *The Imagery of Surrealism*, 1977
Motherwell, Robert, ed., *The Dada Painters and Poets: An Anthology*, 1951
Nadeau, Maurice, *The History of Surrealism*, trans. Richard Howard, 1965
Orenstein, Gloria Fernan, *The Theatre of the Marvelous: Surrealism and the Contemporary Stage*, 1975
Ray, Paul, *The Surrealist Movement in England*, 1971
Raymond, Marcel, *From Baudelaire to Surrealism*, 1949
Read, Herbert E., ed., *Surrealism*, 1971
Richter, Hans, *Dada: Art and Anti-Art*, 1965
Rubin, William, *Dada and Surrealist Art*, 1969
Rye, Jane, *Futurism*, 1972
Sandrow, Nahma, *Surrealism: Theater Arts, Ideas* 1972
Shattuck, Roger, *The Banquet Years: The Arts in France, 1885–1918*, 1959
Tzara, Tristan, *Seven Dada Manifestos and Lampisteries*, trans. Barbara Wright, 1977
Waldberg, Patrick, *Surrealism*, 1965

Alfred Jarry
  — *Selected Works*, trans. Roger Shattuck and Simon W. Taylor, 1965
  — *The Ubu Plays*, trans. Cyril Connelly and Simon W. Taylor, 1968

La Belle, Maurice, *Alfred Jarry: Nihilism and the Theatre of the Absurd*, 1980

Jean Cocteau
  — *Antigone, The Eagle Has Two Heads* (*L'Aigle a deux têtes*), *The Human Voice* (*La Voix humaine*), *The Infernal Machine, Oedipus Rex, Orpheus*, etc., trans. Carl Wildman, 1933–63
  — *Children of the Game* (*Les Enfants terribles*), trans. Rosamond Lehmann, 1955
  — *The Eagle Has Two Heads*, trans. Ronald Duncan, 1948
  — *Enfants Terribles*, trans. Samuel Putnam, 1930
  — *Intimate Relations* (*Les Parents terribles*), trans. Charles Frank, 1956
  — *Call to Order*, trans. Rollo H. Myers, 1927
  — *The Journals*, trans. Wallace Fowlie, 1957
  — *On the Film*, trans. Vera Traill, 1954
  — *Professional Secrets*, trans. Richard Howard, 1970

Brown, Frederick, *An Impersonation of Angels:A Biography of Jean Cocteau*, 1968
Knapp, Bettina Liebowitz, *Jean Cocteau*, 1970
Oxentrandler, Neal, *Scandal and Parade: The Theatre of Jean Cocteau*, 1957
Sprigge, Elizabeth and Kihm, Jean Jacques, *Jean Cocteau: The Man and the Mirror*, 1968
Steegmuller, Francis, *Cocteau*, 1970

André Breton
  — *Manifestoes of Surrealism* (*Les Manifestes du surréalisme*, 1930–72), trans. Richard Seaver and Helen R. Lane, 1974
  — *Manifesto*, trans. Brian Pearce and Dwight Macdonald, 1975
  — *What Is Surrealism?: Selected Writings*, ed. Franklin Rosemont, 1978

Balakian, Anna, *André Breton, Magus of Surrealism*, 1971
Browder, Clifford, *André Breton, Arbiter of Surrealism*, 1967
Caws, Mary A., *André Breton*, 1971
  — *Surrealism and the Literary Imagination: A Study of Breton and Bachelard*, 1966
Matthews, J. H., *André Breton*, 1967
Sheringham, Michael, *André Breton: A Bibliography*, 1972

W. B. Yeats
  — *Autobiographies*, 1953
  — *The Cutting of an Agate*, 1912

— *Essays and Introductions*, 1961
— *Explorations*, 1962
— *Four Plays for Dancers* [with notes], 1926
— *The Letters*, ed. Allan Wade, 1954
— *Plays and Controversies*, 1923

Bushrui, Suheil Badl, *Yeats's Verse-plays: The Revisions, 1900–1910*, 1965
Donoghue, Denis, ed., *The Integrity of Yeats*, 1964
Eddins, Dwight, *Yeats: The Nineteenth Century Matrix*, 1971
Ellmann, Richard, *The Identity of Yeats*, 1954
— *Yeats, the Man and the Masks*, 1949
Engelberg, Edward, *The Vast Design: Patterns in W. B. Yeats's Aesthetic*, 1964
Flannery, James W., *W. B. Yeats and the Idea of a Theatre*, 1976
Gordon, D. J., *W. B. Yeats: Images of a Poet*, 1961
Hall, James and Steinmann, Martin, eds., *The Permanence of Yeats*, 1950
Harper, George Mills, *The Mingling of Heaven and Earth: Yeats's Theory of Theatre*, 1975
Henn, T. R., *The Lonely Tower*, 1950
Hone, J. M., *W. B. Yeats, 1865–1939*, 1942
Ishibashi, Hiro, *Yeats and the Noh*, 1969
Jeffares, A. Norman, *W. B. Yeats, Man and Poet*, 1949
Jeffares, A. Norman and Knowland, A. S., *A Commentary on the Collected Plays of W. B. Yeats*, 1975
Kermode, Frank, *The Romantic Image*, 1957
Marcus, P. L., *Yeats and the Beginnings of the Irish Renaissance*, 1970
Maxwell, D. E. S. and Bushrui, S. B., *W. B. Yeats, 1865–1965*, 1965
Melchiori, Georgio, *The Whole Mystery of Art*, 1960
Miller, Liam, *The Noble Drama of W. B. Yeats*, 1977
Moore, John Rees, *Masks of Love and Death: Yeats as Dramatist*, 1971
Nathan, Leonard E., *The Tragic Drama of William Butler Yeats*, 1963
O'Driscoll, Robert, *Symbolism and Implications: Yeats in the 1890s*, 1975
O'Driscoll, Robert and Reynolds, Lorna, eds., *Yeats and the Theatre*, 1975
Oshima, Shotahara, *W. B. Yeats and Japan*, 1965
Qanber, Akhtar, *Yeats and the Noh*, 1974
Saul, George Brandon, *Prolegomena to the Study of Yeats's Plays*, 1958
Skene, Reg, *The Cuchulain Plays of W. B. Yeats: A Study*, 1974
Taylor, Richard, *The Drama of W. B. Yeats: Irish Myth and the Japanese Nō*, 1976
Ueda, Makoto, *Zeami Busho, Yeats, Pound: A Study in Japanese and English Poetics*, 1956
Ure, Peter, *Yeats the Playwright*, 1963
Vendler, Helen Hennessy, *Yeats's Vision and the Later Plays*, 1953
Wilson, F. A. C., *W. B. Yeats and Tradition*, 1958
— *Yeats' Iconography*, 1960

T. S. Eliot and Modern Verse Drama

— *Essays on Elizabethan Drama*, 1956
— *Notes towards a Definition of Culture*, 1968
— *On Poetry and Poets*, 1957
— *Poetry and Drama*, 1951
— *The Sacred Wood*, 1920
— *Selected Essays, 1917—1932*, 1932
— *The Use of Poetry and the Use of Criticism*, 1933

Bergonzi, Bernard, *T. S. Eliot*, 1972
Birje-Patil, J., *Beneath the Axel-Tree: An Introduction to Eliot's Poems, Plays and Criticism*, 1977
Browne, E. Martin, *The Making of T. S. Eliot's Plays*, 1969
Cahill, Audrey F., *T. S. Eliot and the Human Predicament*, 1967
Chiari, Joseph, *T. S. Eliot, Poet and Dramatist*, 1973
Clarke, David R., ed., *Twentieth Century Interpretations of 'Murder in the Cathedral'*, 1971
Donoghue, Denis, *The Third Voice: Modern British and American Verse Drama*, 1957
Frye, Northrop, *T. S. Eliot*, 1963
Gardner, Helen, *The Art of T. S. Eliot*, 1949
George, A. G., *T. S. Eliot: His Mind and Art*, 1962
Hinchliffe, Arnold P., *Modern Verse Drama*, 1977
Howarth, Herbert, *Notes on Some Figures behind T. S. Eliot*, 1965
Jones, David E., *The Plays of T. S. Eliot*, 1960
Kenner, Hugh, *The Invisible Poet*, 1965
— ed., *T. S. Eliot: A Collection of Critical Essays*, 1963
Kirk, Russell, *Eliot and His Age: T. S. Eliot's Moral Imagination in the Twentieth Century*, 1972
Litz, A. Walton, ed., *Eliot in His Time*, 1973
Macrombie, Margery C., *Modern Religious Drama in the Secular Theatre*, 1970
March, Richard, and Tambimuttu, eds., *T. S. Eliot: A Symposium*, 1948
Margolis, John D., *T. S. Eliot's Intellectual Development, 1922—1939*, 1972
Martin, Graham, Jr, ed., *Eliot in Perspective*, 1970
Matthews, T. S., *Great Tom: Notes towards a Definition of T. S. Eliot*, 1974
Mattiessen, F. O., *The Achievement of T. S. Eliot*, 3rd edn, 1958
Maxwell, D. E. S., *The Poetry of T. S. Eliot: A Symposium*, 1952
Schneider, Elizabeth, *T. S. Eliot: The Pattern in the Carpet*, 1975
Smidt, Kristian, *Poetry and Belief in the Work of T. S. Eliot*, 1961
Smith, Carol H., *T. S. Eliot's Dramatic Theory and Practice from 'Sweeney Agonistes' to 'The Elder Statesman'*, 1963
Smith, Grover Cleveland, Jr, *T. S. Eliot's Poetry and Plays: A Study in Sources and Meaning*, 1956
Spanos, William V., *The Christian Tradition in Modern British Verse Drama*, 1967

Spender, Stephen, *T. S. Eliot*, 1975
Tate, Allen, ed., *T. S. Eliot: The Man and His Work*, 1967
Unger, Leonard, ed., *T. S. Eliot: A Selected Critique*, 1948
Ward, David, *T. S. Eliot between Two Worlds*, 1973
Weales, Gerald, *Religion in Modern English Drama*, 1961
Williamson, George, *A Reader's Guide to T. S. Eliot*, 1955
Wilson, Frank, *Six Essays on the Development of T. S. Eliot*, 1948

Luigi Pirandello

- *Three Plays* (*Right You Are! — If You Think So*, etc.) trans. Edward Storer, 1923
- *Each in His Own Way and Two Other Plays*, trans. Arthur Livingston, 1925
- *Henry IV*, etc., ed. E. Martin Browne, 1969
- *Right You Are! (If You Think So)*, etc., ed. E. Martin Browne, 1962
- *The Rules of the Game*, etc., ed. E. Martin Browne, 1959
- *Naked Masks*, ed. Eric Bentley, 1952

- *On Humor* [*Umorismo*], trans. Antonio Illiano and Daniel P. Testa, 1974
- Preface to *Six Characters in Search of an Author* in *Naked Masks*

Bishop, Thomas, *Pirandello and the French Theatre*, 1960
Büdel, Oscar, *Pirandello*, 1966
Cambon, Glauco, ed., *Pirandello: A Collection of Critical Essays*, 1967
Giudice, Gaspare, *Pirandello: A Biography*, trans. Alastair Hamilton, 1975
Kennard, Joseph Spencer, *The Italian Theatre*, 2 vols., 1932
MacClintock, Lander, *The Age of Pirandello*, 1951
Matthaei, R., *Luigi Pirandello*, 1973
Moestrup, Jorn, *The Structural Pattern of Pirandello's Work*, 1972
Nardelli, Federico Vittore, *L'Uomo segreto: vita e croci di Luigi Pirandello*, 1932
Oliver, Roger W., *Dreams of Passion: The Theater of Luigi Pirandello*, 1979
Paolucci, Anne, *Pirandello's Theatre: The Recovery of the Modern Stage for Dramatic Art*, 1974
Starkie, Walter, *Luigi Pirandello, 1867–1936*, 3rd edn, 1965
Vittorini, Domenico, *The Drama of Luigi Pirandello*, 1935

Federico García Lorca

- *From Lorca's Theatre*, ed. Richard L. O'Connell and James Graham-Luján, 1941
- *Selected Poems*, ed. Francisco García Lorca and Donald M. Allen, 1958
- *Three Tragedies of Federico García Lorca*, ed. Richard L. O'Connell and James Graham-Luján, 1947

Barea, Arturo, *Lorca: The Poet and His People*, trans. Ilsa Barea, 1949
Brenan, Gerald, *The Literature of the Spanish People*, 1953
Campbell, Roy, *Lorca*, 1959
   — *Lorca: An Appreciation of His Poetry*, 1952
Cobb, Carl, *Federico García Lorca*, 1967
Crow, James, *Federico García Lorca*, 1947
Duran, Manuel, ed., *Lorca: A Collection of Critical Essays*, 1962
Higginbotham, Virginia, *The Comic Spirit of Federico García Lorca*, 1976
Honig, Edwin, *García Lorca*, 1944
Ilie, Paul, *The Surrealist Mode in Spanish Literature*, 1968
Lima, Robert, *The Theatre of García Lorca*, 1963
Nadal, Rafael Martínez, *Federico García Lorca and 'The Public'*, 1974
Spicer, Jack, *After Lorca*, 1959
Trend, John Brande, *Lorca and the Spanish Poetic Tradition*, 1956

MODERN FRENCH DRAMA

Bablet, Denis, *Les Révolutions scéniques du XXe sièle*, 1977
Batchelor, John, *Existence and Imagination in the Theater of Henry de Montherlant*, 1967
Baty, Gaston, *Le Masquet et l'encensoir: introduction à une esthétique du théâtre*, 1926
   — *Théâtre nouveau: notes et documents*, 1927
Chandler, Frank W., *The Contemporary Drama of France*, 1920
Chiari, Joseph, *The Contemporary French Theatre: The Flight from Naturalism*, 1958
Dullin, Charles, *Souvenirs et notes de travail d'un acteur*, 1946
Fletcher, John, *Twentieth Century French Drama*, 1972
Forkey, L. O., 'The Theatres of Paris during the Occupation' in *The French Review*, February 1949
Fowlie, Wallace, *Dionysus in Paris: A Guide to Contemporary French Theatre*, 1961
Ghelderode, Michel de, 'The Ostend Interviews', trans. George Hauger, *Tulane Drama Review*, March 1959
Grossvogel, David I., *The Self-Conscious Stage in Modern French Drama*, 1958; revised as *Twentieth Century French Drama*, 1961
Guicharnaud, Jacques and June, *Modern French Theatre from Giraudoux to Genêt*, revised edn., 1975
Hainaux, René, ed., *Stage Design throughout the World since 1935*, 1956
   — ed., *Stage Design throughout the World since 1950*, 1964
Hobson, Harold, *The French Theatre of Today*, 1953
Kemp, Robert, *La Vie du théâtre*, 1956
Knowles, Dorothy, *French Drama of the Interwar Years, 1918–1939*, 1967
Marcel, Gabriel, *L'Heure théâtrale*, 1960
O'Connor, Garry, *French Theatre Today*, 1975
Pitoëff, Georges, *Notre théâtre, textes et documents*, 1949

Pronko, Leonard C., *Avant-Garde: The Experimental Theatre in France*, 1962
Pucciani, Oreste F., ed., *The French Theatre since 1930*, 1954
Saint-Denis, Michel, *Theatre: The Rediscovery of Style*, 1960
Smith, H. A., *Main Currents of Modern French Drama*, 1925
Vilar, Jean, *De la tradition théâtrale*, 1955
    — *Textes de Vilar*, etc., ed. Claude Roy, 1968
Wellwarth, George E., *The Theatre of Protest and Paradox*, 1964

Jacques Copeau
    — *Études d'art dramatique, critiques d'un autre temps*, 1923
    — *Notes sur le métier de comédien*, 1955
    — *Souvenirs du Vieux-Colombier*, 1931

Waldo, Frank, *The Art of the Vieux Colombier*, 1918

Louis Jouvet
    — *Molière et la comédie classique: extraits des cours de Louis Jouvet au Conservatoire, 1939–1940*, 1965
    — *Réflexions du comédien*, 1938
    — *Témoignages sur le théâtre*, 1952

Knapp, Bettina Liebowitz, *Louis Jouvet, Man of the Theatre*, 1958

Jean Giraudoux
    — *Amphitryon 38*, trans. S. N. Behrman, 1938
    — *The Apollo de Bellac*, trans. Maurice Valency, 1954; Ronald Duncan, 1958
    — *Duel of Angels (Pour Lucrèce)*, trans. Christopher Fry, 1958
    — *Electra*, trans. Winifred Smith, 1957; Merlin Thomas and Simon Lee, 1961
    — *The Enchanted (Intermezzo)*, trans. Maurice Valency, 1950
    — *The Madwoman of Chaillot (La Folle de Chaillot)*, trans. Maurice Valency, 1947
    — *Ondine*, trans. Maurice Valency, 1956
    — *Tiger at the Gates (La Guerre de Troie n'aura pas lieu)*, trans. Christopher Fry, 1955
    — *The Virtuous Island (Supplément au voyage de Cook)*, trans. Maurice Valency, 1956

    — *Littérature*, 1941
    — *Visitations*, 1943

Cohen, Robert, *Giraudoux: Three Faces of Destiny*, 1968
Inskip, Donald, *Jean Giraudoux: The Making of a Dramatist*, 1958
Le Sage, Laurence, *Jean Giraudoux: His Life and Works*, 1959
    — *Jean Giraudoux, Surrealism and the German Romantic Ideal*, 1952
Mankin, Paul A., *Precious Irony: The Theatre of Jean Giraudoux*, 1971

Jean-Louis Barrault

— *Memories for Tomorrow*, trans. Jonathan Griffin, 1974
— *Phèdre de Jean Racine, mise en scène et commentaires*, 1946
— *Reflections on the Theatre*, trans. Barbara Wall, 1951
— *The Theatre of Jean-Louis Barrault* (*Nouvelles réflexions sur le théâtre*), trans. Joseph Chiari, 1961

Antonin Artaud

— *Collected Works*, trans. Victor Corti, 1968—
— *Antonin Artaud Anthology*, ed. Jack Hirschman, 1965
— *The Cenci*, trans. S. Watson Taylor, 1969
— *Lettres à Jean-Louis Barrault*, 1952
— *Selected Writings*, ed. Susan Sontag, trans. Helen Weaver, 1976
— *The Theater and Its Double*, trans. Mary Caroline Richards, 1958

Bermel, Albert, *Artaud's Theatre of Cruelty*, 1978
Esslin, Martin, *Antonin Artaud*, 1976
Greene, Naomi, *Antonin Artaud: Poet without Words*, 1970
Hayman, Ronald, *Artaud and After*, 1977
Jung, C. G., *Symbols of Transformation*, trans. R. F. C. Hull, 1956
Knapp, Bettina Liebowitz, *Antonin Artaud, Man of Vision*, 1971
Marowitz, Charles, *Artaud at Rodez*, 1977
Sellin, Eric, *The Dramatic Concepts of Antonin Artaud*, 1968
Tulane Drama Review, 8 (Artaud issue), winter 1963
Virmaux, Alain, *Antonin Artaud et le théâtre*, 1970

Peter Brook

— *The Empty Space*, 1969

Heilpern, John, *Conference of the Birds: The Story of Peter Brook in Africa*, 1977
Smith, A. C. H., *Orghast at Persepolis*, 1971
Trewin, J. C., *Peter Brook: A Biography*, 1971

Jean-Paul Sartre

— *Three Plays*, trans. Kitty Black, 1949
— *Two Plays*, trans. Stuart Gilbert, 1946

— *Being and Nothingness* (*L'Être et le néant*, 1949), trans. Hazel E. Barnes, 1957
— *Existentialism and Humanism* (*L'Existentialisme est un humanism*, 1946), trans. Philip Mairet, 1948
— *Sartre on Theatre*, trans. Frank Jellinck, ed. Michael Contat and Michael Rybalka, 1976
— *What Is Literature?* (*Qu'est-ce que la littérature?*, 1948), trans. Bernard Frechtman, 1950

Andereth, Maxwell, *Commitment in Modern French Literature: A Brief Study of 'littérature engagée' in the Works of Jean-Paul Sartre*, 1967
Barnes, Hazel E., *The Literature of Possibility: A Study of Humanistic Existentialism*, 1959
Champigny, Robin, *Stages on Sartre's Way*, 1959
Cranston, Maurice, *Sartre*, 1962
Curtis, Anthony, *New Developments in the French Theatre: A Critical Introduction to the Plays of Jean-Paul Sartre*, 1948
Grene, M., *Sartre*, 1973
Jameson, Fredric, *Sartre: The Origins of a Style*, 1961
Kern, Edith, ed., *Sartre: A Collection of Critical Essays*, 1962
McCall, Dorothy Kaufmann, *The Theatre of Jean-Paul Sartre*, 1969
Murdoch, Iris, *Sartre, Romantic Rationalist*, new edn., 1961
Suhl, Benjamin, *Jean-Paul Sartre: The Philosopher as a Literary Critic*, 1970
Thody, Philip, *Jean-Paul Sartre: A Literary and Political Study*, 1960
Warnock, Mary, *The Philosophy of Sartre*, 1966

Albert Camus
    — *Caligula and Three Other Plays*, trans. Stuart Gilbert, 1958
    — *The Myth of Sisyphus*, trans. Justin O'Brien, 1955

Brée, Germaine, ed., *Camus: A Collection of Critical Essays*, 1962
    — *Camus: A Critical Study*, rev. edn., 1964
Cruikshank, John, *Albert Camus and the Literature of Revolt*, 1959
Freeman, Edward, *The Theatre of Albert Camus: A Critical Study*, 1971
Hanna, Thomas, *The Thought and Art of Albert Camus*, 1958
King, Adele, *Camus*, 1964
Maquet, Albert, *Albert Camus: The Invincible Summer*, 1958
Parker, Emmett A., *Albert Camus: The Artist in the Arena*, 1965
Scott, Nathan A., *Albert Camus*, 1963
Thody, Philip, *Albert Camus: A Study of His Work*, 1957
    — *Albert Camus, 1913–1960*, 1961

Jean Anouilh
    — *Antigone*, trans. Lewis Galantière, and *Eurydice*, trans. Lothian Small, 1951
    — *Ardèle* (*Ardèle, ou la Marguérite*), trans. Lucienne Hill, 1951
    — *Becket, or The Honour of God* (*Becket, ou l'Honneur de Dieu*), trans. Lucienne Hill, 1961
    — *Cécile, or The School for Fathers* (*Cécile, ou l'École des pères*), trans. Luce and Arthur Klein, 1956
    — *Colombe*, trans. Denis Cannan, 1952
    — *Dinner with the Family* (*Le Rendezvous de Senlis*), trans. Edward Owen Marsh, 1958
    — *The Ermine*, trans. Miriam John, 1956

— *The Fighting Cock* (*L'Hurluberlu, ou le Réactionnaire amoureux*), trans. Lucienne Hill, 1967

— *The Lark* (*L'Alouette*), trans. Christopher Fry, 1955

— *Medea*, trans. Lothian Small, 1957

— *Point of Departure* (*Eurydice*), trans. Kitty Black, 1951

— *Poor Bitos* (*Pauvre Bitos, ou le dîner de têtes*), trans. Lucienne Hill, 1964

— *The Rehearsal* (*La Répétition, ou l'Amour puni*), trans. Pamela Hansford Johnson and Kitty Black, 1961

— *Restless Heart* (*La Sauvage*), trans. Lucienne Hill, 1957

— *Ring round the Moon* (*L'Invitation au château*), trans. Christopher Fry, 1950

— *Thieves' Carnival* (*Le Bal des voleurs*), trans. Lucienne Hill, 1952

— *Time Remembered* (*Léocadia*), trans. Patricia Moyes, 1955

— *Traveller without Luggage* (*Le Voyageur sans bagages*), trans. John Whiting, 1959

— *The Waltz of the Toreadors* (*La Valse des toréadors*), trans. Lucienne Hill, 1956

Fazia, Alba Della, *Jean Anouilh*, 1972

Harvey, John, *Anouilh: A Study of Theatrics*, 1964

Marsh, Edward Owen, *Jean Anouilh, Poet of Pierrot and Pantaloon*, 1953

Pronko, Leonard, *The Work of Jean Anouilh*, 1961

Thody, Philip, *Anouilh*, 1968

THEATRE OF THE ABSURD

Esslin, Martin, *The Theatre of the Absurd*, 1961

Hayman, Ronald, *Tom Stoppard*, 1977

Hinchliffe, Arnold P., *The Absurd*, 1969

Lahr, John, *Prick Up Your Ears* [on Joe Orton], 1978

Styan, J. L., *The Dark Comedy: The Development of Modern Comic Tragedy*, 2nd edn, 1968

Wellwarth, George E., *The Theatre of Protest and Paradox*, 1968

Samuel Beckett

Bair, Deirdre, *Samuel Beckett: A Biography*, 1978

Calder, John, ed., *Beckett at Sixty*, 1967

Coe, Richard N., *Beckett*, 1964

Cohn, Ruby, *Casebook on 'Waiting for Godot'*, 1967

— ed., *Samuel Beckett: A Collection of Criticism*, 1975

— *Samuel Beckett: The Comic Gamut*, 1962

Esslin, Martin, ed., *Samuel Beckett: A Collection of Critical Essays*, 1965

Federman, Raymond and Fletcher, John, *Samuel Beckett, His Works and His Critics: An Essay in Bibliography*, 1970

Fletcher, John, *Samuel Beckett's Art*, 1967

Fletcher, John and Spurling, John, *Beckett: A Study of His Plays*, 1972
Friedman, Melvin J., ed., *Samuel Beckett Now*, 1964
Hayman, Ronald, *Samuel Beckett*, 1968
Hoffman, Frederick J., *Samuel Beckett: The Language of Self*, 1962
Jacobsen, Josephine, and Mueller, William R., *The Testament of Samuel Beckett*, 1964
Journal of Beckett Studies, winter 1976—
Kenner, Hugh, *Samuel Beckett: A Critical Study*, 1961
Knowlson, James, *Catalogue of the Samuel Beckett Exhibition*, 1971
Mercier, Vivian, *Beckett/Beckett*, 1977
Modern Drama [Beckett issue], December 1966
Pilling, John, *Samuel Beckett*, 1976
Robinson, Michael, *The Long Sonata of the Dead*, 1969
Scott, Nathan A., *Samuel Beckett*, 1965
Simpson, Alan Patrick, *Beckett and Behan and a Theatre in Dublin*, 1962
Webb, Eugene, *The Plays of Samuel Beckett*, 1973
Worth, Katharine, ed., *Beckett the Shape Changer*, 1975

Harold Pinter
Baker, William and Tabachnick, Stephen E., *Harold Pinter*, 1973
Burkman, Katharine H., *The Dramatic World of Harold Pinter: Its Basis in Ritual*, 1971
Esslin, Martin, *The Peopled Wound: The Work of Harold Pinter*, 1970
Gale, Steven H., *Butter's Going Up: A Critical Analysis of Harold Pinter's Work*, 1977
Ganz, Arthur, ed., *Pinter: A Collection of Critical Essays*, 1972
Gordon, Lois G., *Stratagems to Uncover Nakedness: The Drama of Harold Pinter*, 1968
Hayman, Ronald, *Harold Pinter*, 1973
Hinchliffe, Arnold P., *Harold Pinter*, 1967
Hollis, James R., *Harold Pinter: The Poetics of Silence*, 1970
Kerr, Walter, *Harold Pinter*, 1967
Lahr, John, ed., *A Casebook on Harold Pinter's 'The Homecoming'*, 1971
Quigley, Austin E., *The Pinter Problem*, 1975
Schroll, Herman T., *Harold Pinter: A Study of His Reputation, 1958—1969, and a Checklist*, 1971
Sykes, Alrene, *Harold Pinter*, 1970
Taylor, John Russell, *Harold Pinter*, 1969
Trussler, Simon, *The Plays of Harold Pinter*, 1973

Eugène Ionesco
— *Plays*, trans. Donald Watson, 1958—
— *Notes and Counter Notes*, trans. Donald Watson, 1964

Coe, Richard N., *Ionesco: A Study of His Plays*, new edn, 1971

Hayman, Ronald, *Eugène Ionesco*, 1972
Pronko, Leonard C., *Eugène Ionesco*, 1965
Tulane Drama Review, 19, spring 1963

Edward Albee
Amacher, Richard E., *Edward Albee*, 1969
Bigsby, C. W. E., *Albee*, 1969
Debusscher, Gilbert, *Edward Albee: Tradition and Renewal*, 1967
Hayman, Ronald, *Edward Albee*, 1971
Rutenberg, Michael E., *Edward Albee: Playwright in Protest*, 1969

Jean Genêt
   — *Plays*, trans. Bernard Frechtman, 1957–63
   — *Letters to Roger Blin: Reflections on the Theater*, trans. Richard Seaver,
     1969

Cella, Lewis T., *Profane Play, Ritual, and Jean Genêt*, 1974
Coe, Richard N., *The Theatre of Jean Genêt: A Casebook*, 1970
   — *The Vision of Jean Genêt*, 1968
Driver, Tom, *Jean Genêt*, 1966
Jacobsen, Josephine and Mueller, William R., *Ionesco and Genêt*, 1968
Knapp, Bettina Liebowitz, *Jean Genêt*, 1968
McMahon, Joseph H., *The Imagination of Jean Genêt*, 1963
Sartre, Jean-Paul, *Saint Genêt, Actor and Martyr* (*Saint Genêt, comédien
     et martyr*, 1952), trans. Bernard Frechtman, 1963
Thody, Philip, *Jean Genêt: A Critical Appraisal*, 1968 [in America, *Jean
     Genêt: A Study of His Novels and Plays*, 1969]
Tulane Drama Review, 19, spring 1963

THE AVANT-GARDE
Ansorge, Peter, *Disrupting the Spectacle: Five Years of Experimental and
     Fringe Theatre in Britain*, 1975
Brecht, Stefan, 'Peter Schumann's Bread and Puppet Theatre', *Tulane
     Drama Review*, vol. XIV, no. 3, 1970
Brustein, Robert, *Revolution as Theatre: Notes on the New Radical Style*, 1971
Cage, John, *Silence*, 1961
   — *A Year from Monday*, 1969
Croyden, Margaret, *Lunatics, Lovers and Poets: The Contemporary Experi-
     mental Theatre*, 1974
Davies, R. G., *The San Francisco Mime Troupe: The First Ten Years*, 1975
Dukore, Bernard F. and Gerould, Daniel C., eds., *Avant-Garde Drama:
     A Casebook, 1918–1939*, 1976
Epstein, John, and others, *The Black Box*, 1970
Henri, Adrian, *Total Art*, 1974
Kirby, E. T., ed., *Total Theatre: A Critical Anthology*, 1969

Knowles, Alison, and others, *Four Suits*, 1965
Kostelanetz, Richard, *Metamorphoses in the Arts*, 1973
  — ed., *Moholy-Nagy*, 1970
  — *The Theatre of Mixed Means*, 1968
Kramer, Hilton, *The Age of the Avant-Garde*, 1973
Kulterman, Udo, *Art and Life*, 1971
Leswick, Henry, ed., *Guerrilla Street Theatre*, 1973
Little, Stuart, *Enter Joseph Papp: In Search of a New American Theatre*, 1974
Marowitz, Charles, *Confessions of a Counterfeit Critic: A London Theatre
  Notebook, 1958–1971*, 1973
Nyman, Michael, *Experimental Music*, 1974
Poggioli, Renato, *The Theory of the Avant-Garde*, trans. Gerald Fitzgerald,
  1968
Pronko, Leonard Cabell, *Theater East and West, Perspectives toward a Total
  Theater*, 1974
Roose-Evans, James, *Experimental Theatre*, 1971
Sainer, Arthur, *The Radical Theatre Notebook*, 1975
Scherill, James, *Breakout! In Search of New Theatre Environments*, 1972
Taylor, Karen M., *People's Street Theatre in America*, 1973
Tomkins, Calvin, *The Bride and the Bachelors*, rev. edn, 1968
Ziegler, Joseph Wesley, *Regional Theatre: The Revolutionary Stage*, 1973

Jerzy Grotowski
  — *Towards a Poor Theatre*, ed. Eugenio Barba, 1969

Temkine, Raymond, *Grotowski*, 1972

THE LIVING THEATRE
Beck, Julian, 'How to Close a Theatre' and 'The Living Theatre and
  Larger Issues' in *Tulane Drama Review*, 8, spring 1964
  — *The Life of the Theatre*, 1972
  — 'The Return of the Living Theatre', *The Drama Review*, 13, spring
  1969
Biner, Pierre, *The Living Theatre*, 2nd edn., 1972
Gottlieb, Saul, 'The Living Theatre in Exile', *Tulane Drama Review*, 10,
  summer 1966
Lebel, Jean-Jacques, *Entretiens avec le living théâtre*, 1969
Renfreu, Neff, *The Living Theatre: USA*, 1970
Rostagno, Aldo, with Julian Beck and Judith Malina, *We, the Living
  Theatre*, 1970
Schechner, Richard, 'Interviews with Judith Malina and Kenneth M.
  Brown', *Tulane Drama Review*, 8, spring 1964
  — 'The Living Theatre' in *Yale/Theatre*, vol. ii, no. 1, spring 1969
Silvestro, Carlo, ed., *The Living Book of the Living Theatre*, 1971

HAPPENINGS
Kaprow, Allan, *Assemblages, Environments and Happenings*, 1966
Kirby, Michael, *The Art of Time*, 1969
  — *Futurist Performance*, 1971
  — *Happenings*, 1965
  — ed., *The New Theatre: Performance Documentation*, 1974
Lebel, Jean-Jacques, *Le Happening*, 1966
Tulane Drama Review, 10 [Happenings issue], winter 1965

THE OPEN THEATRE
Chaikin, Joseph, 'The Open Theatre', *Tulane Drama Review, 9, winter 1964*
  — *The Presence of the Actor*, 1972
Parolli, Robert, *A Book on the Open Theatre*, 1970

THE PERFORMANCE GROUP
Schechner, Richard, ed., *Dionysus in 69*, 1970
  — *Environmental Theatre*, 1973
  — *Essays on Performance Theory, 1970—1976*, 1977
  — *Public Domain: Essays on the Theatre*, 1969
  — and Schuman, Mady, eds., *Ritual, Play and Performance*, 1976

Index